ARCHON INVASION

THE RISE, FALL AND RETURN OF THE NEPHILIM

ROB SKIBA

Archon Invasion *The Rise, Fall and Return of the Nephilim*

www.babylonrisingblog.com and www.babylonrisingbooks.com

Cover art & design by Rob Skiba II
Book design & layout by Sheila Skiba

Edited by [**not yet edited**]

Unless otherwise indicated, all Scripture quotes are from the King James Version of the Bible. Anytime a Scripture reference is made bold, it represents emphasis added by the author.

Sctipture quotations marked as (LXX) are taken from the Septuagint version of the Bible and are in the public domain.

First printing, 2012
ISBN-10: 0985098171
ISBN-13: 978-0-9850981-7-9
Printed in the United States of America

My wife and I dedicate this book to all who hunger and search for truth in the Scriptures.

TABLE OF CONTENTS

TABLE OF FIGURES

Acknowledgements

My first book, *Babylon Rising: And The First Shall Be Last* had perhaps the longest *Acknowledgements* section of any book on the planet. Many of the names listed there I would apply to this book too, so I will refrain from giving them all again here. For now, I am just going to single out those individuals whose work inspired this book and who helped to make it possible.

First and foremost, as always, I must thank my Lord and Savior, Yeshua (Jesus) for saving me and providing for my every need. Without Him, I am nothing.

A special thanks goes out to my wife, Sheila and to Sheryl Finn, and Brian and Melissa Frink who each pitched in to review this book for typos and errors and who provided helpful feedback during the writing process. Thank you so much for your input, insights and help.

In the last week of December of 2009, the Lord led me to the desert of Arizona, two hours north of Tucson. There, He escorted me on an amazing journey of discovery, which ultimately led to the development of ***SEED** the series*. Some time shortly before going on that trip, I had stumbled across Raiders News Update's *Supernatural: The Ultimate Collection* special deal for $60.[1] It included the book *The Omega Conspiracy* by Dr. I.D.E. Thomas, Tom Horn's books, *Nephilim Stargates: The Year 2012 and the Return of the Watchers* and *The Ahriman Gate* as well as the *Conspiracy Theory Special Edition* and *Psychotronic Warfare* CD box sets—all of which blew my mind! I then had to buy the *Days of Noah* CD box set to add to my "ultimate collection."

While on that journey, I must have listened to the *Days of Noah* and *Conspiracy Theory Special Edition* CD box sets at least three or four times each. Those two incredible sets of radio interviews between Tom Horn and Steve Quayle and Tom Horn and Spencer Bennett (respectively), really made me hungry to learn more about the days of Noah and about the mysterious creature the Bible calls the "Nephilim." Tom, Steve and Spencer, thank you so much for keeping me company in the Arizona desert, for all of your research into the Nephilim giants of the Bible, and for revealing the very real possibility that they may return in our day.

It wasn't long after that trip that I discovered the works of L.A. Marzulli, Patrick Heron, Dr. Ken Johnson, Douglas Hamp, Dr. Chuck Missler, David Flynn, Jim Wilhelmsen, Russ Dizdar, Derek and Sharon Gilbert, Gary Stearman, Joseph B. Lumpkin, Dr. A. Nyland, King and Keith Wells, Daniel Duval, Minister Dante Fortson, Dr. Michael Heiser, Dr. Michael Bennett, Dr. Judd Burton and James R. Spillman. Each of these individuals in some way led me to deeper revelations concerning the Nephilim. To each of you, although we all don't agree on everything, I give you my thanks and appreciation for your contributions to my understanding of the various subjects that will be covered in this book.

As I began to do my own research, I often came to the same conclusions as those who have gone before me. There were a few times, however, when my research took me in different directions,

1. Available at: http://survivormall.com/supernaturaltheultimatecollection.aspx

leading me to different conclusions. In such cases, I found it incredibly helpful to post my thoughts on Facebook in some of the many Nephilim-related forums. No shortage of extremely lengthy and sometimes very passionate debates resulted from those posts. My biggest challengers were King and Keith Wells, Minister Dante Fortson and C.K. Quarterman. They (along with a few others) strongly disagree with my thesis concerning how I believe the Nephilim returned after the Flood. Nevertheless, I am extremely grateful for our friendship and the opportunity for us to act as "iron sharpening iron." Every one of our debates helped me to further develop my thesis and for that I am thankful. I'd also like to thank Simon Trommestad, Jared Chrestman, Larry Scott, Chris McCombs, Don Veley and the many members of the Facebook groups, *NEPHILIM - Friend or Foe, Fallen Alien Resistance,* and *PID Radio Cafe*. There is never a dull moment and always interesting posts and dialogue taking place in there, my favorite — friendly — discussion groups on the Internet! Thanks for keeping it real.

Sheila and I also wish to thank the many men and women who have supported us financially as well as those intercessors who have kept us covered in prayer since we stepped out in faith to start our ministry. There are too many people to list here, and most would not want public recognition anyway. Without mentioning names, please know that you are all loved and your support has been *greatly* appreciated! We could not have accomplished as much as we have without you.

When it came to helping us get our message out to the masses, we are most grateful to Gary Stearman and Bob Ulrich of *Prophecy in the News.* Thank you for believing in us and for providing us with a launch platform through your magazine, TV show and of course the *Prophecy Summit 2012.*

We'd also like to thank *Cutting Edge Ministries* for their continued support in promoting our products as well. You are so appreciated.

Thank you, once again, David Hitt for giving me such an amazing platform to speak at *Future Congress 1* and *2*.

My wife and I wish to give a ***very big*** thank you to Albert and Michele Moffat for enabling us to bring our message to the beautiful country of South Africa, for hosting our trip, for sharing your home with us and putting on an incredible event in Pretoria. We were blessed "beyond expectations." Thank you Allen d'Agnel (and Colette) for listening to and passing our materials along to so many in Cape Town and for graciously opening up your home to us while we were there. Thank you Morné Theunissen for being my M.C. in Cape Town and for taking the time to introduce us (and ***SEED***) to the South African movie industry. To all of our new friends in South Africa, we love and appreciate you!

Finally, I owe a *great deal* of thanks, gratitude and appreciation to my wonderful, beautiful and loving wife, Sheila. Thank you for believing in me and for being so incredibly supportive as I continued to work on this book series. It is so amazing to be married to someone who "gets it" and who shares all the same passions, dreams and visions. You were of great assistance in helping with this research and working with me to design and produce books, flyers, brochures, labels, websites, videos and just about anything else we could think of doing. It is so much fun working together, building the dream and traveling on this journey of discovery with you. Your faith knows no limits and your support means the world to me. You are my soulmate, and I constantly thank God for bringing you into my life. I love you more than words can say.

Rob Skiba II

The Colony, Texas
December 2012

Preface

It all started with writing my first blog back in January of 2011. That one blog grew into a lengthy series of blogs[1] until one day I realized that I had written over 1,000 pages of content — and there was much more yet to come! So, I decided to reorganize those blogs into chapters and divide the content up into four books, which I called the *Babylon Rising* series. This book is part 1 of what will eventually become a two-part *Archon Invasion* series,[2] which when combined into one volume, will constitute Sections I and II of Book 2 in the *Babylon Rising* series.

- **Archon Invasion Book 1** deals with the rise, fall and return of the Nephilim in Biblical times.
- **Archon Invasion Book 2** will deal with the return of the Nephilim now and in the future.

1. See: http://www.babylonrisingblog.com
2. The ***Archon Invasion*** books are meant to go with the Archon Invasion DVDs, parts 1 & 2, which are available at www.babylonrisingbooks.com

FIRST DRAFT EDITION

The book you hold in your hands was rushed to print for the purposed of having it ready for *Future Congress 2*. Although several have reviewed it, my editor is still working on the final draft. Therefore, I apologize in advance for any typos, grammatical and/or formatting errors you may find within this edition.

AUDIO BOOK (COMING SOON)

I recorded myself reading the blogs on my Internet radio show[3] and found that people were very interested in being able to listen to the content. Therefore, in addition to the books, I will be producing all new audio recordings of each of them (in MP3 format) and making them available through my websites[4] as purchasable data CDs.

HOW TO GET THE MOST FROM THIS BOOK

Since this material came out of my online blog, it is written in first person, very much the way I talk. I have tried to clean it up a bit and reformat it for the book, but for the most part, just like in my previous book, I want this content to come across as if I were sitting in front of you, telling you what I have learned and believe to be true. My goal is simply to provide you with something that is easy to read and full of useful information that will hopefully challenge you to do your own research into these subjects.

Nearly everything I do is meant to work synergistically together. You will get a lot out of this book by itself, but if you combine it with the online blogs and the videos I've produced on DVD,[5] you will get even more out of it.

I have included a large number of footnotes throughout the book to help you find more information; thus enabling you to dig deeper into the various subjects I'll be covering here. In this day and age, that means using the print medium along with the digital,

3. The Revolutionary Radio Project: http://www.blogtalkradio.com/revolutionaryradio
4. http://www.babylonrisingblog.com and http://www.babylonrisingbooks.com
5. See *Appendix C* for a list of DVDs available for purchase.

therefore a lot of the footnotes will be URLs to online sources of information. Each URL provided was valid at the time of this writing. I cannot guarantee they will always remain valid, but while they are, I would encourage you to look them up in order to better understand the material contained in this book.

Additionally, because I do believe "a picture is worth a thousand words," I've tried to include as many as possible to aid in the telling of this story. I have included references and links to videos throughout this book as well, because as I like to say in my line of work, *"If a picture is worth a thousand words, how much more can you say at 24-30 frames per second?"* To make it even easier, I have organized and embedded most of the videos related to this study on my website for you to view (organized by chapter) at:

www.babylonrisingbooks.com/book2/videos.html

At the end of this book, I have also included *Appendix B* for your benefit. There, you will find books, videos and a selection of online radio programs and audio CD box sets that have all contributed to my understanding of the content I am presenting here. For those of you who are familiar with using Quick Response (QR) Codes, I have also placed a few of them at the back of the book in *Appendix B, C* and *D.* Please be sure to take full advantage of these resources in order to get the maximum benefit of this material.

MY METHOD OF RESEARCH

I once heard William Henry[6] refer to himself as an "investigative mythologist." While I don't agree with a lot of his research, I did like that title. In my case, I suppose I'm more of an "investigative Nephilim mythologist," or perhaps, I could coin a new term and say I'm an "investigative Nephilologist." At any rate, I will be approaching this material as sort of an investigative reporter, or a detective looking for clues.

6. William Henry is a New Age author and researcher. http://www.williamhenry.net

I have chosen to adhere to the following self-imposed rules:

1. I will ***re***-search: approaching the subject with an open mind, starting from scratch (as opposed to basing conclusions on those already made by others).
2. I will look for solid empirical data.
3. I will look for evidence that supports the data.
4. I will try to limit speculation to only what is supported by the data and evidence found.
5. I will try *not* to speculate from a position of biblical (or extra-biblical) silence.
6. In the mouth of two or three witnesses,[7] I will seek to establish truth.
7. I will develop my thesis based on the above criteria.

I've chosen to create these rules for myself because whenever the Scriptures are silent about a particular subject, we are left with the need to make certain assumptions when coming up with theories to explain what is not directly observable in the text. In that regard, we all have the same problem. Therefore, my position is that if we are going to make assumptions about biblical topics, they need to be reasonable ones based on a **literal interpretation** of Scripture.

Can we find Scriptures that *reasonably* support our hypothesis? What do we know about the culture and other writings of those who wrote the Scriptures? Can we find external, cultural clues and references that may have been known by the biblical authors and/or their audience? Do the Scriptures give us enough information to piece the puzzle together, without having to manufacture new pieces out of thin air? If so, then I believe we can make *reasonable assumptions* to support our view. This will be an important principle to understand concerning the return of the Nephilim, both in biblical times and in the days ahead.

7. See: Deut. 17:6 and 19:15; Matt. 18:16; 2 Cor. 13:1; 1 Tim. 5:19; Heb. 10:28

When it comes to the canonized Scriptures, I will use the *King James Version* for the majority of my Bible references, primarily because I consider it to be one of the more accurate translations available to us in English, but also because I was raised using that version. However, there are times when other versions of the English Bible do provide a clearer rendition of the text in support of what I am trying to say. In those cases, I will use other translations simply to help you better understand a point and/or as a comparison to the KJV or other extra-biblical text.

When using the Bible, I always approach it with the belief that we should take it *literally* wherever possible. There are times when it uses metaphorical and symbolic language, but I believe in those cases, the Bible usually tells you that it is doing so and shows you what the symbols, allegories, metaphors and parables mean in the text itself. Therefore, unless the Bible specifically tells me to take it any other way, I will be using a literal interpretation of the text. I believe when we do that, all of the pieces fall right into place and everything becomes so much clearer.

THE SYNCHRONIZED, BIBLICALLY ENDORSED, EXTRA-BIBLICAL TEXTS

Regarding extra-biblical texts, I do read and often quote from such books; primarily the books of 1 Enoch, Jubilees and Jasher. I do not consider these books to be canon, but I do consider them to be valuable sources of information, which can serve as ancient commentaries that elaborate on the canonized Scriptures as well as provide added insight into the beliefs of those who wrote the books we now consider canon. Essentially, I prefer to view them as "synchronized, biblically endorsed, extra-biblical texts."

I say "synchronized" because they follow the same chronological order of events. I say "biblically endorsed" because the Bible itself either quotes from, references and/or in some cases even mentions them by name. If you believe as I do that the Bible was divinely inspired and written by men, then under the inspiration of the

Holy Spirit, God told men to refer to those books, thus endorsing them. Of course, they are considered "extra-biblical texts" because they are not found in the current canon of Scripture.

These ancient books are useful in helping us to understand what is being said in the Bible and provide many added details for the stories contained within it. Wherever these texts conflict with Scripture, I'll toss that information out. Where it agrees and/or elaborates in a way that does not contradict canon, I will treat it as trustworthy.

MY INTENT

My intent in writing this book is to focus on a topic few teachers of eschatology talk about: the Nephilim. The reason for this is because Yeshua (Jesus) said that the Last Days would be like one very specific time in history:

> *"But as the days of Noah were, so shall also the coming of the Son of man be."* (Matthew 24:37)

The one thing that differentiates the days of Noah from any other time in history is the mixing of seed, resulting in the creation of hybrids. According to Genesis 6, a race of creatures known as the "Nephilim" were originally created when angels mixed their seed with that of humans. The Bible speaks of giants in the land both before and after the Flood who "were of old, great men of renown." I believe that last statement refers to the many characters from the mythologies of ancient cultures, which all speak of gods, demigods, heroes and giants. This work will focus on who/what they were and how they got here.

There are many scholars and researchers who have come before me and have done extensive work in the subject matter we'll be covering here. Much of what I know, I learned from them. That is why I call myself a researcher. By that I mean, I *re*-search that which has already been searched by those who have gone before me. Indeed, I freely admit that I have gleaned much insight, wisdom and knowledge from many sources over the years, and I believe I should give credit where credit is due. Therefore, wherever and whenever I can recall the sources of my information, I will endeavor to make those sources known, either in the body of text or with footnotes.

Over the nearly two decades that I have been studying the various topics in this work, the Holy Spirit has given me revelation and new insights as well. Some of those insights build upon the works of others, and some (as far as I know) are insights that originate with me—given, I believe, by God. Wherever I am giving my own opinion and/or interpretation of information, I will try to make that obvious and give my reasoning for it.

It is not my intent nor my desire to plagiarize anyone else's material. If anything, it is my desire to compliment and weave stories and ideas together in an effort to discover and relay truth. Essentially, my desire is to take what I've learned from others and thread it together with what I have learned on my own, in order to "connect the dots" as best I can for you the reader.

To my many friends and fellow researchers who share the same passion for the subjects that will be presented in this book, please do not be offended by any references I may make to your work in which I may have a difference of opinion. I have the **utmost respect** for all of you. I only wish to present different points of view and provide other ways of looking at these subjects for the reader to consider.

SEARCH AND SEE WHETHER THESE THINGS BE TRUE

I am not a theologian, historian, scientist or scholar. I am simply a filmmaker who is a Christian with a passion for research. That said, I do not claim to have the corner on truth. I do, however, confess that I have strong, and what I consider to be well-informed opinions. But that's all it is. I am also not a prophet. Therefore, when talking about things to come, I will be writing speculatively. Please take what I've written here for whatever you feel it is worth, but do not trust my words as being any kind of authority on truth. I could be wrong about some or all of the content in this book. I encourage you to be a "good Berean" and study these things out for yourself.

When it's all said and done, my hope is that you will have found this book fun, interesting, exciting, thought-provoking and maybe even a little challenging. I want to stimulate your mind and create in you a desire to know more and to search the Scriptures, history and even current events, checking them out for yourself in order to find answers to the many questions this work is sure to raise. If in that way, I can cause even one person to find the Truth that sets men free, I will consider that a victory.

CONTACT ME

Please feel free to visit my two related websites:

www.babylonrisingblog.com

www.babylonrisingbooks.com

There you can leave comments and/or e-mail me.

I am also available to come and present this material to anyone you think might be interested. I have extensive public speaking experience and always enjoy sharing information with anyone who is willing to listen. If you can assemble a minimum of 30 people, we'll be happy to come and do a ***free*** seminar in the venue of your choice. All my wife and I ask is that you pay for our transportation and lodging while we're there. For more information, please go to:

www.babylonrisingbooks.com/bookrob.html

Introduction

In Greek mythology, the Muses were the goddesses responsible for the inspiration of literature, science and the arts. In Roman times, it was believed that if you were to write a song, story, poetry or other form of literature, then you were inspired by one or more of the Muses to do so, based on these attributes:

Muse's name	Sphere of influence
Calliope	Epic poetry
Clio	History
Euterpe	Flutes and lyric poetry
Thalia	Comedy and pastoral poetry
Melpomene	Tragedy
Terpsichore	Dance
Erato	Love poetry
Polyhymnia	Sacred poetry
Urania	Astronomy

Table 1

Almost as if to set the record straight concerning the writing of Scripture however, the Apostle Paul told Timothy that it was divinely inspired by God Himself.

> *All scripture is given by inspiration of God, and is profitable for doctrine, for reproof, for correction, for instruction in righteousness:* (2 Timothy 3:16)

This is also confirmed by the Apostle Peter:

> *For the prophecy came not in old time by the will of man: but holy men of God spake as they were moved by the Holy Ghost.* (2 Peter 1:21)

Here we have both biblical and pagan accounts that state that our inspiration comes from elsewhere. Is this always the case? Could it really be that human inspiration does indeed come from the spirit realm — some receiving inspiration from God, others from entities known as Muses, which are probably better known (at least in biblical terms) as demons?

What I find most interesting about this idea is, if we go back to what I wrote in Book 1, *Babylon Rising: And The First Shall Be Last,* concerning the identity of Apollo, we see that he is Nimrod, the lawless one, the man of sin, the Antichrist. According to Plato, Apollo is the leader of the Muses![1] According to the Bible, Jesus was the Word that was made flesh and dwelt among us.[2] Is it just a coincidence that Jesus is considered the "Word" of God? Could it be that there is a "word" of the devil too? At least in the minds of ancient men, it would seem so. Here again we see the principle of Christ vs Antichrist, but this time in terms of the origin—or "spirit"—of human inspiration.

In modern times, it is not uncommon for artists, musicians, writers and filmmakers to say that they were inspired by unseen forces. In

1. Plato, ***Laws Book 2*** Sections 653d, and 653e. See also ***Homeric Hymn 25 To Apollo and the Muses***
2. John 1:14

fact, many openly admit to "channeling" entities in order to write songs, scripts, books and create other forms of art. Take Stephanie Meyer, the writer of the wildly popular Twilight series for instance. She says the idea for Twilight came to her in a dream back in 2003. The dream was apparently about a girl, and a vampire who loved her — but thirsted for her blood.

> *"I woke up (on that June 2nd) from* ***a very vivid dream****. In my dream, two people were having an intense conversation in a meadow in the woods. One of these people was just your average girl. The other person was fantastically beautiful, sparkly, and a vampire. They were discussing the difficulties inherent in the facts that A) they were falling in love with each other while B) the vampire was particularly attracted to the scent of her blood, and was having a difficult time restraining himself from killing her immediately. For what is essentially a transcript of my dream, please see Chapter 13 ("Confessions") of the book."*
>
> * * *
>
> *"All this time,* ***Bella and Edward were, quite literally, voices in my head. They simply wouldn't shut up.*** *I'd stay up as late as I could stand trying to get all the stuff in my mind typed out, and then crawl, exhausted, into bed (my baby still wasn't sleeping through the night, yet) only to have another conversation start in my head. I hated to lose anything by forgetting, so I'd get up and head back down to the computer. Eventually, I got a pen and notebook for beside my bed to jot notes down so I could get some freakin' sleep. It was always an exciting challenge in the morning to try to decipher the stuff I'd scrawled across the page in the dark."*
>
> — Stephanie Meyer, Author, Twilight series[3]

3. From: http://www.stepheniemeyer.com/twilight.html

The wikipedia article on her states:

> *Based on the* [above mentioned] *dream, Meyer wrote the transcript of what is now chapter 13 of the book.*[4] *Despite having very little writing experience, in a matter of three months she had transformed that dream into a completed novel.*[5] *After writing and editing the novel, she signed a three-book deal with Little, Brown and Company for $750,000, an unusually high amount for a first time author. Megan Tingley, the editor who signed Meyer, says that halfway through the reading manuscript she realized that she had a future bestseller in her hands. The book was released in 2005.*
>
> *Following the success of Twilight, Meyer expanded the story into a series with three more books: New Moon (2006), Eclipse (2007), and Breaking Dawn (2008). In its first week after publication, the first sequel, New Moon, debuted at #5 on the New York Times Best Seller List for Children's Chapter Books, and in its second week rose to the #1 position, where it remained for the next eleven weeks. In total, it spent over 50 weeks on the list. After the release of Eclipse, the first three "Twilight" books spent a combined 143 weeks on the New York Times Best Seller List. The fourth installment of the Twilight series, Breaking Dawn, was released with an initial print run of 3.7 million copies. Over 1.3 million copies were sold on the first day alone, setting a record in first-day sales performance for the Hachette Book Group USA. Upon the completion of the fourth entry in the series, Meyer indicated that Breaking Dawn would be the final novel to be told from Bella Swan's perspective. In 2008 and 2009, the four books of the series claimed the top four spots on*

4. Walker, Michael R. (2007). ***A Teenage Tale With Bite.*** BYU Magazine. Retrieved 2008-08-01.
5. Grossman, Lev (April 24, 2008). ***Stephenie Meyer: A New J.K. Rowling?*** Time. Retrieved December 12, 2008.

USA Today's year-end bestseller list, making Meyer the first author to ever achieve this feat. The series then won the 2009 Kids' Choice Award for Favorite Book, where it competed against the Harry Potter series.

The *Harry Potter* series was of course written by J.K. Rowling, which absolutely portrays (and in fact teaches) *real* witchcraft.[6] Are these wildly popular books-to-movies coming with demons attached to them? Is the dark spirit realm responsible for channeling these stories into previously obscure "wanna-be" authors? Is Lucifer responsible for their meteoric rise to success and popularity?

Time and time again, we read about and hear testimony of "inspiration" coming from elsewhere. If this is indeed true, we might do well to look at and listen to what "they" are saying through the artists, authors, poets, musicians and filmmakers of our day. Could it be that through the arts *they* are expressing *their* hopes and dreams — and plans — for the future? If so, it is certainly a sobering idea.

For instance, have you noticed how many movies and television shows are coming out these days depicting mutants and super-human hybrids saving the world? It seems like nearly every other month another superhero movie comes out, glorifying the "beneficial mutation" of that which God already declared perfect. Though ironically enough, these same "good" mutated superheroes always seem to be fighting mutated "bad" super-villains. This sends mixed signals to the audience. On the one hand, mutation can make you into a powerful good guy capable of saving humanity. On the other hand, mutation can also make you into an incredibly evil bad guy. This dichotomy is perhaps most notably revealed in the latest comic book-to-movie offering of *The Amazing Spider-man.*

6. Before turning her life around for the cause of Christ, my own sister got heavily involved in Wicca and other "dark arts" as a teenager. When she saw the *Harry Potter* movies, her comment to me was, *"A lot of that stuff is real."*

In this movie [spoiler alert!], Dr. Curt Connors is a brilliant scientist who is missing part of his right arm. According to his fictional history, he was a gifted surgeon who enlisted in the U.S. Army. While in combat, his arm was injured in a blast that resulted in it having to be amputated from the elbow down. From that point on, he became obsessed with understanding the biological secrets of limb regeneration in lizards. Once he understood how it worked at the genetic level, he concocted a serum using lizard DNA and injected himself with it. The serum worked and his arm grew back. But there was an unforeseen side effect. He began to mutate into a large reptilian monster, known to Spider-man fans as *The Lizard.*

Along with his physical mutations, he (like Spider-man) gained new abilities. Now this once-crippled scientist has:

- Superhuman strength, speed, agility, reflexes, stamina, and durability.
- Telepathic control over reptiles, capable of bringing out nearby creatures' primitive reptilian instincts.
- The ability to quickly heal from wounds.
- Hardened scale-like skin.
- Razor-sharp teeth and claws.
- Ability to leap vast distances.
- Ferocious hand-to-hand combat abilities.
- A 6-foot-long tail capable of shattering concrete.

How interesting that according to ancient literature, the Nephilim were said to have had many of the same attributes, including (but not limited to):

- Superhuman strength, speed, agility, reflexes, stamina and durability.
- Telepathic mind-control and psychic abilities.

- The ability to heal (and possibly resurrect).[7]
- Extreme intelligence; being well acquainted with all forms of science such as astronomy, biology, molecular engineering and architecture.
- The forbidden knowledge of "smiting spirits" and the killing of embryos in the womb (abortion).[8]
- Ferocious hand-to-hand combat abilities.
- 6 fingers and toes, and double rows of teeth.

That sounds like your typical comic book super-villain, doesn't it?

Going back to *The Amazing Spider-man*, what interested me the most about the way Dr. Conners was depicted in the movie is the fact that almost immediately after he injected himself with the DNA of another creature, he went from being a friendly, altruistic, humanitarian scientist, to becoming a *giant*, viciously evil monster. Is that what happened to Nimrod in Genesis 10:8,9? Or perhaps even more sobering, could something like that have been what caused Genesis 6:5?

> *And God saw that the wickedness of man was great in the earth, and that* ***every imagination of the thoughts of his heart was only evil continually***. (Genesis 6:5)

What else could cause men to have ***only*** evil continually in their hearts and minds? As I was doing my research for the *Archon Invasion And The Return of the Nephilim*[9] Parts 1 & 2 DVD presentations (which are both based on the content of this book), I began to see a pattern, which was perfectly illustrated by the titles of two books that were sitting on my desk arranged in this order: *Corrupting the Image* by Douglas Hamp on the left and *Forbidden*

7. Note that the Hebrew word often used in reference to giants in the Bible is Raphaim, which comes from the word rapha (Strong's # 7495), which means: *to heal, to cure, become fresh, repaired and reappeared.*
8. See 1 Enoch 69:12
9. Available at www.babylonrisingbooks.com/store.html

Gates by Tom and Nita Horn on the right. Looking at the two books sitting together side-by-side like that, I thought to myself, *"Wow. There it is!* Corrupting the Image *leads to opening* Forbidden Gates, *which ultimately produces something God never intended to exist: Nephilim."*

With that idea in mind, I began to speculate that Nephilim may simply be that which has become corrupted from the image God originally created. In other words, when we mix "kinds" that were never meant to be mixed, it appears that we open up "forbidden gates" or portals through which something other than the God-given soul (or *nephesh*)[10] meant for a creature may enter and indwell the resulting hybrid. It then becomes essentially "fallen" from its previously created "perfect" state, and thus it is far more susceptible to being predisposed to evil. Seeing what happened to Dr. Conners in *The Amazing Spider-man* movie only seemed to confirm that belief.

Of course, I am not basing my thesis on Marvel comic book characters and movies. But I do find it very interesting that the concepts being portrayed in these fictional stories seem to align quite well with what ancient Hebrew texts have to say concerning the days of Noah. Could it be that the same entities who died in the Flood are now providing the inspiration for stories that may illustrate their return?

Contrary to what many scholars believe and teach concerning the Nephilim, the Hebrew texts (including those of canonized Scripture) do *not* support the idea of multiple incursions, but rather that the return of the Nephilim actually came about through other means, such as through the mixture of animals and humans. Indeed, the ancient texts testify that the days of Noah had more to do with transhumanism than angels having sex with human women (which happened in the days of his great, great grandfather, Jared). Along similar lines, have you been watching the news lately? In fulfillment of the prophecy Jesus gave in

10. See Genesis 2:7 and the Hebrew word nephesh (Strong's #5315)

Matthew 24:37, every year we are hearing more and more about the creation of animal-human hybrids, which is *exactly* what was going on in the days of Noah.

Just like the fictional Dr. Conners, many real-life scientists support the practice of mixing species as a way of curing the many sicknesses, diseases and crippling ailments that plague mankind. When you add the fact that transhumanists like doctors Kevin Warwick, Nick Bostrom, Hugo de Garis and Michio Kaku among others are actively promoting the idea of "becoming like the gods" by mixing humanity with both animals and machines, you quickly begin to see that there may be ulterior motives for such practices. This is nothing new. As you will soon see in this book, it all happened before, and it didn't end well for those who participated in such activity.

I wrote this book to expose what I believe is essentially a Fallen Angel/Nephilim agenda that is actively at work in the earth today. I believe it is an agenda to corrupt all flesh (Genesis 6:12) just as it was in the days of Noah. According to the synchronized, biblically endorsed, extra-biblical texts, this was specifically done in order to "provoke the Lord."[11] My goal is to share with you what I believe the Scriptures and current events are revealing to be true and to show you just how accurate Jesus' prophecy concerning the Last Days really is.

> *But as the days of Noah were, so shall also the coming of the Son of man be.* (Matthew 24:37)

THE GIANTS WERE REAL

> *There were giants in the earth in those days; and also after that, when the sons of God came in unto the daughters of men, and they bare children to them, the same became mighty men which were of old, men of renown.*
> (Genesis 6:4)

11. See Jasher 4:18 and Jubilees 7:24

If you have ever been interested in this subject, you've probably already read and heard a lot of people talking about the post-Flood Nephilim giants returning based on the *usual* interpretation of the above Bible verse — that being the idea that angels came down and mated with women *again* after the Flood. I call that the "Multiple Incursions Theory." While this may be the mainstream, dominant view, I am going to present some other viewpoints here for your consideration.

I have been told that what I am proposing is not a new theory, but I confess I have never read nor heard anything about this theory before. It is a conclusion I came to on my own. If what I am saying is in fact an old theory, then I suggest we pull it out from behind the books on the bottom shelf of the bookcase in the back of the library, dust it off and re-examine it, elaborate on it and at least weigh its merits against the more established, mainstream view once again. Even though I know I am in the minority in my acceptance of this particular view, and may take a lot of heat from my peers (in fact, I already have), that is exactly what I am going to do here; I'm going to dust it off and do an in-depth study of its merits throughout this book.

I'm not stating the following as absolute fact. **This is just my opinion - a theory I have developed as a result of my research.** As with any theory, it must be tested, peer reviewed and validated before being declared something other than just a theory. I am simply presenting my findings here for your consideration. It is my hope that you will test my "facts" and do your own research in order to discover the truth for yourself.

There can be no doubt about it, the giants of the Bible and of ancient folklore, myth and legend were real. They walked this earth. They built megalithic structures and cities all over the planet. They left many things behind that testify to the truth of their wisdom, knowledge and powerful abilities. Initially, they were the offspring of fallen angels and human women. According to the ancient texts, the first generation were completely destroyed within 500 years of their births. Then the giants returned. The question is, how?

Let's find out together.

SECTION I

THE PRE-FLOOD NEPHILIM HYBRIDS

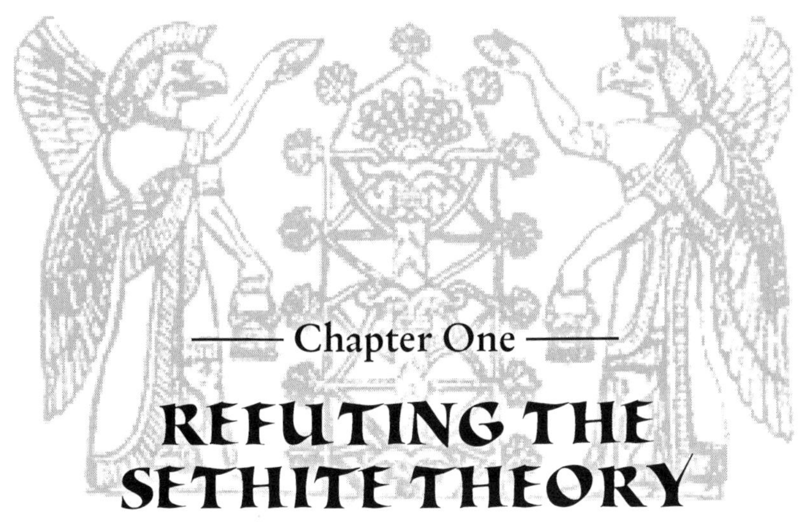

Chapter One

Refuting the Sethite Theory

"Julius Africanus (AD c. 160? - c. 240?) was the first to tentatively suggest that the "sons of God" might be referring to the descendants of Seth and the "seed of men" could possibly be referring to the descendants of Cain."

— Doug Hamp[1]

Before going into an in-depth study about the Nephilim, there is an issue, which often comes up in this discussion (especially when dealing with seminary-trained individuals), and that is the notion that Genesis 6:1-4 is not even talking about angels at all. Rather, some say the "sons of God" in that passage are the righteous children of Seth and the "daughters of men" are the ungodly children of Cain. This is what is called the Sethite Theory.

> *And it came to pass, when men began to multiply on the face of the earth, and daughters were born unto them, That the* ***sons of God*** *saw the* ***daughters of men*** *that they were fair; and they took them wives of all which they chose.* (Genesis 6:1,2)

1. From ***Corrupting the Image*** by Douglas Hamp (© 2011 Defender Publishing, LLC), page 119

In Chapter Three, I will show you the meaning of the Hebrew phrase that was translated into English as "sons of God" and compare its usage in other Old Testament books of the Bible, clearly showing that phrase to be a reference to angels and not humans. Additionally, the book of Jasher completely annihilates the "Sethite Theory" with the following:

> *And Seth lived one hundred and five years, and he begat a son; and* ***Seth called the name of his son Enosh, saying, Because in that time the sons of men began to multiply, and to afflict their souls and hearts by transgressing and rebelling against God.*** *And it was in the days of Enosh that the sons of men continued to* ***rebel and transgress against God****, to increase the anger of the Lord against the sons of men. And* ***the sons of men went and they served other gods****, and they forgot the Lord who had created them in the earth: and in those days the sons of men made images of brass and iron, wood and stone, and they bowed down and served them. And every man made his god and they bowed down to them, and* ***the sons of men forsook the Lord all the days of Enosh*** *and his children; and the anger of the Lord was kindled on account of their works and abominations which they did in the earth. And* ***the Lord caused the waters of the river Gihon to overwhelm them, and he destroyed and consumed them, and he destroyed the third part of the earth, and notwithstanding this, the sons of men did not turn from their evil ways,*** *and their hands were yet extended to do evil in the sight of the Lord. And in those days there was neither sowing nor reaping in the earth; and there was no food for the sons of men and the famine was very great in those days. And the seed which they sowed in those days in the ground became thorns, thistles and briers; for from the days of Adam was this declaration concerning the earth, of the curse of God, which he cursed the earth, on account of the*

> *sin which Adam sinned before the Lord. And it was when men continued to rebel and transgress against God, and to corrupt their ways, that the earth also became corrupt.* (Jasher 2:2-9)

Concerning the days of Enosh, the Septuagint version of Genesis says:

> *And Seth had a son, and he called his name Enos:* ***he hoped to call on the name of the Lord God****.*
> (Genesis 4:26 LXX)

Here Moses takes a moment to give added detail concerning the naming of a child. But what is that text really saying? Enosh's name means, "mortal." That's an unusual thing to name your kid. Further, according to *Jone's Dictionary of Old Testament Proper Names*, Enosh actually means: "Man frail and miserable." The web site abarim-publications.com gives us more detail:

> *The verb " anash," meaning to be desperate, woeful, very sick (2 Samuel 12:15, Jeremiah 17:9). HAW Theological Wordbook of the Old Testament notes on this verb, "most frequently it is used to describe a wound or pain which is incurable...(Jeremiah 15:18, 30:12)" This may shed some light on the enigmatic Beast From The Sea and the fatal wound of which it was healed - Rev 13:3; if not the healing caused by the Christ - Matthew 8:17/ Isaiah 53:4).*

Was Seth (the "appointed" one), saying something that alludes to sadness regarding the mortality of men? Was Enosh a sick and frail child? How did the rabbis interpret this particular passage? *Clarke's Commentary on the Bible* reveals the traditional understanding of *Genesis* 4:26:

> *Then began men to call upon the name of the Lord - The marginal reading is,* ***Then began men to call themselves by the name of the Lord****; which words are supposed to*

signify that in the time of Enos the true followers of God began to distinguish themselves, and to be distinguished by others, by the appellation of sons of God; those of the other branch of Adam's family, among whom the Divine worship was not observed, being distinguished by the name, children of men. ***It must not be dissembled that many eminent men have contended that " chalal,"[2] which we translate began, should be rendered began profanely, or then profanation began****, and from this time they date the origin of idolatry. Most of the Jewish doctors were of this opinion, and Maimonides has discussed it at some length in his Treatise on Idolatry; as this piece is curious, and gives the most probable account of* ***the origin and progress of idolatry****, I shall insert it here.*

> ***"In the days of Enos the sons of Adam erred with great error, and the counsel of the wise men of that age became brutish, and Enos himself was (one) of them that erred****; and their error was this: they said, Forasmuch as God hath created these stars and spheres to govern the world, and set them on high, and imparted honor unto them, and they are ministers that minister before him; it is meet that men should laud, and glorify, and give them honor. For this is the will of God, that we magnify and honor whomsoever he magnifieth and honoureth; even as a king would have them honored that stand before him, and this is the honor of the king himself. When this thing was come up into their hearts they began to build temples unto the stars, and to offer sacrifice unto them, and to laud and glorify them with words, and to worship before them, that they might in their evil opinion obtain favor of the Creator; and* ***this was the root of idolatry****, etc. And in process of time there*

2. Note: Clark actually spelled it as "huchal," but for the sake of consistency, I have changed it here to match the Strong's Concordance transliteration of # 2490.

stood up false prophets among the sons of Adam, which said that God had commanded and said unto them, Worship such a star, or all the stars, and do sacrifice unto them thus and thus; and build a temple for it, and make an image of it, that all the people, women, and children may worship it. And the false prophet showed them the image which he had feigned out of his own heart, and said it was the image of such a star, which was made known unto him by prophecy. And they began after this manner to make images in temples, and under trees, and on tops of mountains and hills, and assembled together and worshipped them, etc. And this thing was spread through all the world, to serve images with services different one from another, and to sacrifice unto and worship them. So, ***in process of time, the glorious and fearful name (of God) was forgotten out of the mouth of all living, and out of their knowledge, and they acknowledged him not.***

And there was found no people on the earth that knew aught, save images of wood and stone, and temples of stone, which they had been trained up from their childhood to worship and serve, and to swear by their names. And the wise men that were among them, as the priests and such like, thought there was no God save the stars and spheres, for whose sake and in whose likeness they had made these images; but as for the Rock everlasting, there was no man that acknowledged him or knew him save a few persons in the world, as Enoch, Methuselah, Noah, Sham, and Heber. And in this way did the world walk and converse till that pillar of the world, Abraham our father, was born." Maim. in Mishn, and Ainsworth in loco.

— Clarke's Commentary on the Bible (Genesis 4:26)

Here we see Maimonides, a highly respected Jewish philosopher, one that many consider to have been among the greatest Torah scholars of the Middle Ages elaborating on what the ancient book of Jasher stated.

This interpretation is derived from the Hebrew word "chalal" (Strongs # 2490), which means "*to profane, wound, defile, break, etc.*" Thus, Genesis 4:26 may be better rendered:

> *And Seth had a son, and he called his name Enos:* ***because men began to profane and defile the name of YHVH.*** (Genesis 4:26) [emphasis and revision mine]

as opposed to:

> *And to Seth, to him also there was born a son; and he called his name Enos:* ***then began men to call upon the name of the LORD.*** (Genesis 4:26)

The days of Enosh were not good, but rather rebellious. It is not my intent to say whether or not Enosh participated in that rebellion himself. That is not the point I'm trying to make. The point is, this text is usually used to justify the "godly line of Seth," which is typically (erroneously) associated with "the sons of God" in *Genesis* 6:4 as opposed to the "ungodly line of Cain," which is referred to as "the daughters of men" in that same passage. Proponents of the "Sethite Theory" will point to Genesis 4:26 and say, "*See the sons of Seth are worshipping (calling upon) the name of the Lord.*" Clearly that is not what was happening there. It does not say that the sons of Seth are calling upon the Lord, it says that "men" began to. But as we've seen above, this "*calling on the name of the Lord*" is more of a blasphemy—an act of profaning—rather than an act of worship anyway.

Perhaps there was repentance by the time God judged this rebellion and that's why Enosh named his son, Kenan, which means "sorrow." I don't know, but this pre-Flood, Gihon river judgement is very interesting. It would appear that God sent a warning flood. This may have been the deluge that sunk Atlantis. I believe it is what caused the depression we now call the Mediterranean Sea, which may have been one third of the land of Eden. I will address these ideas further in later volumes.

The Sethite Theory is flawed on so many levels that I can hardly believe it is still being taught in seminaries, but it is. Minister Dante Fortson shares my frustration and makes an interesting observation in his book, *As The Days of Noah Were:*

> *Seth's line is the one that seems to be acting against the will of God if we actually read the story. They initiate the disobedience by taking wives of their own choosing. It seems as though the "daughters of Cain" had no say in the matter, and the sons of Cain did not participate in this event. Everyone in Cain's line seems to be completely innocent as far as the text of Genesis 6:1-4 is concerned. The facts seem to support the exact opposite of what the Lines of Seth Theory teaches. According to scripture, Cain's line seems to be neutral in these events and Seth's sons seem to initiate the defiance of God.*
>
> —Minister Dante Fortson[3]

Indeed, if the sons of God are supposed to be a representation of the good sons of Seth mating with the bad daughters of Cain, why is it that the *supposedly* "good-guys" are the ones doing the bad thing? Beyond that, how do "kissing cousins" produce the likes of Og of Bashan or Goliath? I don't care how much spinach you feed someone, incest will never produce 9 to 36 foot[4] tall giants!

The only thing that explains the giants of the Bible is the notion that something supernatural took place. That's exactly what happened according to the canonized Scriptures as well as the ancient Hebrew synchronized, biblically-endorsed, extra-biblical texts. According to the book of 1 Enoch, 200 Watcher class angels landed on Mount

3. ***As the Days of Noah Were***, by Minister Dante Fortson, page 36
4. See Amos 2:9

Hermon in the days of Jared. They mated with women, who gave birth to massive offspring known as the Nephilim. Those wicked creatures killed each other off within 500 years, then their parents, the Watchers were judged. The question now is, did angels continue to mate with women again after that?

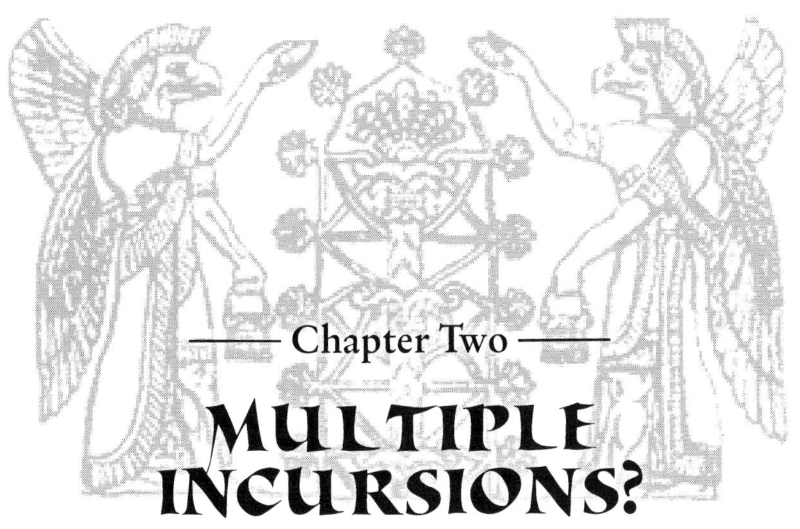

Chapter Two

MULTIPLE INCURSIONS?

"There is a principle which is a bar against all information, which is proof against all argument, and which cannot fail to keep man in everlasting ignorance. That principle is condemnation before investigation."

— Edmund Spencer

Many have asked the question, *"If the Nephilim were destroyed in the Flood, how did they return after it?"* On the surface, it is tempting to think that the easiest answer is, angels came down and mated with women again... and apparently again and again. I once held that view myself, but now I disagree. It is my strong belief that multiple incursions did *not* happen.

As we explore the many reasons why I believe this way, it is my hope that the facts presented in this book will help you to gain a greater understanding of the pre and post-Flood worlds as well as enable you to see the dangers of some of the things taking place in laboratories around the world right now.

If you are open to other possibilities apart from the mainstream view, I ask that you stick with me to the very end. Please hear me out completely before you decide. I know many who believe in the Multiple Incursions Theory are extremely passionate about that belief. If you are one such person, and if you've even bothered to read this far, then I ask that you not tune me out until you have at least heard my **entire thesis** and understand why I am so passionate about this particular viewpoint. We should all remain open to other possibilities (myself included). With that in mind, let's look at a number of problems that come with believing in the Multiple Incursions Theory.

THE EXTREMELY SEVERE JUDGMENT

The two hundred fallen angels known as Watchers who landed on Mt. Hermon in the days of Jared received an extremely severe punishment from God. First, they were forced to watch their children be destroyed:

> *And to Gabriel said the Lord: 'Proceed against the bastards and the reprobates, and against the children of fornication: and destroy [the children of fornication and] the children of the Watchers from amongst men [and cause them to go forth]: send them one against the other that they may destroy each other in battle:* ***for length of days shall they not have. And no request that they make of thee shall be granted unto their fathers on their behalf;*** *for they hope to live an eternal life, and that* ***each one of them will live five hundred years.****'* (1 Enoch 10:9,10)

Then, a promise of no peace nor forgiveness was given by God to these disobedient angels.

> *'Enoch, thou scribe of righteousness, go, declare to the Watchers of the heaven who have left the high heaven, the*

> *holy eternal place, and have defiled themselves with women, and have done as the children of earth do, and have taken unto themselves wives: "Ye have wrought great destruction on the earth: And* ***ye shall have no peace nor forgiveness of sin****: and inasmuch as they delight themselves in their children,* ***The murder of their beloved ones shall they see, and over the destruction of their children shall they lament, and shall make supplication unto eternity, but mercy and peace shall ye not attain.****"*
> (1 Enoch 12:4-6)

The Watchers begged for forgiveness and essentially requested Enoch to be their attorney to plead their case before God. However, they found neither forgiveness nor mercy.

> *I wrote out your petition, and in my vision it appeared thus, that* ***your petition will not be granted unto you*** *throughout all the days of eternity, and that judgment has been finally passed upon you: yea (your petition) will not be granted unto you. And from henceforth* ***you shall not ascend into heaven unto all eternity, and in bonds of the earth the decree has gone forth to bind you for all the days of the world****. And (that) previously you shall have seen the destruction of your beloved sons and ye shall have no pleasure in them, but they shall fall before you by the sword.* ***And your petition on their behalf shall not be granted, nor yet on your own: even though you weep and pray*** *and speak all the words contained in the writing which I have written.*
> (1 Enoch 14:4-7)

According to the text, Enoch then takes a tour into the depths of Hades — into Tartarus, the eternal prison that awaits the Watchers. After seeing the *horrors* that are in those places he says:

> *Then Uriel answered me, one of the holy angels who was with me, and said unto me: 'Enoch, why hast thou*

> *such fear and affright?' And I answered: 'Because of this fearful place, and because of the spectacle of the pain.' And he said unto me: '**This place is the prison of the angels, and here they will be imprisoned forever.**'*[1] (1 Enoch 21:9-10)

This is the prison where the angels who choose to mate with women go to be punished. Lucifer is already out-numbered 2-to-1, so do you really believe he'd continue to risk losing more of his army to the prison of Tartarus? I think not. Lucifer played the proverbial "angel incursion card" and lost — big time! Can you imagine him trying to convince another platoon of angels to try that again, especially after what happened to the ones who did it the first time?

This of course raises an interesting question: Do angels and demons fear this judgment? Let's consider what was said even before the Watchers did what they did:

> *And the angels, the sons of heaven, saw and lusted after them, and said to one another: "Come, let us choose us wives from among the children of men and have children with them." And Semjaza, who was their leader, said to them: "**I fear you will not agree to do this deed, and I alone shall have to pay the penalty of this great sin.**"* (1 Enoch 6:2-4)

Notice here that Semjaza, the leader of this entire group was afraid to do what he himself identified as a "great sin," which of course would come with a great consequence. They knew this in advance! After making their mutual oaths (which is why Mt. Hermon is called what it is), they went ahead and committed the great sin of mating with women. Then came the feared judgment. When their sentence was pronounced, we see the following response of the Watchers.

1. See also: 2 Peter 2:4 and Jude 6

> *Then I went and spoke to them all together, and* ***they were all afraid, and <u>fear and trembling</u> seized them****. And they besought me to draw up a petition for them that they might find forgiveness, and to read their petition in the presence of the Lord of heaven. For from thenceforward they could not speak (with Him) nor lift up their eyes to heaven for shame of their sins for which they had been condemned.* (1 Enoch 13:3-5)

Later in the text, we see that even the good angels were terrified by what they saw.

> *On that day Michael answered Raphael and said: "The power of the spirit grips me and* ***makes me tremble because of the severity of the judgment*** *of the secrets, and the judgment of the angels.* ***Who can endure the severe judgment*** *which has been executed, and before which they melt away?" And Michael answered again, and said to Raphael: "Who would not have a softened heart concerning it, and* ***whose mind would not be troubled by this judgment*** *against them because of those who have led them out?"* (1 Enoch 68:2,3)

Here we see both the good and the bad angels were terrified by the severe judgment that comes from mating with human women. Now look at what the mighty Archangel Michael says next:

> *"Therefore all that is hidden shall come on them for ever and ever;* ***<u>for no other angel</u> or man shall have his portion in this judgment****, but* ***they alone have received their judgment*** *for ever and ever."* (1 Enoch 68:5)

Michael is prophesying that *no other angel* will ever be judged for that act again.[2] Based on the context of the previous chapters and verses, the reason is because the hosts of heaven (both good and

---

2. Yet in spite of that prophecy, there is one will dare to mate with women again. However, that will not happen until the Last Days as we will see in the final chapter of this book.

bad) saw how extremely severe that particular act of disobedience was judged by God. This is *the* judgment specifically allotted for those who commit this particular crime (sin) against humanity:

> *For God did not spare angels when they had sinned, but hurling them down to Tartarus consigned them to caves of darkness, keeping them in readiness for judgement.*
> (2 Peter 2:4 Weymouth New Testament)

> *And angels -- those who did not keep the position originally assigned to them, but deserted their own proper abode -- He reserves in everlasting bonds, in darkness, in preparation for the judgement of the great day.*
> (Jude 6 Weymouth New Testament)

I chose to use the *Weymouth New Testament*[3] translation for those two verses because it preserves the original word Tartarus and I believe best conveys what is taking place in those passages of Scripture.

Barnes' Notes on the Bible has the following to say concerning these two parallel verses:

> *But cast them down to hell - Greek tartarōsas - "thrusting them down to Tartarus." The word here used occurs nowhere else in the New Testament, though it is common in the Classical writers. It is a verb formed from Tartaros, Tartarus, which in Greek mythology was the lower part, or abyss of Hades, where the shades of the wicked were supposed to be imprisoned and tormented, and corresponded to the Jewish word Geenna - "Gehenna." It was regarded, commonly, as beneath the earth; as entered through the grave; as dark, dismal, gloomy; and as a place of punishment.*
>
> — Barnes' Notes on the Bible (2 Peter 2:4)

3. ***The Weymouth New Testament*** is Public Domain and available on-line at: http://speedbible.com/weymouth/index.htm

> *Peter says, "chains of darkness;" that is, the darkness encompasses them "as" chains. Jude says that those chains are "everlasting," (desmois aidios. Compare Romans 1:20, "his eternal power and Godhead"). The word does not elsewhere occur. It is an appropriate word to denote that which is eternal; and no one can doubt that if a Greek wished to express that idea, this would be a proper word to use. The sense is, that* ***that deep darkness always endures; there is no intermission; no light; it will exist forever. This passage in itself does not prove that the punishment of the rebel angels will be eternal, but merely that they are kept in a dark prison in which there is no light****, and which is to exist for ever, with reference to the final trial. The punishment of the rebel angels after the judgment is represented as an everlasting fire, which has been prepared for them and their followers, Matthew 25:41.*
>
> — Barnes' Notes on the Bible (Jude 6) [emphasis mine]

Remember this fact: The Tartarus prison judgment is not an *eternal* one. The Lake of Fire is the final eternal judgment for the fallen angels. Some would argue that they know about that eternal judgment and yet continue to practice evil on the earth anyway. So, why should they fear Tartarus? Well, we know from certain passages of Scripture that the demons are aware of an appointed time for final judgment and torment.

> *And, behold, they cried out, saying, What have we to do with thee, Jesus, thou Son of God?* ***Art thou come hither to torment us before the time****?* (Matthew 8:29)

They apparently know about God's seven-thousand-year time clock and that when it runs out after the Millennial Reign of Christ, they will finally be judged and cast into the Lake of Fire that is prepared for the devil and his angels.[4] So, let's boil this down to a simple question: If you knew that at the end of next week, you'd suffer for eternity in everlasting flames of fire, would you want to risk going to an *additional* place of torment *today* and lose what little freedom you have left before the great judgment known as the *Second Death* comes? Of course not. Only a fool would risk losing what little (precious) freedom he has left before suffering for eternity. If we think that way in our human wisdom, why should we think that angels would not reason the same way?

Looking at the history of the world, it would appear that the devil and his angels are free to do just about anything they want. There certainly has been no shortage of horrific evil throughout the last half-dozen millennia or so. Yet, for whatever reason, God draws a line in the sand when it comes to angels mating with humans who were created in His own image. Committing that one particular sin comes with a very distinct and horrible judgment, and God would not be just if He did not impose the same exact judgment on any other angel who committed the same act of disobedience that the Watchers of Genesis 6 did.

The angels fear Tartarus. Based on what the demons (the disembodied spirits of the Nephilim)[5] said when they encountered Jesus, while they were still in possession of the "Maniac of the Gadarenes," it would seem that they too were painfully aware of the horrors of the Abyss:

> *Jesus asked him, "What is your name?"*
>
> *"Legion," he replied, because many demons had gone into him.* ***And they <u>begged</u> Jesus <u>repeatedly</u> not to order them to go into the Abyss.***
> (Luke 8:30,31 NIV)

4. See Matthew 25:41 and Revelation 20:7-15
5. See 1 Enoch 15:8-12 and 1 Enoch 16:1

If the demons really are the disembodied spirits of dead Nephilim, how would they know what the Abyss (a.k.a. Tartarus and the Bottomless Pit) was like? Clearly, they did not take part in the extreme judgment that was imposed upon their parents, so how would they know anything about it that it should make them so afraid? There's actually an interesting story given in the book of Jubilees concerning the demons after the Flood, which may shed some light on this situation. It takes place shortly after men began to multiply on the earth and the multitude of demons — the spirits of countless dead Nephilim — began to plague the fledgling population.

> *And in the third week of this jubilee* ***the unclean demons began to lead astray the children of the sons of Noah; and to make to err and destroy them.*** [6]
>
> *And the sons of Noah came to Noah their father, and they told him concerning the demons which were leading astray and blinding and slaying his sons' sons. And he* [Noah] *prayed before the Lord his God, and said:*
>
> *"God of the spirits of all flesh, who hast shown mercy unto me, and hast saved me and my sons from the waters of the flood, and hast not caused me to perish as Thou didst the sons of perdition; For Thy grace hath been great towards me, and great hath been Thy mercy to my soul; Let Thy grace be lift up upon my sons, and let not wicked spirits rule over them lest they should destroy them from the earth. But do Thou bless me and my sons, that we may increase and multiply and replenish the earth. And Thou knowest how Thy Watchers, the fathers of these spirits, acted in my day: and as* ***<u>for these spirits which are living,</u> imprison them and hold them fast in the place of condemnation****, and let them not bring destruction on the sons of thy*

6. If we are to take Jesus' words in Matthew 24:37 literally, some speculate that there could have been as many as 7 billion people (or more) on the planet in the days of Noah, just as there are today. Since Genesis 6:12 states that <u>all flesh</u> had become corrupted, that would mean there were over 7 billion disembodied spirits of dead Nephilim tormenting just a few generations of humans after the Flood.

> *servant, my God; for these are malignant, and created in order to destroy. And let them not rule over the spirits of the living; for Thou alone canst exercise dominion over them. And let them not have power over the sons of the righteous from henceforth and for evermore."*
>
> *And the Lord our God bade us* [the good angels] *to bind all.*
>
> *And the chief of the spirits, Mastêmâ,* [who is Satan] *came and said: "Lord, Creator, let some of them remain before me, and let them hearken to my voice, and do all that I shall say unto them; for if some of them are not left to me, I shall not be able to execute the power of my will on the sons of men; for these are for corruption and leading astray before my judgment, for great is the wickedness of the sons of men."*
>
> *And He said:* ***"Let the tenth part of them remain before him, and let nine parts descend into the place of condemnation."*** (Jubilees 10:1-9)

Here we see Satan (described as Mastêmâ) asking God to let him keep ten percent of the demons to do his bidding on earth. Strangely enough, God grants him this wish. He then banishes the other ninety percent to Tartarus to join their parents in the prison of the Abyss. The remaining ten percent witnessed this. So, it is easy to understand why, after seeing Jesus coming their way, they were terrified that their time had come to join the others in that judgment. Therefore, I think it is *extremely* unlikely that any other angel in Heaven or in the company of Lucifer would dare to even think about doing what they saw their brothers the Watchers do!

Again, we know that YHVH is just, holy and changes not. Therefore, if the above represents the official punishment or sentence for committing the crime (sin) that was committed in Genesis 6:1-4, **God would not be just if He were to allow another "incursion" and not impose the same judgment on those who participated**.

Lucifer is not bound in chains. He is free to go *"to and fro on the earth,"*[7] making his rounds *"as a roaring lion, walking about, seeking whom he may devour."*[8] He also apparently still has access to Heaven where he is known as the *"accuser of the brethren"* who *"accuses men day and night before God."*[9] He would not have access to Heaven if he had done what the Watchers did. He would be *"bound in everlasting chains of darkness"*[10] like Semjâzâ and the rest of the Watchers. How could he have the power to work freely on this earth, and be the *"prince of the power of the air"*[11] if he were bound in chains inside of it!?

No. I do not believe Lucifer, nor any other fallen angels have tried a repeat of *The Genesis Six Experiment* (at least not in biblical times), and I would challenge anyone who disagrees with that statement to present Scriptural proof that angels once again mated with women, producing offspring. The best anyone can come up with is Genesis 6:4 and Numbers 13:33—but as you will soon see, neither of those work as a ready defense for the multiple incursion argument.

Some have tried to point to the fact that the men of Sodom wanted to mate with the angels who visited Lot's home as proof of post-Flood angel sex.

> *But before they retired for the night, all the men of Sodom, young and old, came from all over the city and surrounded the house. They shouted to Lot, "Where are the men who came to spend the night with you? Bring them out to us so we can have sex with them!"* (Genesis 19:4,5 NLT)

Note however that {A} the text only shows that they *attempted* to, it does not say that they did and {B} even if those *men* could mate

7. See: Job Chapters 1 and 2
8. 1 Peter 5:8
9. Revelation 12:10
10. 1 Enoch 10:12, Jubilees 5:6-11, 2 Peter 2:4 and Jude 6
11. Ephesians 2:2

with the *male* angels, they would not have produced offspring. So, that argument is invalid and does not support the Multiple Incursions Theory either.

The bottom line is, the judgment on the Watchers was extremely severe. Lucifer knows he is already outnumbered 2-to-1. Therefore, as a master tactician who has dedicated himself to opposing all that is good, I do not believe he would risk losing any more of his evil, angelic troops to the prison of the Abyss. That would be a poor military strategy by any earthly standard.

Any military commander who has decided to wage a war against a superior enemy while already being outnumbered 2-to-1 is going to be more interested in finding ways to *increase* his numbers, not decrease them! Since Lucifer is smarter than humans who would not take the chance of losing valuable troops in such a situation, I do not believe he would take the risk either. A smart tactician would maximize the use of his available troops and look for other ways of gaining any advantage he could find with the resources available to him. Losing troops while already outnumbered is not an advantage.

Therefore, I suggest the Nephilim must have returned another way.

THERE ARE NO CONFIRMING SCRIPTURES

NOTE: It is bad practice to base any belief, theory, dogma or doctrine on only one verse in Scripture. Keep that in mind when considering Genesis 6:4. Scripture *always* self-authenticates and confirms itself. It is my contention that those who hold to the Multiple Incursions Theory have *no* other validating Scripture to confirm their interpretation of that verse.

If we are to believe that Scripture always confirms and interprets itself, then it must be noted that there is *not one* confirming

Scripture in support of Genesis 6:4 that *specifically states* that angels ever mated with women again. Not one! As far as I can tell, we don't even find evidence of such activity in any other extra-biblical Hebrew texts either, at least not in the books of Jasher, Jubilees nor 1 Enoch — three books that give us tremendous detail about the activities of the Fallen Ones. Even Josephus fails to give support to the idea of multiple incursions in any of his works on the history of the Jews.

Still, a common line of thought amongst believers in the Multiple Incursions Theory can be seen in the following excerpt from an e-mail newsletter I recently received titled, <u>LESSON 5</u> *"And Also Afterward: Giants in the Old Testament"* by my friend and fellow Nephilim researcher Dr. Judd Burton. As a historian, archaeologist and the director of the Institute of Biblical Anthropology, Dr. Burton certainly has *far* more academic credentials than I do. I greatly admire him and his work, so I certainly intend no disrespect when I quote him here. Some of the things he wrote in that newsletter merely reflect what the vast majority of researchers in this field believe. Therefore, with his permission, I am using some of his work here simply as an example of what has become the mainstream view concerning the return of the Nephilim in the post-Flood world. He states:

> *If the Nephilim died in the flood, how is it that they appear in later passages of the Old Testament? The passage of Genesis 6:4 suggests the answer.*
>
> > *"The Nephilim were on the earth in those days — and also afterward — when the sons of God went to the daughters of men and had children by them."*
>
> *Here "also afterward"* ***<u>implies</u> after the flood,*** *and the subsequent phrase* ***<u>suggests</u> that not only were there Watcher angel incursions before the flood, but also after it****, when additional rebellious angels mated with human females to produce additional generations of giants.* [emphasis mine]

Dr. Burton is certainly not alone in that view. Again, that is essentially the majority view of virtually every scholar I know in this field of interest. However, that view is based solely on speculation, arguing from biblical silence. Thus, he is quite correct in his use of words like "***implies***" and "***suggests***" because the text itself does not specifically say this was so. It is an assumption with no further biblical support. My contention is that a number of equally valid implications exist and will become evident as we continue to explore the Scriptures and the synchronized, biblically endorsed, extra-biblical texts.

Those who hold to the multiple incursions view subscribe to the notion that Genesis 6:4 is saying, "*There were giants* [Nephilim] *on the earth in those days and also afterward* ***when*** *the sons of God came* [again and again] *in to the daughters of men....*" Even the well-respected Dr. I.D.E. Thomas, whose seminal work, *The Omega Conspiracy*, spawned a new generation of Nephilim researchers, promoted this idea.

> *In Genesis 6, where the word "Nephilim" is first used, we are told that the Nephilim appeared on the Earth just before the Flood, and that their appearance was the main reason for the Flood. There followed another incursion of these fallen angels at a later date. We read in Genesis 6:4, "The Nephilim were on the earth in those days and also afterward..." (NIV). This data is found in Numbers 13:33: "We saw the Nephilim there (the descendants of Anak come from the Nephilim)" (NIV).*
>
> *This second eruption was probably on a more limited and restricted scale than the first. Nevertheless, God ordered their complete destruction.*
>
> —Dr. I.D.E. Thomas, *The Omega Conspiracy*[12]

12. ***The Omega Conspiracy*** (© 2008 Anomalos Publishing), page 109

I have tremendous respect and admiration for Dr. Thomas as well. His book really opened my eyes to a lot of things (just as it did for many others as well). However, I see a number of flaws in this interpretation, which will become more apparent as we continue our study of both Genesis 6:4 and Numbers 13:33.

I'd like to suggest that an equally valid interpretation of Genesis 6:4 would be: *"**Because** the sons of God came in to the daughters of men and bore children to them, there were giants* [Nephilim] *in the land in those days and also afterward...."*

I changed the order of the sentence and inserted the word "because" in place of "when" simply to make this interpretation easier to understand, but it is not necessary to prove my point, as we'll soon see.

My translation is not all that different from that of the Douay-Rheims Bible, which renders it as:

> *Now giants were upon the earth in those days. For after the sons of God went in to the daughters of men and they brought forth children, these are the mighty men of old, men of renown.* (Genesis 6:4 Douay-Rheims)

Depending on how one word is translated, we can easily come to two different conclusions. The Hebrew word "asher" is the key word in question. In Genesis 6:4, it is the word translated into English as "when." However, it has a number of other meanings that are just as valid. Strong's (#834) renders its meaning as:

> *after, alike, as soon as,* ***because****, every, for, forasmuch, from whence,*

The *NAS Exhaustive Concordance* gives its short definition as "*who, which, that,*" but it lists a variety of other definitions as seen in the following modified screenshot from bible.cc.

<< 833	834. asher	835 >>

who, which, that

Original Word: אֲשֶׁר
Transliteration: asher
Phonetic Spelling: (ash-er')
Short Definition: which

NAS Exhaustive Concordance

Word Origin

a prim. pronoun

Definition

who, which, that

NASB Word Usage

The usual translation of Genesis 6:4 reads:

"The Nephilim were on the earth in those days, and also afterward, *WHEN* the sons of God came in to the daughters of men, and they bore children to them. Those were the mighty men who were of old, men of renown." (NASB)

But **NOTE** how many times "asher" is translated as "BECAUSE" as opposed to how many times it is translated as "WHEN"

although (1), anyone (1), because (45), because* (73), before* (3), concerning* (1), deadly* (1), everything* (2), everywhere* (2), how (24), how* (6), if (8), inasmuch (1), inasmuch* (2), just (1), just* (6), much (1), powder* (1), reason (1), set (1), since (3), since* (5), so (9), so* (1), steward* (4), storehouses (1), such (8), such* (2), than* (1), therefore (1), these (2), this (1), though* (1), unless* (1), until* (35), what (166), what* (8), whatever (16), whatever* (40), when (44), when* (1), whenever (1), where (49), where you how (1), where* (136), whereas* (1), whereby (1), wherein (1), wherever (4), wherever* (27), which (1925), which he and how (1), which* (1), whichever (1), while (1), while those who (1), who (1), who (850), whoever (4), whoever* (13), whom (345), whom* (1), whomever (1), whomever* (3), whose (80), whose remains when (1), why (2).

Figure 1

Looking at **Figure 1**, you will notice that "asher" is translated more often (at least in the NASB) as "because" rather than "when." Thus, for me this becomes more of a "**first cause**" issue, rather than a "**repeat offense**" issue. In my opinion, those are the two dominant views concerning how the Nephilim returned: A first cause with lasting genetic effects versus repeat offenses through multiple incursions.

The bottom line is, with only this *one word* in *one verse* (that could be interpreted at least two different ways) to go on, both camps of researchers are making an assumption in order to explain the established fact that there were indeed giants on the earth both before and after the Flood. So, the question then becomes, which *preconceived notion* is correct, logical and verifiable (with Scripture) when considering all of the evidence available to us?

Depending on which idea one subscribes to, both groups of researchers will naturally look at Genesis 6:4 differently — much like the way we may view the optical illusion of **Figure 2**. Are we looking at a candleholder or the profile of two people facing each other? Depending on how you look at it, you can actually see both. So, which answer is correct?

Figure 2

Can I say you're wrong if all you can see is a candleholder? Can you blame me if all I can see are the profiles of two people looking at one another? How are we to determine what is really being depicted there?

The solution is to consult the originator of the artwork. He will tell you what was actually put on that canvas. In this case, I am the artist. I can tell you that I created the profile of a man facing to the left, then I duplicated it and flipped the copied profile horizontally and backed it away from the original just far enough to the left in order to create the illusion that is depicted in the middle. In this and other such examples, no matter what the illusion may be, the solution is to consult the originator of the image.

Likewise, when it comes to Genesis 6:4, no matter what the illusion may appear to be, we must consult the Author of Scripture in order to find truth. One way we can do that is to weigh our perceptions against everything else the Author wrote concerning the same subject. That is all I'm trying to do here in this book. I'm taking the *perception* of what we think we are seeing in Genesis 6:4 and I'm looking for confirmation from the Author to see if it is correct. When looking at the whole of Scripture, the Author has not given us any indication that we are seeing multiple incursions. *It is an illusion.*

Although I can still "see" Genesis 6:4 as a first-cause issue even when *asher* is translated as "when," I think the meaning becomes much clearer when translated as "because" as seen below in my revised version of the text:

> *"The Nephilim were on the earth in those days, and also afterward,* ***because*** *the sons of God came in to the daughters of men, and they bore children to them. Those were the mighty men* ***who*** *were of old, men of renown."* (Genesis 6:4 Rob's Revised NASB Version)

Even though most English versions of Genesis 6:4 use the word "when," I have not done anything with that Scripture that the Hebrew does not fully support by changing it to the more often used (elsewhere) translation of "because." It must also be noted that the same word *asher* is used again in Genesis 6:4, translated as "who" (850 times), which next to the word "which" (1,925 times) appears to be its second most common rendering in the NASB (as seen in **Figure 1**).

Simply changing "when" to "because" makes it very easy to see this as a first-cause issue versus a repeat-offense issue. In other words, it doesn't *have to* mean that there was a second or multiple incursions that created more Nephilim giants after *The Genesis Six Experiment.* It could simply be that all of the giants "who" followed "afterward" were a by-product — *or the result* — of the initial incursion.

Everything else that Dr. Burton wrote in the previously mentioned newsletter built upon a preconceived notion of an ***implied*** "second incursion." In Chapter Five of his book, *The Omega Conspiracy,*[13] Dr. Thomas also admits that this idea is based on speculation. In

13. ***The Omega Conspiracy,*** (© 2008 Anomalos Publishing House), page 69.

fact, this is almost universally the case amongst believers in that theory because there are no definitive Scriptures that would state there were indeed multiple incursions. It is an argument from biblical silence, based on assumptions derived from the fact that Nephilim were on the earth both before and after the Flood.

Further, the *reason* given for these other incursions generally involves an assumed attempt to prevent the Messiah's birth. If that's the case, then more questions immediately come to mind: Like why did this supposed return of the fallen angels center *only* on Ham's children — when prophetically speaking, the Messiah was to come through Shem's offspring? If the goal was to wipe out the Messiah, why mess with tribes that had nothing to do with His ancestry? Dr. Burton explains:

> ***The giants relocated themselves in the Levant to keep the Jews out, to pollute or destroy (as in the case of David) the bloodline of Messiah, and to oppress and lead astray the Jews.*** *In terms of culture, it is evident that the giants established their Watcher and Nephilim forebears as the gods of ancient polytheism.* [emphasis mine]

I agree with the notion that this strategy worked, in terms of setting up a polytheistic system, which would lead much of the world into the worship of false gods. In fact, that's the foundational principle of my whole *Babylon Rising* series. I covered it in my *Mythology and the Coming Great Deception*[14] DVD and will be examining it much closer in Book 3[15] as well. Still, I must differ with the opening statement in the above paragraph.

Figure 3

14. Available at www.babylonrisingbooks.com/store.html
15. You can read a fair amount of Book 3's content in blog format on my website, www.babylonrisingblog.com under the "God vs god" section.

Dr. Burton goes on to say, "*Their entire culture was built upon preventing the arrival of Messiah.*" OK, but if the goal is to prevent the arrival of Messiah, why not totally obliterate the fledgling nation through polluted genetics *within* the lineage of Shem? Why focus on Ham? Why not scoop up all of Shem's women, have sex with them and be done with the whole affair? Or why not infect the offspring of all three of Noah's sons? Why not have them totally devour the land as they did before the Flood, only this time prevent anyone else from building a boat or any other structure of safety. Destroy everything once again! They came close last time. Maybe they could try harder this time. Seems to me, that would have been a far more effective strategy. However, they could not do that because it appears — when taking all of the available facts into consideration — that they were either not able or willing to repeat what they did in Genesis 6.

In my opinion, the Multiple Incursions Theory is full of holes and is based on *pure speculation*. The Scriptures do not give us any indication that any angels mated with humans again after the Flood.

Therefore, I suggest the Nephilim must have returned another way.

SIZE BEGAN TO DROP DRAMATICALLY

If the account given in 1 Enoch and other ancient texts are to be believed, the immediate offspring — the first generation of Nephilim — were massively huge! They grew to upwards of 300 cubits or more.

> *And all the others together with them took unto themselves wives, and each chose for himself one, and they began to go in unto them and to defile themselves with them, and they taught them charms and enchantments, and the cutting of roots, and made them acquainted with plants. And they became pregnant, and* ***they bare great giants, whose***

> ***height was three thousand ells:***[16] *Who consumed all the acquisitions of men. And when men could no longer sustain them, the giants turned against them and devoured mankind. And they began to sin against birds, and beasts, and reptiles, and fish, and to devour one another's flesh, and drink the blood. Then the earth laid accusation against the lawless ones.* (1 Enoch 7)

An ancient text known as *The Kebra Nagast,*[17] or the *Book of the Glory of the Kings* [of Ethiopia], has been held in the highest regard throughout Abyssinia for at least a thousand years. According to the introduction[18] of this text, which was translated by E.A. Wallis Budge in 1932, it explains that *"even today it is believed by every educated man in that country to contain the true history of the origin of the Solomonic line of kings in Ethiopia, and is regarded as the final authority on the history of the conversion of the Ethiopians from the worship of the sun, moon, and stars to that of the Lord God of Israel."* As if to put an interesting spin on the Sethite Theory[19] it has this to say concerning the first-generation offspring of the Watchers:

> *And the daughters of Cain with whom the angels had companied conceived, but they were unable to bring forth their children, and they died. And of the children who were in their wombs some died, and some came forth; having split open the bellies of their mothers they came forth by their navels. And when they were grown up and reached man's estate* ***they became giants, whose height reached unto the clouds****;* (Kebra Nagast 100)

We have trouble imagining giants that big, but the Greeks didn't. They called them the Titans. Even Josephus confirms this.

---

16. Dr. A. Nyland translates the "three thousand ells" of Enoch 7:2 as 300 cubits in his book, ***Complete Books of Enoch,*** page 20
17. See: http://en.wikipedia.org/wiki/Kebra_Nagast
18. See: http://www.sacred-texts.com/chr/kn/kn000-5.htm
19. The theory that the *"sons of God"* in Genesis 6:1-4 are the "good" sons of Seth and the *"daughters of men"* are the "bad" offspring of Cain.

> *For many angels of God accompanied with women, and begat sons that proved unjust, and despisers of all that was good, on account of the confidence they had in their own strength; for the tradition is, that* ***these men did what resembled the acts of those whom the Grecians call giants*** [Titans].
>
> — Flavius Josephus, *Antiquities of the Jews 1.3.1*

The Bible seems to confirm the enormous size of some of these hybrids as well — even when referring to those who came after the Flood:

> *Yet I destroyed the Amorites* (who were descendants of Canaan) *before them, though they were* ***tall as the cedars and strong as the oaks.*** (Amos 2:9a NIV)

Most scholars refer to post-Flood Nephilim in terms of 9- to 18-foot giants, but YHVH, through the prophet Amos refers to giants who were as tall as cedar trees! This is very interesting when considering the cedars of Lebanon, which were often referenced in the Bible as being renowned for their enormous height. They can grow to over 100 feet tall, but even a modest cedar grows to between 30 and 50 feet in height. Giants of 30+ feet in height have apparently been found in the past,[20] and those of this stature would certainly explain the comments made by the Hebrew spies when they first scouted out the land of Canaan:

> *They gave Moses this account: "We went into the land to which you sent us, and it does flow with milk and honey! Here is its fruit. But the people who live there are powerful, and the cities are fortified and very large.* ***We even saw descendants of Anak there. The Amalekites live in the Negev; the Hittites, Jebusites and Amorites live in the hill country; and the Canaanites live near the sea and along the Jordan."*** (Number 13:27-29 NIV)

20. Steve Quayle has done a masterful job of collecting stories, pictures and evidence from all around the world concerning the giants,compiling them all together in one book, ***Genesis 6 Giants,*** available at: www.stevequayle.com.

Take careful note of the names listed there because we're going to come back to them soon. There's a reason they are naming specific people groups, with no mention of any angels being involved with the sons and "ites" that Moses wrote about here.

Despite their great size, Caleb was ready to go and take them out.

> *But the men who had gone up with him said, "We can't attack those people; they are stronger than we are." And they spread among the Israelites a bad report about the land they had explored. They said, "The land we explored devours those living in it.* ***All the people we saw there are of great size. We saw the Nephilim there (the descendants of Anak come from the Nephilim). We seemed like grasshoppers in our own eyes, and we looked the same to them.*** *"* (Number 13:31-33 NIV)

I would suggest that nothing smaller than 24- to 36-foot tall giants would make someone describe themselves as feeling like a "grasshopper" by comparison. We know from verses 28 and 29, that the spies are specifically identifying entire people groups who were known to be giants. They reiterate this fact in verse 32, stating that "***all*** *the people we saw there are of* ***great size****."* They then associate these giants with the Nephilim, stating that the sons of Anak were offspring of *other* Nephilim (not of angels). Finally, they use an idiom that denotes size comparison. This same idiom is actually used in Isaiah 40 to describe how much bigger *God* is than man:

> *It is He that sitteth upon the circle of the earth, and* ***the inhabitants thereof are as grasshoppers****; that stretcheth out the heavens as a curtain, and spreadeth them out as a tent to dwell in:* (Isaiah 40:22)

Isaiah is saying God sits above the earth and that people are as grasshoppers compared to him. This is one way the idiom was used. Another way it was used was in reference to vast numbers.

> *And the Midianites and the Amalekites and* ***all the children of the east lay along in the valley like grasshoppers for multitude****; and their camels were without number, as the sand by the sea side for multitude.* (Judges 7:12)

The usage in Numbers 13 would seem to indicate both size and number (as in a vast multitude). Indeed, according to the account given by the Hebrew spies to Moses, we can easily deduce that the land of Canaan was literally *loaded* with giants!

For the sake of illustration I have created the following graphic to show you what the various sizes of men and giants would look like if standing side by side:

Figure 4

Figure 4 shows their body mass as well as their height. They weren't just tall, they were also "as strong as the oaks."

Consider also the fact that when the (normal-sized) Hebrew spies went into the land of Canaan, they brought back a single cluster of grapes that was so large it took two men to carry it on a pole! That really got me thinking. As I was writing this, I actually had a bowl of grapes sitting on my desk that my wife had brought to me. I grabbed a cluster and went into the bathroom and held it up to my head to get a sense of scale. If we are to take the Scriptures literally, and just imagine a single cluster of grapes like we might buy at the supermarket, scaled to the head of some giants, the following graphic illustrates an approximate scale of the size of the grapes and the corresponding size of a giant that might have been eating them:

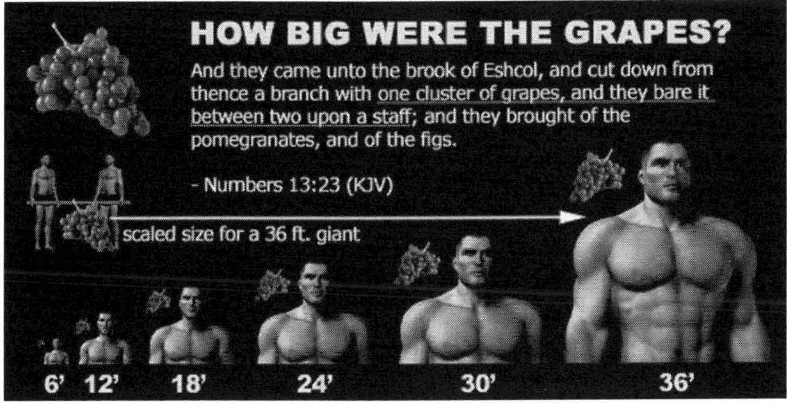

Figure 5

Big people need big food or *lots and lots* of small food. Personally, I have no problem believing that genetic modification of food may have been taking place in the land of Canaan (just as it is in our world today). Clearly, when looking at the historical record, ancient people had advanced technological and scientific abilities. Could it be that they were just as advanced in the science of genetics as they were in astronomy, mathematics and architecture? If so, the creation of "big food" is not beyond the realm of possibility.

If this assumption is valid, looking at **Figure 5**, we can see that a six foot man would have no problem carrying a single cluster of grapes that was scaled to anything smaller than what a 30 foot tall giant might have been eating. Much bigger than that however, would require two people to carry it. Thus, even by the size of the grapes we may deduce that the giants of Canaan were at least 30 to 36 feet tall! No doubt about it, a 36-footer is quite massive. However, even if the Amorites could have possibly grown to be as tall as 100 to 150 feet max (the size of the cedars of Lebanon),[21] that is still only about *one quarter* the size of the first-generation pre-Flood giants. Remember, 1 Enoch says the first-generation hybrids got to be "3,000 ells" or 300 cubits, which equals approximately 450 feet tall—a number that Scripture records as being the same as the length of Noah's Ark. I wonder if that's just a coincidence?

Why the dramatic decrease in size? If angel + human = 450-footers, why do we not see evidence of such massive creatures in the post-Flood world? If the Multiple Incursions Theory were true, there should be multitudes of 450- footers, but that is not what the Scriptures describe. As impressive as the post-Flood giants were, they were still significantly smaller than their pre-Flood ancestors.

Therefore, I suggest the Nephilim must have returned another way.

THE TOTAL CORRUPTION OF ALL FLESH

> *And God looked upon the earth, and, behold, **it was corrupt; for all flesh had corrupted his way upon the earth**.* (Genesis 6:12)

The activity of the Nephilim from the days of Jared until the Flood caused ***all flesh*** to become completely corrupted. By my reckoning, they were on the earth for nearly 1,200 years prior to the Flood. Look at what they were able to do in that amount of time! Surely, if there had been multiple incursions, we would not be here today—after nearly five thousand years.

21. I realize this sounds too incredible to be true, but that is what the ancient texts actually say when understood with a literal interpretaion.

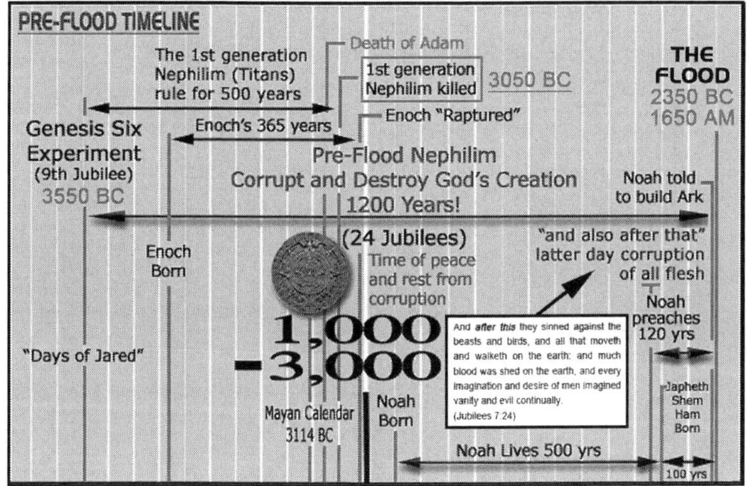

Figure 6

According to 1 Enoch, the first generation of the pre-Flood Nephilim only lived for 500 years.[22] Judging from the writings of the Hebrews as well as other ancient cultures, it would appear there were second, third, and other generations that were on the earth in one form or another for a total of roughly 1,200 years from the days of Jared leading up to the Flood. In that time, Genesis tells us that they were able to thoroughly corrupt all flesh.

Genesis, 1 Enoch, Jubilees and Jasher all agree that the ***whole earth*** and ***everything*** on it had been thoroughly corrupted by the effects of *The Genesis Six Experiment*. It got so bad that the only thing God could do was wipe everything out and start over!

If we were to look at this from a strategic perspective, we'd have to say that was a very effective military campaign launched by the Fallen Ones. If Lucifer's goal was to wipe out the seed, he did a pretty amazing job with just 200 angels in 1,200 years! If Lucifer's **angel+human=TOTAL CORRUPTION** strategy was so successful (starting with just 200 angels), and if he had the ability to continue

22 See Enoch 10:10

to use that strategy after the Flood (with all of the other angels within the 1/3 of Heaven's hosts available to him), don't you think he would have? Proponents of the Multiple Incursions Theory say he did. So I ask, why didn't the whole earth become *completely corrupted* again and again and again and again and again? That's right, they've had nearly ***five times*** the amount of time since the Flood as they did before the Flood to continue their previously effective plans. So, what happened? Why are they not *still* doing it? Why is there no further mention of giants after the time of David in Scripture? If they had the ability—or willingness—to continue to mate with women *as* they did in Genesis 6, how do we answer those questions? How do we account for the lack of evidential and Scriptural support for that position? We can't.

Therefore, I suggest the Nephilim must have returned another way.

SCIENCE INSTEAD OF SEX

I believe that there is abundant evidence in support of a very real and ongoing so-called scientific "*alien-human-hybrid breeding program.*" However, this may be because Satan and his angels can't do what they did in Genesis 6. If they could, I don't believe we would have "Alien Greys" to contend with today. There would be no need for them, or for Satanic Ritual Abuse (SRA) to create "portals" nor any of the other demonic activity that we are seeing these days.. I believe those are all tactics the Devil *has* to use today in order to do what he originally attempted in *The Genesis Six Experiment.*

Figure 7

The events of Genesis 6 were a direct response to the prophecy of Genesis 3:15.

> *"And I will put enmity between you and the woman, and between your offspring and hers; he will crush your head, and you will strike his heel."* (Genesis 3:15 NIV)

Ever since then, Lucifer has tried to corrupt the seed of the woman. He failed to do so, and the Messiah was born and did what He came to do. So, that plan failed.

Enoch 15:6-12 tells us that the disembodied spirits of the Nephilim became known as "evil spirits" (demons). According to some researchers, the so-called Greys are nothing more than biological constructs — corporeal suits if you will — that the disembodied spirits of the Nephilim can inhabit.

Since the time of Christ, they have been subject to His authority and that of His Believers.[23] We can cast them out of bodies. So, in response, it appears they may have created their own bodies out of genetic material, in order to use these physical bodies to interact with the three-dimensional world.

Others disagree and believe that the Greys are actually one form of the fallen angels. In either case, they aren't known for having sex. Rather, they are known for abduction and performing scientific experimentation on their victims. According to researchers like Dr. David Jacobs, there is clearly a breeding program taking place — the goal of which is to create a hybrid that looks fully human.[24]

My friend and fellow researcher L.A. Marzulli claims to have held actual "alien implants" in his hand. In his *Watchers* DVD series, he shows how these devices have been removed from the bodies of people who claim to have been abducted by alien beings. He believes that those implants are directly related to some sort of hybridization breeding program. He further speculates that these things may be directly linked to the coming "Mark of the Beast"

23. Mark 16:17
24. See: http://www.babylonrisingbooks.com/book2/videosC101.html

that the Apostle John wrote about in the Book of Revelation, and he's not the only one who believes these things. In fact, I completely agree with those ideas myself, as I had come to similar conclusions based on my own research concerning Nimrod. However, all of that evidence seems to point more toward laboratory experiments than it does sexual intercourse with angels. Therefore, such things only serve to further illustrate the points I'm making here against the Multiple Incursions Theory.

In reference to so-called "alien abductions," the current alien-human-hybrid breeding program does not involve marriage and mating. It involves abduction and the extraction and implantation of bodily fluids through surgical means. I do not believe the fallen angels would have to resort to medical procedures if all they had to do was take women, have sex with them and produce offspring like they did in the days of Jared.

Perhaps this is the meaning behind Daniel 2:42,43?

> *And as the toes of the feet were part of iron, and part of clay, so the kingdom shall be partly strong, and partly broken. And whereas thou sawest iron mixed with miry clay, **they shall mingle themselves with the seed of men: <u>but they shall not cleave one to another</u>,** even as iron is not mixed with clay.* (Daniel 2:42,43)

The text is clearly referring to the mixture of seed. We know that the phrase "***shall <u>not</u> cleave one to another***" is a Hebrew idiom being used for marriage, the ritual of which is always consummated by having sex. In this way, the two become one flesh.

> *Therefore shall a man leave his father and his mother, and shall **cleave** unto his wife: and **they shall be one flesh**.* (Genesis 2:24)

> *And said, For this cause shall a man leave father and mother, and shall **cleave** to his wife: and **they twain shall be one flesh**?* (Matthew 19:5)

> *What? know ye not that **he which is joined to an harlot is one body? for two, saith he, shall be one flesh**.* (1 Corinthians 6:16)

By saying they "*shall **not** cleave one to another*," Daniel is clearly stating that although seed is being mingled, it is not happening via copulation. Thus, it must be happening another way. As we see in any number of online video interviews with Dr. David Jacobs,[25] that is exactly what the "abduction testimonies" reveal: hybrid offspring are being produced via scientific experimentation, not sexual intercourse with angels.

Even secular theorists and the ancient Sumerian texts point to so-called "ancient aliens" or "gods" genetically *manipulating* DNA in order to produce modern humans:

> *Create primeval man, that he may bear the yoke!*
>
> * * *
>
> *Nintu shall mix clay with his hands and his blood. Then a god and a man will be mixed together in clay. Let us hear the drumbeat forever after. Let a ghost come into existence from the god's flesh, let her proclaim it as his living sign, and let the ghost exist so as not to forget (the slain god).*
>
> *They answered 'Yes!' in the assembly, the great Anunnaki who assign the fates.*
>
> *On the first, seventh, and fifteenth of the month he made a purification by washing. Ilawela who had intelligence, they slaughtered in their assembly. Nintu mixed clay*

25. See: http://www.babylonrisingbooks.com/book2/videosC101.html

> *with his flesh and blood.*[26] *They heard the drumbeat forever after.*
>
> *A ghost came into existence from the god's flesh. And she (Nintu) proclaimed it as his living sign. The ghost existed so as not to forget (the slain god). After she had mixed that clay, she called up the Anunnaki, the great gods. The Igigi, the great gods, spat spittle upon the clay. Mami made her voice heard and spoke to the great gods, 'I have carried out perfectly the work you ordered of me. You have slaughtered a god together with his intelligence. I have relieved you of your hard work, I have imposed your load on man. You have bestowed noise on mankind. I have undone the fetter and granted freedom.'*
>
> —Atrahasis I[27]

How interesting that this is essentially the way the movie *Prometheus* actually begins. [Spoiler Alert!] A spaceship lands on early earth and a god sacrifices himself. His blood and DNA then falls into a primitive ocean and the implication is that this is how mankind "evolved" into being. The premise of course is that ancient aliens are our true parents and that evolution got a kick-start via pan-spermia; life came about as a result of "intelligent design" but the intelligence was not God (as in YHVH) but rather the gods of Sumerian mythology.[28]

The ancient Sumerian texts refer to the Anunnaki as "gods" who were themselves the product of other higher gods before them—a concept that further supports the idea that they are not the fallen angels, but rather the offspring thereof. Even the word itself seems to strongly indicate what type of being they are: Anunnaki means something akin to "those of royal blood"[29] or "princely

26. Is this the process that is being referred to in Daniel 2:43?
27. ***Myths From Mesopotamia: Creation, The Flood, Gilgamesh, and Others*** by Stephanie Dalley (© 2008 Oxford Word's Classics) pages 15 & 16
28. See: http://www.babylonrisingbooks.com/book2/videosC102.html
29. See: ***A Dictionary of Ancient Near Eastern Mythology*** by Gwendolyn Leick (NY: Routledge, © 1998), page 7

offspring."[30] I find no evidence in Scripture that supports the notion that angels are born, nor that they have blood or can be killed as *Ilawela* apparently was when he was slaughtered in order to create men using his DNA.

According to the ancient texts, these Anunnaki were said to have *genetically engineered* life here on earth. Here again, we are talking about lab experiments and not sex with fallen angels. Thus, all evidence suggests that they were in fact *Nephilim* who were highly advanced scientists engaging in the science of genetically engineering humanoid offspring.

Yes, there certainly are ancient texts (but not the Bible) that also mention gods mating with women, but how are we to define these gods? In the Bible, gods were everything from wood and stone, to the sun, moon and stars, and just about anything in between. Just because we see the word "god" it doesn't necessarily mean a being from Heaven. Based on Genesis 6:4, I believe these so-called "gods," who were mating with women in the Greek myths for example, were themselves Nephilim, and not the fallen angels. They were the "mighty **men**" or "heroes of old" who became "great **men** of renown."

Take Zeus for instance. To the ancient Greeks, he was regarded as the king of the gods. His sexual exploits were legendary. He mated both with goddesses as well as human women. Some try to use this as proof for angel incursions. After all, here is a "god" who descends from the sky and mates with humans. The problem is, the Bible makes no mention of female angels and boldly proclaims that angels do not participate in marriages in heaven.[31] So, if Zeus was supposedly an angel married to other angels (goddesses), how can one reconcile that story with the truth of Scripture? To further complicate matters, the Greek myths also talk about Zeus' *birth*. There are no Biblical references for angels being born. They appear

30. See: ***Gods, Demons and Symbols of Ancient Mesopotamia: An Illustrated Dictionary*** by Jeremy Black and Anthony Green (© 1992 University of Texas Press), page 34.
31. See Matthew 22:30

to have been created mature and all male. Apart from appearing to arrive from the heavens, no Biblical definition of an angel fits Zeus.

Zeus was the offspring of the Titans. Where did the Titans end up? Tartarus. Coincidentally, that's the same place both the Bible, 1 Enoch and Jubilees mention as being the prison of the Watchers and at least 90% of their first generation Nephilim offspring's spirits.[32] As we've already learned, the Titans were another name for the early generation Nephilim. Therefore, Zeus can not be an angel. Rather he is at best a second or third generation Nephilim offspring.

Both 1 Enoch and the writings of Peter and Jude indicate that there was only one incursion and that the angels who participated in it were severely judged and bound in "everlasting chains of darkness" in a terrible place known as Tartarus.

Therefore, I suggest the Nephilim must have returned another way.

Now that we've eliminated multiple incursions as a possibility for the return of the Nephilim in biblical times, let's go back to Genesis 6, reexamine it and see where the clues lead.

32. See: Jubilees 10:5-10

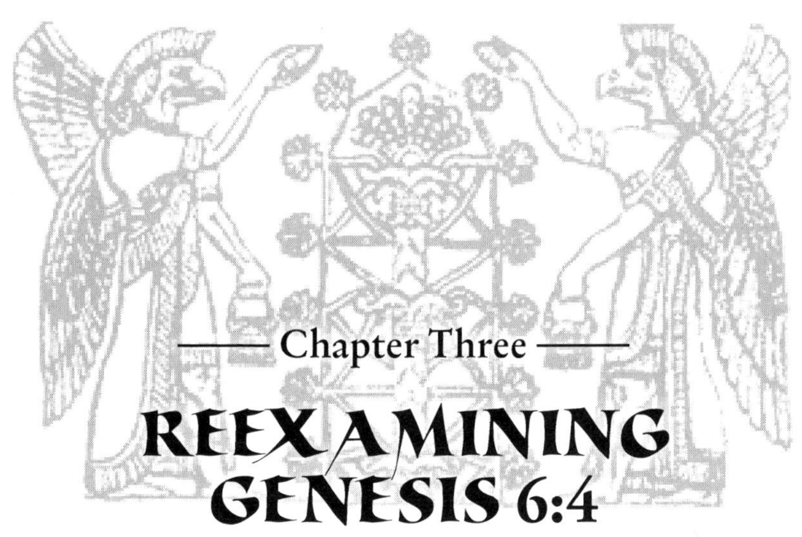

— Chapter Three —

REEXAMINING GENESIS 6:4

"Sometimes we stare so long at a door that is closing that we see too late the one that is open."

— Alexander Graham Bell

I chose the above quote because I think that for too long, scholars have looked at Genesis 6:4 in only one way and as such they are (in my opinion) missing the bigger picture — especially when it comes to identifying the real connection of the days of Noah with those of our day. Noah's day was not just about violence and blatant sin. That has existed ever since Cain killed Abel. Noah's day did not involve the act of angels mating with humans either. That happened way back in the early days of Jared and was put to a stop within 500 years of the first (and I believe only) "incursion" of fallen angels. So, what was really going on in the days after the first generation Nephilim were completely destroyed? What specifically differentiates the days of Noah from those of Jared? Why did Jesus tie the Last Days to the days in which Noah lived (all 950 years worth)? I believe the answer lies in both the context as well as the sub-text of Genesis 6:4. If I may encourage you to take your eyes off the closing door of an old doctrine, I will try to escort you through

an open door that I believe will reveal much truth concerning the Last Days and how they relate to Genesis 6:4.

First and foremost, I must emphasize once again that I do not believe it is proper to base any doctrine, belief or theory on only one Scripture in the Bible, and especially not on only one word in such a reference. As we saw in the previous chapter, the Hebrew word in question is *asher* and the Scripture I am referring to is of course, Genesis 6:4.

Many who subscribe to the Multiple Incursions Theory believe that the word *asher*, which was translated into English as "when," means to infer the concept of a perpetual *whenever*, thus implying that more incursions happened in the post-Flood time period further assumed by the phrase "and also after that" in this same passage. Let's reexamine this controversial text in order to see if these premises are justified and true.

THE NEPHILIM

> *The **Nephilim** were on the earth in those days, and also afterward, when the sons of God came in to the daughters of men, and they bore children to them. Those were the mighty men who were of old, men of renown.*
> (Genesis 6:4 NASB)

I chose to use the NASB here because it preserves the original word, *Nephilim* instead of translating it as *giant* like the KJV does. Notice it says that these Nephilim were on the earth as a result of the "sons of God" coming in to the daughters of men. The very structure of this sentence leads us to believe there is a difference between the sons of God (in this case, the "Watcher" class of fallen angels)[1] and their offspring, called the Nephilim. Thus, contrary to what some believe, I do not subscribe to the idea that the Nephilim *are*

1. Both ***Jubilees 4:15*** and the ***1 Enoch 10:9*** refer to these fallen angel parents as, "the Watchers"

the fallen angels, but rather that they are the offspring thereof. In addition to the accepted canon of Scripture, both 1 Enoch and the book of Jubilees seem to bear this out as well:

> *And all of them [the Watchers] together went and took wives for themselves, each choosing one for himself, and they began to go in to them and to defile themselves with sex with them. And the angels taught them charms and spells, and the cutting of roots, and made them acquainted with plants. And the women became pregnant, and they bare great giants, whose height was three thousand ells:*[2]
> (1 Enoch 7:1-3 Ethiopic version)

According to the footnotes in Dr. A. Nyland's edition of 1 Enoch, the author states:

> *Here the Greek texts differ from the Ethiopic. One Greek manuscript adds to this section, "And the women bore to the Watchers three races:* ***first, the great giants who brought forth the Nephilim, and the Nephilim brought forth the Elioud****. And they existed and their power and greatness increased."* [emphasis mine]
>
> — Dr. A. Nyland[3]

The book of Jubilees makes a similar set of comparisons:

> *For owing to these three things came the flood upon the earth, namely, owing to the fornication wherein the Watchers against the law of their ordinances went a whoring after the daughters of men, and took themselves wives of all which they chose: and they made the beginning of uncleanness.* ***And they begat sons the Nâphîdîm****, and they were all unlike, and they devoured one another:* ***and the Giants slew the Nâphîl, and the Nâphîl***

2. Or 300 cubits
3. ***Complete Books of Enoch***, by Dr. A. Nyland, footnote #14, page 242

> ***slew the Eljô, and the Eljô mankind****, and one man another. And every one sold himself to work iniquity and to shed much blood, and the earth was filled with iniquity.* (Jubilees 7:21-23)

Here in both the 1 Enoch passge as well as the Jubilees passage we see several different *types* of giants. I believe the first generation giants were the massively huge, 450 footers (3,000 ells, or 300 cubits tall) — the ones the Greeks called, the Titans. According to the Greek myths, the Titans were overthrown by the Olympians and imprisoned in Tartarus. Like many other cultures before them, the Greeks clearly had several "classes" of gods, which may be reflected in the Jubilees differentiation of giants, Nâphîdîm (a derivative spelling of Nephilim) and the Eljô. Notice also what Josephus had to say:

> *For* ***many angels of God accompanied with women, and begot sons*** *that proved unjust, and despisers of all that was good, on account of the confidence they had in their own strength; for the tradition is, that these men did what resembled the acts of those* ***whom the Grecians call giants*** [Titans].
>
> — Flavius Josephus[4]

Many scholars say that the Titans were the Nephilim and that the Nephilim were the fallen angels. Take G.H. Pember for instance:

> *Through a misapprehension of the Septuagint, which we will presently explain, the English version renders Nephilim as "giants." But the form of he Hebrew word indicates as verbal adjective or noun, of passive or neuter signification, from Naphal, to fall: hence it must mean "the fallen ones," that is, probably the fallen angels. Afterwards, however, the terms seems to have been transferred to their offspring,*

4 . From ***Antiquities of the Jews 1.3.1***

as we may gather from the only other passage in which it occurs. In the evil report which the ten spies give of the land of Canaan, we find them saying: "All the people which we saw in it were men of great stature. And there we saw the Nephilim, the sons of Anak, descended from the Nephilim: and we seemed to ourselves as grasshoppers, and so we did to them. (Numb. xxiii. 32,33).

It was doubtless the mention of the great stature of these men, together with the Septuagint rendering of 'gigantes' that suggested our translation "giants." The root of the Greek 'gigas' have, however, no reference to great stature, but point to something very different. The word is merely another form of 'geegenees': it signifies "earth-born" and was used of the Titans, or sons of Heaven and Earth—Coelus and Terra—because, though superior to the human race, they were, nevertheless, of partly terrestrial origin. The meaning of "giants" in our sense of the term, is altogether secondary, and arose from the fact that these beings of mixed birth were said to have displayed a monstrous growth and strength of body. It will, therefore, be apparent that the rendering of the Septuagint correctly expresses the idea which was in the mind of the translator, since he appears to have taken 'Nephilim' in each case to signify the offspring of the sons of God and the daughters of men. We however, as we have explained above, prefer understanding the word primarily of the fallen angels themselves.

—G.H. Pember[5]

I'm perplexed by Pember's conclusions because even the word *Titan* itself and the myths associated with them indicate that they were indeed "earth-born" entities. Ancient literature and modern scholars often link the Titans with the Nephilim, but remember,

5 . ***Earth's Earliest Ages*** by G.H. Pember (© 1975 Kregel Publishing),pages.132,133

we just established that angels are not earth-born. In fact, there is no indication that they are even born at all! According to Scripture, it would appear that they were created mature just as Adam was. Further complicating the issue for people who believe as Pember did, according to the Greek myths, there were both male and female Titans who mated to produce other Titans and the Olympians. Yet, we find no mention of female angels in Scripture and we know that Jesus said angels in heaven do not marry. So even if there were female angels, if they can't marry what are we talking about here with regard to all that we know concerning the Titans of mythology? Fornication in Heaven? God forbid. No. While the Titans may be synonymous with the first-generation Nephilim, they cannot be synonymous with the fallen angels.

It must also be noted that, as Pember pointed out, the word Nephilim comes from the Hebrew word, *nephal.* But what he neglects to say is that this word has a *variety* of meanings beyond simply "the fallen." It's usage in the NASB includes:

> **abandon** (1), allot (1), allotted (2), anyone falls (1), apportioned (2), attacked (2), **born** (1), bring down (1), burst (1), came down (1), cast (16), **cast down** (5), casts (1), collapse (1), come (3), dash down (1), defect (1), **defected** (3), deserted (3), deserters (3), did (1), dismounted (1), divide by lot (2), divide it by lot (1), downfall (1), dropped (1), fail (1), fail* (1), failed (4), fall (130), fall down (4), **fallen** (55), fallen away (1), fallen down (4), falling (3), falling down (2), falls (22), falls away (1), fell (98), fell down (8), felled (1), felling (1), give birth (1), go over (1), going over (2), gone over (3), **inferior** (2), **killed** (1), knocks (1), lay (1), lay down (1), lay flat (1), lie down (1), look (1), lost (2), lying (5), making (1), **perish** (1), present (1), presenting (3), prostrating (1), remains (1), settled (1), surely fall (1), throw (2), topple (1), turns (1), void (1), **waste away** (3).

Clearly the word, "*fallen*" applies, but so also does "*born*" and "*abandon*" — both of which would certainly be descriptive of the offspring of the Watchers, who grew up essentially as fatherless orphans. These "*fallen*" were also "*killed*" and "*perished*" and "*wasted away*" as ones "*cast down*" by God for being the "*inferior,*" "*defected*" abominations that were never meant to exist in the first place. See how all of those words can apply to the Nephilim? It is therefore my conclusion that we are not talking about fallen angels, but rather their offspring.

1 Enoch states that the first generation angel-human-hybrid Nephilim were destroyed within 500 years of their birth:

> *And to Gabriel said the Lord: 'Proceed against the bastards and the reprobates, and against the children of fornication: and destroy [the children of fornication and] the children of the Watchers from amongst men [and cause them to go forth]:* ***send them one against the other that they may destroy each other in battle****: for length of days shall they not have. And no request that they (the Watchers) make of thee shall be granted unto their fathers on their behalf; for* ***they hope to live an eternal life, and that each one of them will live five hundred years****.*
>
> (1 Enoch 10:9,10)

Presumably, if the Titan Nephilim had five hundred years to fight, they also had five hundred years to procreate as their parents did. This would have produced second, third, fourth... generation hybrids of beings mixed with both their own seed as well as the seed of men. This, according to the ancient texts, created a variety of giants by different names, sizes and characteristics as stated above in Jubilees and in the Greek version of 1 Enoch. These all existed in the pre-Flood world.

In the Sumerian texts, I believe the second generation Nephilim are the *Anunnaki* (I say second generation because 1 Enoch disqualifies the first generation by virtue of the fact that they killed each other off within 500 years) and the later generations were known as the *Igigi*. This will become more important to understand as we begin to bring this whole story into our present day. Suffice it to say, I truly believe that there is a reason why the History Channel's *Ancient Aliens* series and so many other shows and books are promoting the whole concept of the Anunnaki and their possible return in the near future. I don't know what (if anything) is going to happen on December 21, 2012, but with all of the hype about it in nearly every form of media — from a strategic, military perspective — I would have to say that it would be the perfect time for the enemy to launch a *Coming Great Deception* involving the return of the "gods." For now, all we can do is wait and see.

Figure 8

IN THOSE DAYS AND ALSO AFTERWARD

> *There were giants in the earth* ***in those days; and also after that****, when the sons of God came in unto the daughters of men, and they bare children to them, the same became mighty men which were of old, men of renown.* (Genesis 6:4)

The Nephilim giants were the offspring of the angels and according to Genesis 6:4 they were on the earth *"in those days,"* which naturally begs the question, "Which days?" I'm of the opinion that Moses is writing a chronological tale, meaning that he is following a linear progression of events. The entire Torah is written that way. The author is telling us a story from Creation until the conquest of Canaan after 40 years of wandering in the desert following the Exodus. There is nothing in Mose's style of writing that would indicate that he is in the habit of writing a non-linear story. Genesis 6:4 is no exception. The entire chapter is in a *pre*-Flood context. Thus, the "those days" referred to in verse 4 are related to the events spoken about in verses 1-2.

> *And it came to pass, when men began to multiply on the face of the earth, and daughters were born unto them, That the sons of God saw the daughters of men that they were fair; and they took them wives of all which they chose.* (Genesis 6:1,2)

Comparing Genesis 6:1,2 with the synchronized, biblically endorsed, extra-biblical texts, we may easily understand *"those days"* to be a reference to the days of Jared when the 200 Watchers (sons of God) came down and mated with the daughters of men. Moses then makes the statement that they were also around, *"after that."* This is where many scholars think he is making a non-linear statement in an otherwise completely linear context. Unfortunately, the Hebrew word used for "after" betrays that belief. The word is *achar* (Strong's # 310). It simply means *"afterward, after, following, subsequent..."* and is therefore a term essentially used for the next thing that happened. It is not a reference to something far off in the future. Moses was writing about the days of Noah that preceded the Flood, which came after the days of Jared, Noah's great, great grandfather. For a better sense of context, please observe the timeline chart once again depicted in **Figure 9**.

If my calculations are correct, we see that *The Genesis Six Experiment* took place in roughly 3550 BC. Enoch 10:10 says the first generation Nephilim were completely destroyed within 500 years, which brings us up to roughly 3050 to 3000 BC. That is the *"those days"* spoken about in Genesis 6:1-4. The *"and also after that"* is therefore referring to the time period of roughly 3000 BC to 2350 BC. It covers a duration of roughly 650 to 700 years leading up to the Flood, during which there was a return of the Nephilim. It is not talking about the

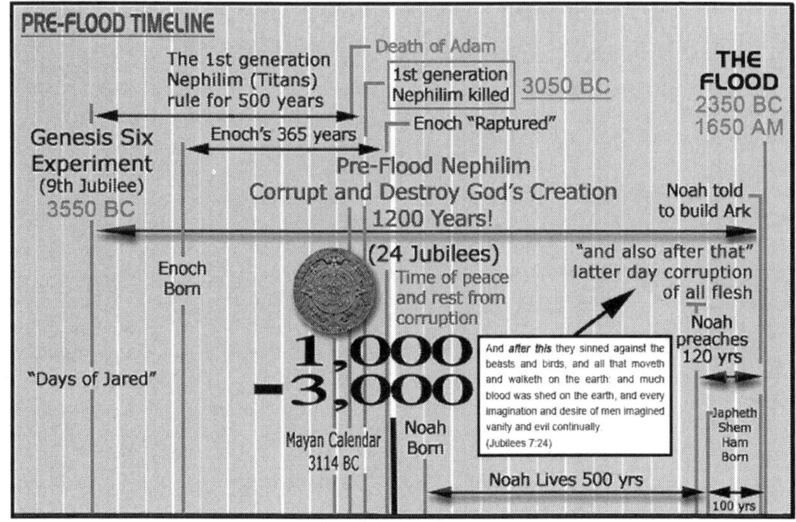

Figure 9

time period of (or just prior to) the time of Moses and the conquest of Canaan, which was about 1400 years later! The Hebrew word *achar* does not in any way support that notion.

In fact, while in Branson, MO at the *Prophecy Summit 2012,* I shared a stage with L.A. Marzulli and Doug Hamp (who like many others both believe in the Multiple Incursions Theory). We were being interviewed by Derek Gilbert in front of a live audience. In the second half of the show (after L.A. left), Doug and I had a friendly, moderated debate facilitated by Derek on the issue of the return of the Nephilim. When it came to the discussion of Genesis 6:4, Doug had a Bible translation that actually emphasized the word "after" as meaning *immediately* after that. He was using, the *International Standard Version* of the Bible, which he endorsed as being a really good and accurate translation, but (with all due respect to him), I'd say it really did not work too well in favor of his argument.[6]

6. You can listen to the debate in Derek Gilbert's View From The Bunker radio archives under the title: ***VFTB Live at the Prophecy Summit: The Nephilim*** at http://vftb.net/?p=4547 (the specific discussion referred to here begins at 48 min.)

> *The Nephilim were on the earth at that time (and also* ***immediately*** *afterward), when those divine beings were having sexual relations with those human women, who gave birth to children for them. These children became the heroes and legendary figures of ancient times.*
> (Genesis 6:4 ISV)

Using this translation, it was quite easy for me to point out that we aren't talking about a time period that was over a thousand years later. No, the *"after that"* of Genesis 6:4 is a reference to something that occurred *shortly* after the events of Genesis 6:1-3 and entirely in a pre-Flood context. The synchronized, biblically endorsed, extra-biblical texts become quite useful at this point in helping us to understand what is really being said here. Moreover, those texts lead us into an understanding that there was actually a return of the Nephilim *before* the Flood. We'll explore that idea a lot more in Chapter Five.

WHEN OR BECAUSE?

> *There were giants in the earth in those days; and also after that,* ***when*** *the sons of God came in unto the daughters of men, and they bare children to them, the same became mighty men which were of old, men of renown.*
> (Genesis 6:4)

Moving forward in Genesis 6:4, we come to the seemingly insignificant word "when," which as we've already learned is translated from the Hebrew word *asher* (Strong's # 834).

Since I've already dealt with this word in the previous chapter, I won't spend much more time on it here. Suffice it to say, I believe "because" would be a better translation here than "when." If properly understood as "because," we may think of Genesis 6:4 as referring to a first cause issue, rather than a repeat offense issue. I believe this is not only justified by the Hebrew word itself, but also by the context of the events taking place in that time period according to Genesis as well as the books of 1 Enoch, Jasher and Jubilees.

THE SONS OF GOD
(OFFERING A COUNTERFEIT SALVATION)

> *There were giants in the earth in those days; and also after that, when **the sons of God** came in unto the daughters of men, and they bare children to them, the same became mighty men which were of old, men of renown.*
> (Genesis 6:4)

The term "sons of God" comes from the Hebrew phrase *be·nei ha·'e·lo·him* which is the exact same phrase used in the book of Job as a reference to angels:

> *Now there was a day when the **sons of God** came to present themselves before the LORD, and Satan also came among them.* (Job 1:6)

> *Again there was a day when the **sons of God** came to present themselves before the LORD, and Satan came also among them to present himself before the LORD.*
> (Job 2:1)

As you can see, the Bible itself tells us how we should interpret "sons of God." They are angels. This is attested to in the Scriptures as well as in the ancient extra-biblical texts.[7] Even Josephus acknowledges this truth. But just what exactly were these fallen angels really doing in Genesis 6:1-4? We are told they lusted after the daughters of men because they found them to be attractive, but was that the only reason? Would they really risk so great a punishment simply due to lust?

---

7 . See also: ***Babylon Rising: And The First Shall Be Last*** by Rob Skiba, (© 2012 King's Gate Media, LLC, Revised Edition), Chapter One, *The Genesis Six Experiment* page 26.

Going back a few centuries to the time of Adam and Eve, we see that one of the three promises the Serpent in the Garden made was that they could become divine:

> *And the serpent said unto the woman,* ***Ye shall not surely die*** [promise of immortality]*: For God doth know that in the day ye eat thereof, then* ***your eyes shall be opened*** [promise of "illumination" - greater understanding], *and* ***ye shall be as gods*** [promise of divinity], *knowing good and evil.* (Genesis 3:4,5)

Lucifer truly is the "Father of Lies." Adam and Eve were already immortal. Death did not come until after they ate of the Forbidden Fruit. Their eyes were already open. They walked with God and saw Him as He is, in all His glory. If they lacked any understanding, all they had to do was ask YHVH for it in one of their regular times of conversation. Also, they already were "as God" for we know that Adam was made in His image and likeness. So, in reality the Serpent promised them what they already had and thus stole from them those very things when they accepted his offer!

Here we find that in addition to corrupting the seed of God's previously approved, "very good" creation, another motive of the fallen "sons of God" appears to have been to offer a *counterfeit* of what *the* Son of God offers to us.

In addition to being an attempt at wiping out the seed that would one day crush the Devil's head,[8] I believe the fallen angels were also offering a false salvation. When Adam and Eve ate the fruit, they fell from a previously perfect existence into a fallen state. Just like the Hegelian dialectic, it would appear that the Devil had his own "Luciferian dialectic" in which he created a problem, which caused a reaction to which he then offered a solution. When fallen humans mated with fallen angels, the result was a counterfeit "son of god," called the Nephilim. This is the direct antithesis of what Yeshua did for us:

8. See Genesis 3:15

> *But as many as received Him,* ***to them gave He power to become the sons of God****, even to them that believe on His name:* (John 1:12)

> *For* ***you are all sons of God*** *through faith in Christ Jesus.* (Galations 3:26)

> *Jesus answered and said to them, "The sons of this age marry and are given in marriage. But those who are counted worthy to attain that age, and the resurrection from the dead, neither marry nor are given in marriage; nor can they die anymore, for* ***they are equal to the angels and are sons of God****, being sons of the resurrection."* (Luke 20:34-36)

Through Yeshua (Jesus) — who is the only begotten Son of God — we are given the power to become *sons of God*. That is the truth the Devil and his Fallen Ones apparently hoped to counterfeit.

Note in the Luke passage that our Lord says we become "*equal to the angels and are sons of God.*" He is saying that the angels are the sons of God and that we can become like them — if we do it His way. When we except Yeshua as our Savior, we become "born again" of incorruptible (or immortal) seed — which in this case, is *His* seed:

> *Being born again,* ***not of corruptible seed, but of incorruptible****, by the word of God, which liveth and abideth for ever.* (1 Peter 1:23)

The alternative way of doing it produced Nephilim (fallen ones of fallen seed) who became the "mighty men" of renown.

CAME IN UNTO THE DAUGHTERS OF MEN

> *There were giants in the earth in those days; and also after that, when the sons of God* ***came in unto the daughters of men****, and they bare children to them, the same became mighty men which were of old, men of renown.*
> (Genesis 6:4)

I almost didn't bother to include a breakdown of this phrase because I thought it was pretty obvious what was taking place there. But after looking at the Hebrew words used, and the order in which they are given, I'm not so sure now. The word translated as *"came in"* is *yabo'u* in Hebrew. Strong's # 935 defines its root *bo* as:

> *abide, apply, attain, be, befall, besiege, bring forth, in,*
>
> *A primitive root; to go or come (in a wide variety of applications) -- abide, apply, attain, X be, befall, + besiege, bring (forth, in, into, to pass), call, carry, X certainly, (cause, let, thing for) to come (against, in, out, upon, to pass), depart, X doubtless again, + eat, + employ, (cause to) enter (in, into, -tering, -trance, -try), be fallen, fetch, + follow, get, give, go (down, in, to war), grant, + have, X indeed, (in-)vade, lead, lift (up), mention, pull in, put, resort, run (down), send, set, X (well) stricken (in age), X surely, take (in), way.*

While this is a word used to describe "going into" a woman in a sexual sense (see Genesis 30:4 for example), it also could mean entering into in another sense as well (see Genesis 7:7 for example). The Hebrew word *el* (Strong's # 413) is a preposition meaning "to" which simply supports the word *yabo'u* (came in) in Genesis 6:4. So, we see that these fallen angel Watchers definitely entered women in order to produce offspring. But author, researcher and lecturer Dr. Thomas Horn has an interesting take on the matter that doesn't necessarily involve sexual intercourse.

> *According to Enoch, two hundred of these powerful angels departed "high heaven" and used human DNA to extend their progeny into humankind's place of existence. The Interlinear Hebrew Bible offers an interesting interpretation of Genesis 6:2 in this regard. Where the King James Bible says, "The sons of God saw the daughters of men that they [were] fair" (brackets in original), the IHB interprets this as, "The benei Elohim saw the daughters of Adam, that they were fit extensions." The term "fit extensions" seems applicable when the whole of the ancient record is understood to mean that the Watchers wanted to leave their proper sphere of existence in order to enter Earth's three-dimensional reality. They viewed women — or at least their genetic material — as part of the formula for accomplishing this task.*
>
> — Dr. Thomas Horn[9]

Dr. Horn thus appears to believe that even the first incursion did not involve sex, but rather some sort of manipulation of genetic materials, involving women who were viewed as "fit extensions" through which the fallen angels could incarnate themselves. He later goes on to quote a *Mysterious World* article by Douglas Elwell, who apparently holds to a similar view. His quote is abbreviated, so I will give an extended version of what Elwell wrote here:

> *The Nephilim were the gigantic offspring that resulted from the union of the fallen angels and "the daughters of men", that grew to be of a tremendous stature and possessed of a titanic arrogance and will-to-power that rivaled that of their Satanic fathers. As Stephen Quayle explains in his seminal work, Genesis 6 Giants,*
>
> > *The Nephilim that were produced by the angel/ mankind marriage were much different from either of their parents. This, too, went against God's plan*

9. Excerpt from ***Pandemonium's Engine*** (© 2011 Defender Publishing), pages 39,40

> *for the Earth in which each animal and human being was to reproduce "after its own kind". [Genesis 1:24] This is perhaps the best demonstration that the parents of these creatures were not simply descendants of Cain and Seth. Had they been, they would have produced human offspring, rather than the Nephilim. The Nephilim were more than simply large beings or giants in the way giants are normally thought of today. When the Greek Septuagint was created, the Hebrew word Nephilim was translated into Greek as gegenes. This is the same word used in Greek mythology for the "Titans", creatures created through the interbreeding of the Greek gods and human beings. The English words "genes" and "genetics" are built around the same root word as gegenes; genea meaning "breed" or "kind". Thus, the choice of this word again suggests a genetic component to the creation of these giants.*[10]

Though Quayle appears to promote the idea that the Nephilim were actually formed by combining the DNA of the fallen angels and human women, since angels are spirit and thus do not have DNA, we hold to the thesis that the Nephilim were genetically manufactured beings created from the genetic material of various pre-existing animal species. Thus, to fit them into our scientific paradigm, we should officially term the Nephilim as a subclass of homo artificialis: homo artificialis nephili.

Thus, the fallen angels did not personally interbreed with the daughters of men, but used their godlike intellect to delve into the secrets of YHWH's Creation and manipulate it to their own purposes. And the key to creating or recreating man, as we have (re)discovered in the twentieth century, is the human genome — DNA.

10. Quoted from Stephen Quayle, ***Genesis 6 Giants*** (© 2002 End Time Thunder Publishers, Bozeman, MT), page 128.

> *Quayle points out that the Greek antecedent of the word "giants" is the word gegenes, from which was derived the Greek word gigantes (Genesis 6:4, LXX), from which we in turn derive the English word "giant". Moreover, gegenes, besides being the root of the word "giant", is also the root of the words "genes", "genetics", "geneology", and so forth. Thus, the concept of genetic manipulation was "spliced in" to the ancient conception of giants.*
>
> — Douglas Elwell[11]

As you will see later in this book, my thesis is a bit of "hybrid" of what these scholars have described. I do believe that there is a spiritual component to DNA, thus I have no problem believing that angel seed can mix with a human female's egg. After all, we have the perfect example of such a thing revealed in the incarnation of Christ:

> *Now the birth of Jesus Christ was on this wise: When as his mother Mary was espoused to Joseph, before they came together, **she was found with child of the Holy Ghost**.* (Matthew 1:18)

Matthew's Gospel tells us that Mary became pregnant by the Holy Ghost (which is a spirit). Luke's Gospel gets a little bit more specific:

> *Then said Mary unto the angel, How shall this be, seeing I know not a man?*
>
> *And the angel answered and said unto her, **The Holy Ghost shall come upon thee, and the power of the Highest shall overshadow thee:** therefore also that holy thing which shall be born of thee shall be called the Son of God.* (Luke 1:34,35)

11. See Doug Elwell's entire article here: http://www.mysteriousworld.com/Journal/2003/Spring/Giants/

In an interview I did with Douglas Hamp regarding his book, *Corrupting the Image*, he made a statement concerning DNA that brought everything into focus for me. He said, *"DNA is information."*[12] If DNA is indeed simply a storage system for information, then it is not hard to imagine all sorts of beings having such a mechanism within them — even those in the so-called "spirit realm." Clearly the Holy Spirit delivered an information package in the form of a seed that impregnated Mary with our Savior. Is it therefore such a stretch to imagine the same thing being possible with other "spirits" too?

Oddly enough, in an episode of the ABC Family mini series called *Fallen*, the character who played the recently released Fallen Angel Azazel saw a church sign that said something about Jesus. When he asked the person he was with who this Jesus was, the person told him that He was the son of God. Azazel then laughed to himself and said, *"Do as I say not as I do, huh?"* thus revealing his frustration over having been so severely punished for doing the very thing God apparently later did Himself.

I do believe that the phrase *"came in unto the daughters of men"* in Genesis 6:4 could be seen as a reference to sexual intercourse during the first incursion. This appears to be strongly supported by the synchronized, biblically endorsed, extra-biblical texts, by Josephus and other ancient sources as well. However, looking at the sentence structure of Genesis 6:4, it appears to be referring to the *"after that"* pre-Flood scenario. If so, I'd be more inclined toward Tom Horn's thesis, which is actually nearly identical to a theory I developed on my own, before I ever read any of his materials on the subject. I'll explain more about that in the following chapters.

THE SAME BECAME MIGHTY MEN

> *There were giants in the earth in those days; and also after that, when the sons of God came in unto the daughters of*

12. http://www.blogtalkradio.com/revolutionaryradio/2012/03/29/nephilim-corrupting-the-image

> *men, and they bare children to them,* ***the same became mighty men*** *which were of old, men of renown.* (Genesis 6:4)

The phrase "mighty men" in the above passage comes from the Hebrew word, *gibbor*. In *The Man of Many Names* chapter of my book, *Babylon Rising: And The First Shall Be Last*[13] I stated that this word (like so many other Hebrew words) requires context whenever it is to be interpreted—especially if interpreting it as "giant." The word *gibbor* (Strong's # 1368) means:

> *champion, chief, excel, giant, man, mighty man, one, strong man,*

Whether we're talking about great men of valor like David's "mighty men" or a giant, the word certainly applies either way. Great men of valor are mighty just as much as a giant is. Therefore, we need to look at the context in order to determine whether we are talking about a brave man or a giant man. In this case, I believe the text clearly lends itself to the interpretation of "giant"—especially when you take the extra-biblical texts into consideration. The Septuagint version of Genesis 6:4 agrees:

> *Now the giants* [**Nephilim**] *were upon the earth in those days; and after that when the sons of God were wont to go in to the daughters of men, they bore children to them, those were the giants* [**gibborim**] *of old, the men of renown.* (Genesis:6:4 LXX)

The Hebrew word, *raphaim* is the much more common term for "giant" in the Old Testament Scriptures, but in addition to Genesis 6:4, there are at least three other times where the word *gibbor* seems to be used in the same way:

---

13. ***Babylon Rising: And The First Shall Be Last*** by Rob Skiba (© 2012 King's Gate Media, LLC, Revised Edition), Chapter Two, *The Man of Many Names* pg. 26

> *And Chus begot Nebrod:* ***he began to be a giant*** *upon the earth. He was a giant hunter before the Lord God; therefore they say, As Nebrod* ***the giant hunter*** *before the Lord.* (Genesis 10:8,9 LXX)

> *He breaketh me with breach upon breach, he runneth upon me like a* ***giant****.* (Job 16:14)

> *Therefore David ran and stood upon the Philistine* [Goliath] *and took his sword and drew it out of the sheath thereof and slew him and cut off his head therewith And when the Philistines saw their* ***champion*** *was dead they fled.* (1 Samuel 17:51)

We all know who and what Goliath was. In the 1 Samuel passage, we see the word translated as "champion" and it comes as no surprise that in context, the word *gibbor* is used in reference to a giant.

As the oldest book in the Bible, I do find the Job passage rather interesting. The *Amplified Bible* places that Scripture in the context of attacks unleashed on Job by Satan. Thus, I find the association of a "giant" there to be quite enlightening as well.

The situation with Nimrod is even more fascinating. It appears that through some sort of (sexual?) defilement Nimrod began to become a *gibbor*. There are at least three ways to look at this:

1. Nimrod simply became a strong and powerful man (though other cultures say he was much more than that).
2. Nimrod began to become a giant himself (through some sort of defilement).
3. Nimrod began to become a giant hunter (as in a hunter of giants).

I suspect all three of the above possibilities concerning Nimrod are probably true. The Septuagint provides some extremely interesting insights concerning the way the (Hebrew) translators treated the same Hebrew word *gibborim* in Genesis 6:4, Genesis 10:8,9 and in 2 Samuel 10:7 (concerning David's "mighty men").

> *When David heard of it, he sent Joab and all the army, the* ***mighty men****.* (2 Samuel 10:7)

In both of the Genesis examples, the Septuagint's translators chose to translate the Hebrew *gibborim* into the Greek *gigas* or *gigantes* (from which we get words like, "gigantic"), which was translated in both cases into "giant" in English. However, in the 2 Samuel passage, the Greek is *tous dynatous.* Clearly, they were demonstrating that they knew and understood the reality of who was a giant and who was just a strong, valiant man.

It's all in the context. The Septuagint uses *gigantes* in Genesis 6:4 for the Hebrew *Nephilim*, which helps you understand the context of the *hoi gigantes* (Hebrew: *gibborim* = English: *giant*) of the latter half of that verse. When the translators chose to use the same derivative word *gigas* for Nimrod, they were clearly stating that he had indeed become a giant. The Septuagint then makes a distinct contrast between that case (as well as the one in Genesis 6:4) and the use of the words *tous dynatous* in 2 Samuel 10:7 or the *ton dynaton,* which is also translated as "mighty men" in 2 Samuel 23:8 and elsewhere. In short, they obviously knew the difference.

> *These be the names of the* ***mighty men*** *whom David had: The Tachmonite that sat in the seat, chief among the captains; the same was Adino the Eznite: he lift up his spear against eight hundred, whom he slew at one time.*
>
> (2 Samuel 23:8)

Nimrod was the inspiration for many mythological characters throughout ancient cultures. He was a mighty warrior, giant and possibly a hunter and subduer of giants as well. In fact, according to some, giants were said to have helped Nimrod build the Tower of

Babel. Ancient Arabic legends speak about the giant races being dispersed across the lands along with the people whose languages were confounded.[14] According to an Arabic manuscript found at Baalbek and quoted by Michael Alouf in his work, "*History of Baalbek*," we see:

> *After the flood, when Nimrod reigned over Lebanon,* ***he sent giants*** *to rebuild the fortress of Baalbek, which was so named in honour of Baal, the god of the Moabites and worshippers of the Sun.*[15]

Apparently, even to this day (though I personally do not share this view), local tradition asserts that the Tower of Babel was actually located at Baalbek.[16] Whether that is true or not, when looking at the megalithic structures that *are* present there, it is easy to imagine that they could have been built by giants. Assuming any of the Arabic legends are true, we've just found evidence of giants who lived almost immediately after the Flood.

The notion that the Tower of Babel was built by giants is also supported in the ancient Mesopotamian texts. The Etemenanki (Sumerian "temple of the foundation of heaven and earth") was the name of a ziggurat dedicated to Marduk in the city of Babylon. According to the Babylonian Creation myth, known as the *Enûma Eliš* (Epic of Creation) Tablet VI, we see that it was the Anunnaki giants who built Etemenaki (as the gate of god):

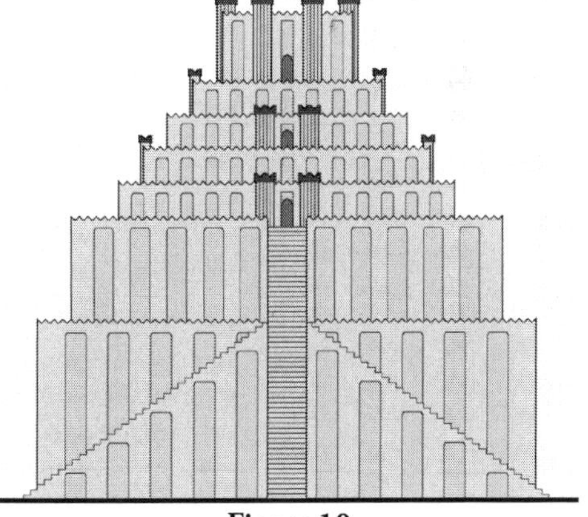

Figure 10

14 See for instance, the works of Berossus, Eupolemus, Alexander Polyhistor and the Sibylline Oracles, as quoted by Cory

15 ***History of Baalbek,*** by Michael Alouf, page 41.

16 Ibid., quoting a traveller named d'Arvieux' from his M moires, Part IIe, Ch. 26, c. 1160

> *The Anunnaki made their voices heard and addressed Marduk their Lord, "Now, O Lord, that you have set us free, what are our favours from you? We would like to make a shrine with its own name..."*
>
> *...When Marduk heard this, his face lit up greatly, like daylight. "Create Babylon, whose construction you requested! Let its mud bricks be molded, and build high the shrine!"*
>
> *The Anunnaki began shovelling. The whole year they made bricks for it. When the second year arrived, they had raised the top of Esagila in front of (?) the Apsu. They founded the dwelling for Anu, Ellil, and Ea likewise.*
>
> * * *
>
> *Indeed, Bab-ili (is) your home too!*
>
> — *The Epic of Creation*[17]

There are more connections as you will soon see, but I'm getting ahead of myself. I just wanted to lay a foundation for what's to come. We'll come back to Nimrod in Chapter Seven. For now, it is important to notice that in this context, Nimrod was a giant and a commander of giants after the Flood, just like the mighty men of renown were before the Flood.

Even a casual analysis of Genesis 6:4 reveals that those *"and also after that"* Nephilim are the *same* ones who became the giants of old, which were regarded as *men* of renown. Here again, contrary to what Pember and others may think, the text clearly reveals that these giant Nephilim were referred to as men (hybrids), and not angels or sons of God. These giant men are the same ones mentioned at the beginning of the sentence, which are not from the post-Flood world, but rather predate it by hundreds of years.

17. Excerpts from Tablet VI of *The Epic of Creation* from ***Myths from Mesopotamia: Creation, The Flood, Gilgamesh, and Others*** by Stephanie Dalley (© 1989 Oxford Classics) pages 262, 263

We may also take note of the fact that it was ***men*** who were the cause of God's anger which led to the Flood.

> *And God saw that the wickedness of* ***man*** *was great in the earth, and that every imagination of the thoughts of his heart was only evil continually.*
>
> *And it repented the Lord that he had made* ***man*** *on the earth, and it grieved him at his heart.*
>
> *And the Lord said, I will destroy* ***man*** *whom I have created from the face of the earth; both man, and beast, and the creeping thing, and the fowls of the air ; for it repenteth me that I have made them.* (Genesis 6:5-7)

The Flood was not a judgment against the Watchers. They had a completely different judgment,[18] which was given a full 600 year+ years before the water judgment. The Flood was a judgment against man and the creatures God created, which had become corrupted. Author James R. Spillman agrees, noting:

> *At this juncture, God is not blaming fallen angels for man's sin. The blame is placed squarely on man, both small size and supernormal giant size. Still, it is apparent that it was the infusion of the nephilim that stained the character of normal man to such an extent that both could be represented by the one onerous word "man." We must discern that the "giants" are a physical manifestation even though in essence they have a spiritual interconnection.*
>
> —James R. Spillman[19]

WHICH WERE OF OLD

> *There were giants in the earth in those days; and also after that, when the sons of God came in unto the daughters of*

18. 1 Enoch 10:9-12, 2 Peter 2:4 and Jude 6
19. From ***A Conspiracy of Angels*** by James R. Spillman (© 2006, 2nd Print Edition, True Potential Publishing, Inc,), page 9

> *men, and they bare children to them, the same became mighty men* ***which were of old****, men of renown.*
> (Genesis 6:4)

The nail in the coffin of the Multiple Incursions Theory is found in the word translated as "old" in English. It is the Hebrew word *olam* (Strong's # 5769). It is a word used to describe something in the *very* distant past. It is translated elsewhere in the Bible as "everlasting" (110 times) and "forever" (136 times)! According to Strong's, the word means:

> *always, ancient time, any more, continuance, eternal, for, everlasting, long time,*
>
> *Or lolam {o-lawm'}; from alam; properly, concealed, i.e. The vanishing point; generally, time out of mind (past or future), i.e. (practically) eternity;*

That is hardly the word Moses would use to describe something fairly recent (as in the post-Flood Nephilim of Canaan). Looking at the structure of the sentence, we see that it is saying the ones who were the product of the union of angels and women were the ones who were produced after that... a long, long, long time ago! Thus, the phrase, *"which were of old"* is extremely telling in the Hebrew — and quite damaging to the Multiple Incursions Theory.

MEN OF RENOWN

> *There were giants in the earth in those days; and also after that, when the sons of God came in unto the daughters of men, and they bare children to them, the same became mighty men which were of old,* ***men of renown****.*
> (Genesis 6:4)

The final phrase in Genesis 6:4 is talking about hybrid ***men***, who were the (Nephilim giant) offspring of the sons of God who had mated with the daughters of men. They were legendary heroes and the inspiration for the gods of the ancient world. Going back to the *International Standard Version* of the Bible, we see this to be true:

> *The Nephilim were on the earth at that time (and also immediately afterward), when those divine beings were having sexual relations with those human women, who gave birth to children for them.* ***These children became the heroes and legendary figures of ancient times.*** (Genesis 6:4 ISV)

I think I'm beginning to like Doug Hamp's preferred translation myself. It really does simplify the story quite a bit, doesn't it?

SUMMARY

First, it must be noted that all of Genesis is in chronological order. It is a linear book, telling a very straight-forward time-line of events from Creation to the Exodus. The same is true for Genesis 6. The entire chapter is talking about the days leading up to the Flood, which occurs in chapter 7. Thus, *all* of Genesis 6 is in a ***pre***-Flood context. The synchronized, biblically endorsed, extra-biblical texts also make this abundantly clear.

The KJV chooses a poor word, "giants" for a translation. As there are a number of other words that are also translated "giant" throughout the Bible, it would have been much better to leave the Hebrew word Nephilim.

The *"those days"* being referred to are those which were spoken of in Genesis 6:1-3. The phrase *"and also after that"* is a big point that needs to be carefully considered and understood. Moses has not yet written about the Flood. His entire line of thinking for the whole of chapter 6 is a build up for the Flood coming in chapter 7.

As an aside, it should also be of extreme importance to note when it was that Moses wrote Genesis in the first place. Did he write it while on Mt. Sinai, *before* discovering there were giants in the land of Canaan? If so, that totally obliterates any notion that he was making a non-linear commentary for what will later be described in Numbers 13:33. How could he be referring to something he had not yet become aware of?

Indeed, while debated extensively, quite a number of ancient Hebrew scholars, rabbis and commentators agree that Moses wrote about everything from Creation up to and including the giving of the Law while he spent his 40 days with God on that mountaintop. That just makes sense. God wrote the 10 commandments on stone, but I am quite sure it did not take Him 40 days to do it. In the meantime, it would appear that God was personally dictating to Moses everything He had done up until that very moment. The rest of the Torah was written as a work in progress from the time Moses came down from the mountain until his death. The 13th century Spanish rabbi Ramban (also known as Nachmanides) agrees:

> *"When Moses came down from the mountain, he wrote from the beginning of the Torah until the end of the story of the Tabernacle, and the conclusion of the Torah he wrote at the end of the 40th year..."*
>
> —Nachmanides[20]

In either case, the Torah reads like a journal. Clearly, Genesis through Leviticus set the stage for what it would be like to be "God's chosen people." Those books contain a *lot* of specific information for how to do everything associated with the sacrifices and keeping of the Law, the practices of the Levitical priests, the functions of the Tabernacle and just general information for living the way God wanted them to live. All of that laid the foundation for the journeys which would follow.

Numbers was probably written as a play-by-play journal, and Deuteronomy is sort of the *Cliff-Notes* recap of the previous 4

20. Ramban, preface to his Torah commentary. See also: http://www.myjewishlearning.com/texts/Bible/Origins_of_the_Bible/Authorship/Torah_of_Moses.shtml

books, wrapping the whole thing up nice and neat for Joshua to take over after Moses' death.

The above is supported by both common sense as well as even the most casual observance of the progression of events in the text itself, and is confirmed by ancient Hebrew sages who have discussed all of that at length and wrote their conclusions down for us long ago.

The Hebrew word used for "after" is *achar* (Strong's # 310). It simply means "afterward, after, following, subsequent" and is a term used for the next *immediate* thing that happened. It is *not* a reference to something far off in the future (like more than 1,400 years from the "in those days" spoken of in the previous verses).

The Hebrew word *asher*, while accurately translated as "when" is more often translated as "because" (73 times verses 44 for when), which if translated as such here would certainly strengthen the argument for a *first cause* rather than a justification for multiple incursions.

The phrase *"came in unto the daughters of men"* is curious as well. While we certainly can assume sexual intercourse, we may also assume genetic manipulation and the insertion of seed into the bodies of women in other fashions, such as through surgical implantation instead of copulation.

The remaining phrases talk of giant offspring being the result, but while we may be tempted to just stick with sex as the means by which that happened, I don't believe the words themselves close the door to any other possibilities for how the giant offspring were produced. Technically speaking, there are no sexual terms used here. There are a variety of more common terms used in numerous other places throughout the Bible when describing sexual activity.

Finally, the Hebrew word that was translated as *"of old"* in English, is *olam* (Strong's # 5769). It is a word used to describe something in the *very* distant past and is translated elsewhere as "everlasting" (110 times), "forever" (136 times). It is hardly the word one would use to describe something fairly recent. Furthermore, looking at the structure of the phrase, *"the **same** became mighty men which were of old,"* we see that it is saying the ones who were the product of the union of angels and women [however that took place] were the ones who were produced after that... a long, long time ago!

Putting all of the information in this chapter together, I believe Genesis 6:4 should be understood as follows:

> *There were giants* [Nephilim] *in the earth in those days* [the days of Jared]*; and also* [immediately] *after that* [in the days after the first generation Nephilim were killed off, but still before the Flood], *when* [or because of the fact that] *the sons of God* [had] *came in* [entered/inserted their seed] *unto the daughters of men, and they bare* [Nephilim] *children to them, the same* [afore mentioned Nephilim] *became mighty men* [giants] *which were of old* [in the very distant past], *men of renown* [the great heroes and gods of myth and legend].
>
> (Genesis 6:4 KJV reexamined and amplified)

Is this reexamined and amplified rendering of Genesis 6 justified? Beyond what I've already written here in this chapter, let's take a look at *The Genesis Six Experiment* again, but this time using the Bible as well as the synchronized, biblically-endoresed, extra-biblical texts to see the bigger picture emerge.

—— Chapter Four ——

THE GENESIS SIX EXPERIMENT SYNCHRONIZED

"The history of evil is found in bits and fragments of ancient text: a line in Jasher, a statement in Jubilees, a page in Enoch, a hint in the Bible."

—Joseph B. Lumpkin[1]

In his book, *Fallen Angels, the Watchers and the Origins of Evil.* Joseph B. Lumpkin used the Bible, 1 Enoch, Jasher and Jubilees to weave together a complete tapestry that nicely reveals the origins of evil using the ancient Hebrew texts. In like manner, this chapter will reveal the origin, rise, fall and return of the Nephilim.

Chapter One of Book 1 in my *Babylon Rising* series dealt with Genesis 6 in a summarized fashion. I will now put the synchronized, biblically endorsed, extra-biblical texts together to illustrate the expanded version of what I called, *The Genesis Six Experiment*. The following ancient texts have been arranged in a chronological order,

1. A quote from the back cover of ***Fallen Angels, the Watchers and the Origins of Evil*** by Joseph B. Lumpkin (© 2006 Fifth Estate)

synchronized to each other in order to give the "bigger picture" of what was captured in but a single chapter of Genesis.

GENESIS 6

1 And it came to pass, when men began to multiply on the face of the earth, and daughters were born unto them,

2 That the sons of God saw the daughters of men that they were fair; and they took them wives of all which they chose.

1 ENOCH 6

3. And Semjâzâ, who was their leader, said unto them: 'I fear ye will not indeed agree to do this deed, and I alone shall have to pay the penalty of a great sin.'

4. And they all answered him and said: 'Let us all swear an oath, and all bind ourselves by mutual imprecations not to abandon this plan but to do this thing.'

5. Then sware they all together and bound themselves by mutual imprecations upon it.

6. And they were in all two hundred; who descended in the days of Jared on the summit of Mount Hermon, and they called it Mount Hermon, because they had sworn and bound themselves by mutual imprecations upon it.

7. And these are the names of their leaders: Sêmîazâz, their leader, Arâkîba, Râmêêl, Kôkabîêl, Tâmîêl, Râmîêl, Dânêl, Êzêqêêl, Barâqîjâl, Asâêl, Armârôs, Batârêl, Anânêl, Zaqîêl, Samsâpêêl, Satarêl, Tûrêl, Jômjâêl, Sariêl.

8. These are their chiefs of tens.

1 ENOCH 7

1. And all the others together with them took unto themselves wives, and each chose for himself one, and they began to go in unto them and to defile themselves with them, and they taught them charms and enchantments, and the cutting of roots, and made

them acquainted with plants.

2. And they became pregnant, and they bare great giants, whose height was three thousand ells:[2]

3. Who consumed all the acquisitions of men. And when men could no longer sustain them,

4. the giants turned against them and devoured mankind.

5. And they began to sin against birds, and beasts, and reptiles, and fish, and to devour one another's flesh, and drink the blood.

6. Then the earth laid accusation against the lawless ones.

JUBILEES 7 (NOAH'S RECAP)

21. For owing to these three things came the flood upon the earth, namely, owing to the fornication wherein the Watchers against the law of their ordinances went a whoring after the daughters of men, and took themselves wives of all which they chose: and they made the beginning of uncleanness.

22. And they begat sons the Nâphîdîm, and they were all unlike, and they devoured one another: and the Giants slew the Nâphîl, and the Nâphîl slew the Eljô, and the Eljô mankind, and one man another.

23. And every one sold himself to work iniquity and to shed much blood, and the earth was filled with iniquity.

1 ENOCH 9

1. And then Michael, Uriel, Raphael, and Gabriel looked down from heaven and saw much blood being shed upon the earth, and all lawlessness being wrought upon the earth.

2. And they said one to another: 'The earth made without inhabitant cries the voice of their crying up to the gates of heaven.

3 And now to you, the holy ones of heaven, the souls of men make their suit, saying, "Bring our cause before the Most High.".'

4. And they said to the Lord of the ages: 'Lord of lords, God of

2. Dr. A. Nyland translates the three thousand ells as three hundred cubits.

gods, King of kings, and God of the ages, the throne of Thy glory (standeth) unto all the generations of the ages, and Thy name holy and glorious and blessed unto all the ages!

5. Thou hast made all things, and power over all things hast Thou: and all things are naked and open in Thy sight, and Thou seest all things, and nothing can hide itself from Thee.

6. Thou seest what Azâzêl hath done, who hath taught all unrighteousness on earth and revealed the eternal secrets which were (preserved) in heaven, which men were striving to learn:

7. And Semjâzâ, to whom Thou hast given authority to bear rule over his associates.

8. And they have gone to the daughters of men upon the earth, and have slept with the women, and have defiled themselves, and revealed to them all kinds of sins.

9. And the women have borne giants, and the whole earth has thereby been filled with blood and unrighteousness.

10. And now, behold, the souls of those who have died are crying and making their suit to the gates of heaven, and their lamentations have ascended: and cannot cease because of the lawless deeds which are wrought on the earth.

11. And Thou knowest all things before they come to pass, and Thou seest these things and Thou dost suffer them, and Thou dost not say to us what we are to do to them in regard to these.'

1 ENOCH 10

1. Then said the Most High, the Holy and Great One spake, and sent Uriel to the son of Lamech, and said to him:

2. 'Go to Noah and tell him in my name "Hide thyself!" and reveal to him the end that is approaching: that the whole earth will be destroyed, and a deluge is about to come upon the whole earth, and will destroy all that is on it.

3. And now instruct him that he may escape and his seed may be preserved for all the generations of the world.'

4. And again the Lord said to Raphael: 'Bind Azâzêl hand and foot, and cast him into the darkness: and make an opening in the desert, which is in Dûdâêl, and cast him therein.

5. And place upon him rough and jagged rocks, and cover him with darkness, and let him abide there for ever, and cover his face that he may not see light.

6. And on the day of the great judgement he shall be cast into the fire. And heal the earth which the angels have corrupted, and proclaim the healing of the earth, that they may heal the plague, and that all the children of men may not perish through all the secret things that the Watchers have disclosed and have taught their sons.

8. And the whole earth has been corrupted through the works that were taught by Azâzêl: to him ascribe all sin.'

9. And to Gabriel said the Lord: 'Proceed against the bastards and the reprobates, and against the children of fornication: and destroy [the children of fornication and] the children of the Watchers from amongst men [and cause them to go forth]: send them one against the other that they may destroy each other in battle: for length of days shall they not have.

10. And no request that they (i.e. their fathers) make of thee shall be granted unto their fathers on their behalf; for they hope to live an eternal life, and that each one of them will live five hundred years.'[3]

11. And the Lord said unto Michael: 'Go, bind Semjâzâ and his associates who have united themselves with women so as to have defiled themselves with them in all their uncleanness. [4]

12. And when their sons have slain one another, and they have seen the destruction of their beloved ones, bind them fast for seventy generations[5] in the valleys of the earth, till the day of their judgement and of their consummation, till the judgement that is for ever and ever is consummated.

---

3. Take note of this fact: The first generation Nephilim were to kill each other off within 500 years of their birth.
4. See 2 Peter 2:4 and Jude 6
5. Note that Psalm 90:10 states that a generation is 70 - 80 years. On the low end, that would mean that the Watchers would remain buried for 4,900 years.

JASHER 3

17 And it was in the year of Adam's death which was the two hundred and forty-third year of the reign of Enoch, in that time Enoch resolved to separate himself from the sons of men and to secret himself as at first in order to serve the Lord.

18 And Enoch did so, but did not entirely secret himself from them, but kept away from the sons of men three days and then went to them for one day.

19 And during the three days that he was in his chamber, he prayed to, and praised the Lord his God, and the day on which he went and appeared to his subjects he taught them the ways of the Lord, and all they asked him about the Lord he told them.

20 And he did in this manner for many years, and he afterward concealed himself for six days, and appeared to his people one day in seven; and after that once in a month, and then once in a year, until all the kings, princes and sons of men sought for him, and desired again to see the face of Enoch, and to hear his word; but they could not, as all the sons of men were greatly afraid of Enoch, and they feared to approach him on account of the Godlike awe that was seated upon his countenance; therefore no man could look at him, fearing he might be punished and die.

21 And all the kings and princes resolved to assemble the sons of men, and to come to Enoch, thinking that they might all speak to him at the time when he should come forth amongst them, and they did so.

22 And the day came when Enoch went forth and they all assembled and came to him, and Enoch spoke to them the words of the Lord and he taught them wisdom and knowledge, and they bowed down before him and they said, May the king live! May the king live!

23 And in some time after, when the kings and princes and the sons of men were speaking to Enoch, and Enoch was teaching them the ways of God, behold an angel of the Lord then called unto Enoch from heaven, and wished to bring him up to heaven to make him reign there over the sons of God, as he had reigned over the sons of men upon earth.

24 When at that time Enoch heard this he went and assembled all the inhabitants of the earth, and taught them wisdom and knowledge and gave them divine instructions, and he said to them, I have been required to ascend into heaven, I therefore do not know the day of my going.

25 And now therefore I will teach you wisdom and knowledge and will give you instruction before I leave you, how to act upon earth whereby you may live; and he did so.

26 And he taught them wisdom and knowledge, and gave them instruction, and he reproved them, and he placed before them statutes and judgments to do upon earth, and he made peace amongst them, and he taught them everlasting life, and dwelt with them some time teaching them all these things.

27 And at that time the sons of men were with Enoch, and Enoch was speaking to them, and they lifted up their eyes and the likeness of a great horse descended from heaven, and the horse paced in the air;

28 And they told Enoch what they had seen, and Enoch said to them, On my account does this horse descend upon earth; the time is come when I must go from you and I shall no more be seen by you.

29 And the horse descended at that time and stood before Enoch, and all the sons of men that were with Enoch saw him.

30 And Enoch then again ordered a voice to be proclaimed, saying, Where is the man who delighteth to know the ways of the Lord his God, let him come this day to Enoch before he is taken from us.

31 And all the sons of men assembled and came to Enoch that day; and all the kings of the earth with their princes and counsellors remained with him that day; and Enoch then taught the sons of men wisdom and knowledge, and gave them divine instruction; and he bade them serve the Lord and walk in his ways all the days of their lives, and he continued to make peace amongst them.

32 And it was after this that he rose up and rode upon the horse; and he went forth and all the sons of men went after him, about eight

hundred thousand men; and they went with him one day's journey.

33 And the second day he said to them, Return home to your tents, why will you go? perhaps you may die; and some of them went from him, and those that remained went with him six day's journey; and Enoch said to them every day, Return to your tents, lest you may die; but they were not willing to return, and they went with him.

34 And on the sixth day some of the men remained and clung to him, and they said to him, We will go with thee to the place where thou goest; as the Lord liveth, death only shall separate us.

35 And they urged so much to go with him, that he ceased speaking to them; and they went after him and would not return;

36 And when the kings returned they caused a census to be taken, in order to know the number of remaining men that went with Enoch; and it was upon the seventh day that Enoch ascended into heaven in a whirlwind, with horses and chariots of fire.

37 And on the eighth day all the kings that had been with Enoch sent to bring back the number of men that were with Enoch, in that place from which he ascended into heaven.

38 And all those kings went to the place and they found the earth there filled with snow, and upon the snow were large stones of snow, and one said to the other, Come, let us break through the snow and see, perhaps the men that remained with Enoch are dead, and are now under the stones of snow, and they searched but could not find him, for he had ascended into heaven.

JASHER 4

1 And all the days that Enoch lived upon earth, were three hundred and sixty-five years.[6]

1 ENOCH 12

1. Before these things Enoch was hidden, and no one of the children

6. See also Genesis 5:23,24

of men knew where he was hidden, and where he abode, and what had become of him.

2. And his activities had to do with the Watchers, and his days were with the holy ones.

3. And I, Enoch was blessing the Lord of majesty and the King of the ages, and lo! the Watchers called me--Enoch the scribe--and said to me:

4. 'Enoch, thou scribe of righteousness, go, declare to the Watchers of the heaven who have left the high heaven, the holy eternal place, and have defiled themselves with women, and have done as the children of earth do, and have taken unto themselves wives: "Ye have wrought great destruction on the earth:

5. And ye shall have no peace nor forgiveness of sin: and inasmuch as they delight themselves in their children,

6. The murder of their beloved ones shall they see, and over the destruction of their children shall they lament, and shall make supplication unto eternity, but mercy and peace shall ye not attain."'

1 ENOCH 13

1. And Enoch went and said: 'Azâzêl, thou shalt have no peace: a severe sentence has gone forth against thee to put thee in bonds:

2. And thou shalt not have toleration nor request granted to thee, because of the unrighteousness which thou hast taught, and because of all the works of godlessness and unrighteousness and sin which thou hast shown to men.'

3. Then I went and spoke to them all together, and they were all afraid, and fear and trembling seized them. [7]

4. And they besought me to draw up a petition for them that they might find forgiveness, and to read their petition in the presence of the Lord of heaven.

7. Note the abject terror the angels felt regarding their pending judgment. This great fear is further depicted and elaborated on in 1 Enoch 68:2-5, with Michael, the mighty archangel expressing *his* terror concerning the severe judgment of the Watchers.

5. For from thenceforward they could not speak (with Him) nor lift up their eyes to heaven for shame of their sins for which they had been condemned.

6. Then I wrote out their petition, and the prayer in regard to their spirits and their deeds individually and in regard to their requests that they should have forgiveness and length of days.

7. And I went off and sat down at the waters of Dan, in the land of Dan, to the south of the west of Hermon: I read their petition till I fell asleep.

8. And behold a dream came to me, and visions fell down upon me, and I saw visions of chastisement, and a voice came bidding (me) I to tell it to the sons of heaven, and reprimand them.

9. And when I awaked, I came unto them, and they were all sitting gathered together, weeping in 'Abelsjâîl, which is between Lebanon and Sênêsêr, with their faces covered.

10. And I recounted before them all the visions which I had seen in sleep, and I began to speak the words of righteousness, and to reprimand the heavenly Watchers.

1 ENOCH 14

1. The book of the words of righteousness, and of the reprimand of the eternal Watchers in accordance with the command of the Holy Great One in that vision.

2. I saw in my sleep what I will now say with a tongue of flesh and with the breath of my mouth: which the Great One has given to men to converse therewith and understand with the heart.

3. As He has created and given to man the power of understanding the word of wisdom, so hath He created me also and given me the power of reprimanding the Watchers, the children of heaven.

4. I wrote out your petition, and in my vision it appeared thus, that your petition will not be granted unto you throughout all the days of eternity, and that judgement has been finally passed upon you: yea (your petition) will not be granted unto you.

5. And from henceforth you shall not ascend into heaven unto all eternity, and in bonds of the earth the decree has gone forth to bind you for all the days of the world.

6. And (that) previously you shall have seen the destruction of your beloved sons and ye shall have no pleasure in them, but they shall fall before you by the sword.

7. And your petition on their behalf shall not be granted, nor yet on your own: even though you weep and pray and speak all the words contained in the writing which I have written.

> And on that day Michael answered Raphael and said: 'The power of the spirit grips me and **makes me to tremble because of the severity of the judgement of the secrets, the judgement of the angels: who can endure the severe judgement which has been executed,** and before which they melt away?" (1 Enoch 68:2)

8. And the vision was shown to me thus: Behold, in the vision clouds invited me and a mist summoned me, and the course of the stars and the lightnings sped and hastened me, and the winds in the vision caused me to fly and lifted me upward, and bore me into heaven.

9. And I went in till I drew nigh to a wall which is built of crystals and surrounded by tongues of fire: and it began to affright me. And I went into the tongues of fire and drew nigh to a large house which was built of crystals: and the walls of the house were like a tesselated floor (made) of crystals, and its groundwork was of crystal.

11. Its ceiling was like the path of the stars and the lightnings, and between them were fiery cherubim, and their heaven was (clear as) water.

12. A flaming fire surrounded the walls, and its portals blazed with fire.

13. And I entered into that house, and it was hot as fire and cold as ice: there were no delights of life therein: fear covered me, and trembling got hold upon me.

14. And as I quaked and trembled, I fell upon my face.

15. And I beheld a vision, And lo! there was a second house, greater than the former, and the entire portal stood open before me, and it was built of flames of fire.

16. And in every respect it so excelled in splendour and magnificence and extent that I cannot describe to you its splendour and its extent.

17. And its floor was of fire, and above it were lightnings and the path of the stars, and its ceiling also was flaming fire.

18. And I looked and saw therein a lofty throne: its appearance was as crystal, and the wheels thereof as the shining sun, and there was the vision of cherubim.

19. And from underneath the throne came streams of flaming fire so that I could not look thereon.

20. And the Great Glory sat thereon, and His raiment shone more brightly than the sun and was whiter than any snow.

21. None of the angels could enter and could behold His face by reason of the magnificence and glory and no flesh could behold Him.

22. The flaming fire was round about Him, and a great fire stood before Him, and none around could draw nigh Him: ten thousand times ten thousand (stood) before Him, yet He needed no counselor.

23. And the most holy ones who were nigh to Him did not leave by night nor depart from Him.

24. And until then I had been prostrate on my face, trembling: and the Lord called me with His own mouth, and said to me: 'Come hither, Enoch, and hear my word.'

25. And one of the holy ones came to me and waked me, and He made me rise up and approach the door: and I bowed my face downwards.

1 ENOCH 15

1. And He answered and said to me, and I heard His voice: 'Fear

not, Enoch, thou righteous man and scribe of righteousness: approach hither and hear my voice.

2. And go, say to the Watchers of heaven, who have sent thee to intercede for them: "You should intercede" for men, and not men for you:

3. Wherefore have ye left the high, holy, and eternal heaven, and lain with women, and defiled yourselves with the daughters of men and taken to yourselves wives, and done like the children of earth, and begotten giants (as your) sons?

4. And though ye were holy, spiritual, living the eternal life, you have defiled yourselves with the blood of women, and have begotten (children) with the blood of flesh, and, as the children of men, have lusted after flesh and blood as those also do who die and perish.

5. Therefore have I given them wives also that they might impregnate them, and beget children by them, that thus nothing might be wanting to them on earth.

6. But you were formerly spiritual, living the eternal life, and immortal for all generations of the world.

7. And therefore I have not appointed wives for you; for as for the spiritual ones of the heaven, in heaven is their dwelling.[8]

8. And now, the giants, who are produced from the spirits and flesh, shall be called evil spirits upon the earth, and on the earth shall be their dwelling.

9. Evil spirits have proceeded from their bodies; because they are born from men, and from the holy Watchers is their beginning and primal origin; they shall be evil spirits on earth, and evil spirits shall they be called.[9]

10. As for the spirits of heaven, in heaven shall be their dwelling, but as for the spirits of the earth which were born upon the earth,

8. This indicates two things: 1) there are no female angels and 2) this explains the statement Jesus made in Matthew 22:30.

9. Here we find the origin of demons. Evil sprits or demons are not fallen angels, but rather the disembodied spirits of dead Nephilim.

on the earth shall be their dwelling.] [10]

11. And the spirits of the giants afflict, oppress, destroy, attack, do battle, and work destruction on the earth, and cause trouble: they take no food, but nevertheless hunger and thirst, and cause offences. And these spirits shall rise up against the children of men and against the women, because they have proceeded from them.[11]

1 ENOCH 16

1. From the days of the slaughter and destruction and death of the giants, from the souls of whose flesh the spirits, having gone forth, shall destroy without incurring judgement--thus shall they destroy until the day of the consummation, the great judgement in which the age shall be consummated, over the Watchers and the godless, yea, shall be wholly consummated."

2. And now as to the Watchers who have sent thee to intercede for them, who had been aforetime in heaven, (say to them): "You have been in heaven, but all the mysteries had not yet been revealed to you, and you knew worthless ones, and these in the hardness of your hearts you have made known to the women, and through these mysteries women and men work much evil on earth."

4. Say to them therefore: "You have no peace."'

JASHER 4

2 And when Enoch had ascended into heaven, all the kings of the earth rose and took Methuselah his son and anointed him, and they caused him to reign over them in the place of his father.

3 And Methuselah acted uprightly in the sight of God, as his father Enoch had taught him, and he likewise during the whole of his life taught the sons of men wisdom, knowledge and the fear of God, and he did not turn from the good way either to the right or to the left.

4 But in the latter days of Methuselah, the sons of men turned from

10. This shows us where the eternal destiny of all earth-born spirits is to be. It is why our ultimate destination is not Heaven but rather the New Jerusalem here on Earth.

11. A perfect description of what demons do to mankind.

the Lord, they corrupted the earth, they robbed and plundered each other, and they rebelled against God and they transgressed, and they corrupted their ways, and would not hearken to the voice of Methuselah, but rebelled against him.[12]

5 And the Lord was exceedingly wroth against them, and the Lord continued to destroy the seed in those days, so that there was neither sowing nor reaping in the earth.[13]

6 For when they sowed the ground in order that they might obtain food for their support, behold, thorns and thistles were produced which they did not sow.

7 And still the sons of men did not turn from their evil ways, and their hands were still extended to do evil in the sight of God, and they provoked the Lord with their evil ways, and the Lord was very wroth, and repented that he had made man.

8 And he thought to destroy and annihilate them and he did so.

9 In those days when Lamech the son of Methuselah was one hundred and sixty years old, Seth the son of Adam died.

10 And all the days that Seth lived, were nine hundred and twelve years, and he died.

11 And Lamech was one hundred and eighty years old when he took Ashmua, the daughter of Elishaa the son of Enoch his uncle, and she conceived.

12 And at that time the sons of men sowed the ground, and a little food was produced, yet the sons of men did not turn from their evil ways, and they trespassed and rebelled against God.

13 And the wife of Lamech conceived and bare him a son at that time, at the revolution of the year.

14 And Methuselah called his name Noah, saying, The earth was in his days at rest and free from corruption, and Lamech his father called his name Menachem, saying, This one shall comfort us in

12. Jasher 4:18 explains how they corrupted the earth and their ways.

13. God is depicted here as destroying "corrupt seed." This is the beginning of a pattern that will play out all through the Scriptures even to today.

our works and miserable toil in the earth, which God had cursed.[14]

15 And the child grew up and was weaned, and he went in the ways of his father Methuselah, perfect and upright with God.

16 And all the sons of men departed from the ways of the Lord in those days as they multiplied upon the face of the earth with sons and daughters, and they taught one another their evil practices and they continued sinning against the Lord.

17 And every man made unto himself a god, and they robbed and plundered every man his neighbor as well as his relative, and they corrupted the earth, and the earth was filled with violence.

18 And their judges and rulers[15] went to the daughters of men and took their wives by force from their husbands according to their choice, and the sons of men in those days took from the cattle of the earth, the beasts of the field and the fowls of the air, and taught the mixture of animals of one species with the other,[16] in order therewith to provoke the Lord; and God saw the whole earth and it was corrupt, for all flesh had corrupted its ways upon earth, all men and all animals.

And God looked upon the earth, and, behold, it was corrupt; for ***all flesh had corrupted his way*** upon the earth. (Genesis 6:12)

14. Genesis says that Lamech named his son Noah. Jasher says he named him Manechem. Is this a contradiction or a synonym? Both mean essentially the same thing: *rest, peace, comfort* from previous chaos. It should also be noted that Lamech died early, having not followed in the ways of his father (Jasher 5:19) thus leaving Noah under the care of his Godly grandfather, Methuselah who was at this time the king of the world (Jasher 4:2). It is therefore more than reasonable to assume that what the king says goes: his name shall be Noah.
15. It is uncertain as to whether these "judges and rulers" are angels (as in archons and kosmokrators) or merely the human leaders of men. Whichever the case may be, we see that abduction and transgenic experimentation was the result — not copulation as seen in the days of Jared.
16. I strongly believe that the mixture of animals and humans (which creates animal-human chimeras such as centaurs, minotaurs and satyrs) is key to understanding the return of the Nephilim both before and after the Flood, as well as potentially in our day too (in fulfillment of Jesus' prophecy in Matthew 24:37).

JUBILEES 7 (NOAH'S RECAP)

24. And after this[17] they sinned against the beasts and birds, and all that moveth and walketh on the earth: and much blood was shed on the earth, and every imagination and desire of men imagined vanity and evil continually.[18]

GENESIS 6

3 And the Lord said, My spirit shall not always strive with man, for that he also is flesh: yet his days shall be an hundred and twenty years.[19]

4 There were giants in the earth in those days; and also after that,[20] when the sons of God came in unto the daughters of men, and they bare children to them, the same became mighty men which were of old, men of renown.

5 And God saw that the wickedness of man was great in the earth, and that every imagination of the thoughts of his heart was only evil continually.[21]

6 And it repented the Lord that he had made man on the earth, and it grieved him at his heart.

JASHER 4

19 And the Lord said, I will blot out man that I created from the face of the earth, yea from man to the birds of the air, together with cattle and beasts that are in the field for I repent that I made them.

---

17. The "after this" written about here is in a pre-Flood context and is the same as the "after that" of Genesis 6:4.
18. This is the parallel verse that goes along with Jasher 4:18, which both explain how Genesis 6:12 came to be.
19. This verse is very telling. During the last 120 years leading up to the Flood, God's spirit could no longer dwell in man. I believe this happened because man's flesh (that the Apostle Paul described as being the "temple of the Holy Spirit) had become corrupted.
20. This is the same as the "after this" of Jubilees 7:24. It is entirely in a pre-Flood context and is therefore not a reference to any post-Flood second incursion.
21. This is further confirmation that it is a parallel to the pre-Flood account of Noah's story given in the recap of Jubilees 7. What made the people get to the point of having every imagination and thought of their hearts being only evil continually? According to these texts, such a state of being came as a result of blending themselves with animals not angels.

20 And all men who walked in the ways of the Lord, died in those days, before the Lord brought the evil upon man which he had declared, for this was from the Lord, that they should not see the evil which the Lord spoke of concerning the sons of men.

21 And Noah found grace in the sight of the Lord, and the Lord chose him and his children to raise up seed from them upon the face of the whole earth.

GENESIS 6

7 And the Lord said, I will destroy man whom I have created from the face of the earth; both man, and beast, and the creeping thing, and the fowls of the air; for it repenteth me that I have made them.

8 But Noah found grace in the eyes of the Lord.

9 These are the generations of Noah: Noah was a just man and perfect in his generations,[22] and Noah walked with God.

10 And Noah begat three sons, Shem, Ham, and Japheth.[23]

11 The earth also was corrupt before God, and the earth was filled with violence.

---

22. The word used for "perfect" is *tamim* in Hebrew, which indicates genetic purity.
23. The context of this verse immediately following the previous one, which described Noah's genetic purity would appear to indicate that the three sons were also genetically pure. Jasher 5:15 reveals to us the fact that Noah's wife Naamah was the daughter of righteous Enoch. She was about 82 years older than Noah and since the corruption of all flesh came much later in her life, it stands to reason that she was pure as well. Noah took her as his wife when he was 498 years old (Jasher 5:16) and we know that he was 500 years old when he started having children (Genesis 5:32). Thus, I believe all of Noah's immediate family was genetically pure.

    Some have tried to suggest that this was the same Naamah of Cain's lineage (Genesis 4:22) and use that to justify a belief in the "Serpent Seed Theory," which states that Cain was the offspring of Lucifer and that his seed perpetuated through Naamah in a marriage to Noah. The biggest problem with this theory (apart from no Biblical support for the Serpent Seed Theory in general) is the timing. Naamah, the daughter of Cain was born nearly 600 years before Noah was born. That would make her approximately 1,200 years old by the time of the Flood. The Bible clearly tells us that Methuselah was the longest lived individual on this planet and he died at 969, which was within a "God day" thus fulfilling God's promise of Genesis 2:17. For Naamah to have lived longer, that would directly contradict God's promise of man's mortality limitations due to the sin of eating from the Tree of the Knowledge of Good and Evil.

12 And God looked upon the earth, and, behold, it was corrupt; for all flesh had corrupted his way upon the earth.[24]

13 And God said unto Noah, The end of all flesh is come before me; for the earth is filled with violence through them; and, behold, I will destroy them with the earth.

14 Make thee an ark of gopher wood; rooms shalt thou make in the ark, and shalt pitch it within and without with pitch.

15 And this is the fashion which thou shalt make it of: The length of the ark shall be three hundred cubits, the breadth of it fifty cubits, and the height of it thirty cubits.

16 A window shalt thou make to the ark, and in a cubit shalt thou finish it above; and the door of the ark shalt thou set in the side thereof; with lower, second, and third stories shalt thou make it.

17 And, behold, I, even I, do bring a flood of waters upon the earth, to destroy all flesh, wherein is the breath of life, from under heaven; and every thing that is in the earth shall die.

18 But with thee will I establish my covenant; and thou shalt come into the ark, thou, and thy sons, and thy wife, and thy sons' wives with thee.[25]

19 And of every living thing of all flesh, two of every sort shalt thou bring into the ark, to keep them alive with thee; they shall be male and female.

20 Of fowls after their kind, and of cattle after their kind, of every creeping thing of the earth after his kind, two of every sort shall come unto thee, to keep them alive.[26]

21 And take thou unto thee of all food that is eaten, and thou shalt gather it to thee; and it shall be for food for thee, and for them.

22 Thus did Noah; according to all that God commanded him, so did he.

---

24. All flesh became corrupted as a result of what we read in Jasher 4:18 and Jubilees 7:24.
25. I maintain that all of Genesis 6 is written in chronological order, in a linear fashion and entirely in a pre-Flood context. If this is true, note that the first mention of the wives of Noah's sons comes *after* the description of all flesh becoming corrupted (through transgenic manipulation according to Jasher and Jubilees).
26. Note that this verse uses the phrase "after their/his kind" <u>three</u> times.

GENESIS 7

1 And the Lord said unto Noah, Come thou and all thy house into the ark; for thee have I seen righteous before me in this generation.

2 Of every clean beast thou shalt take to thee by sevens, the male and his female: and of beasts that are not clean by two, the male and his female.

3 Of fowls also of the air by sevens, the male and the female; to keep seed alive upon the face of all the earth.

4 For yet seven days, and I will cause it to rain upon the earth forty days and forty nights; and every living substance that I have made will I destroy from off the face of the earth.

5 And Noah did according unto all that the Lord commanded him.

6 And Noah was six hundred years old when the flood of waters was upon the earth.

7 And Noah went in, and his sons, and his wife, and his sons' wives with him, into the ark, because of the waters of the flood.

8 Of clean beasts, and of beasts that are not clean, and of fowls, and of every thing that creepeth upon the earth,

9 There went in two and two unto Noah into the ark, the male and the female, as God had commanded Noah.

10 And it came to pass after seven days, that the waters of the flood were upon the earth.

JASHER 6

9 Two and two came to Noah into the ark, but from the clean animals, and clean fowls, he brought seven couples, as God had commanded him.

10 And all the animals, and beasts, and fowls, were still there, and they surrounded the ark at every place, and the rain had not descended till seven days after.

11 And on that day, the Lord caused the whole earth to shake, and the sun darkened, and the foundations of the world raged, and the

whole earth was moved violently, and the lightning flashed, and the thunder roared, and all the fountains in the earth were broken up, such as was not known to the inhabitants before; and God did this mighty act, in order to terrify the sons of men, that there might be no more evil upon earth.[27]

12 And still the sons of men would not return from their evil ways, and they increased the anger of the Lord at that time, and did not even direct their hearts to all this.

---

27. This is an extraordinary text! I believe this event actually describes the *root cause* of the Flood. Building upon the work of Immanuel Velikovsky in his books ***Worlds in Collision, Ages in Chaos*** and ***Earth in Upheaval,*** I have been developing a theory about the mechanism through which God executed the Flood judgment. In this theory, I suggest that a comet or other large object may have hit the earth, most probably in the location now known as Greenland. The secular evolutionist believes the "Extinction Level Event" (E.L.E) that killed the dinosaurs was caused by an impact in the Yucatán Peninsula roughly 65 million years ago. The Chicxulub crater at that location is considered by many to be the largest confirmed impact structure on earth. In recent years, scientists have discovered a number of other craters of about the same age, prompting some to believe the earth experienced multiple impacts, all at about the same time. The collision of *Comet Shoemaker-Levy 9* into Jupiter back in 1994, demonstrated how gravity (the Inverse Square Law) caused the object to break apart into many pieces resulting in multiple impacts over time across the gas giant's surface. With that concept in mind, could it be that Chicxulub is *not* the world's largest impact crater? Perhaps that title may better fit another location? It is my belief that the primary impact crater which caused the Flood is in fact the continent of Greenland (which is tear-drop shaped island covered with an ice sheet that has a volume of approximately 680,000 cubic miles, which is 6,000 feet thick in some places, covering a depressed land basin that descends nearly 1,000 feet below sea level). As the world's largest island, it sits at the top of the mid-Atlantic rift, which separates the Americas from Europe and Africa. The topography of the entire Arctic Circle, extending south into much of the northern hemisphere shows evidence that something massive caused a circular ring of absolute devastation in all directions (see Velikovsky's ***Earth in Upheaval***). When you combine that with the fact that very large creatures such as the Mammoths of Siberia were instantly flash-frozen, it all appears to add up to something extraordinary happening in the planet's northern region, which I have come to believe was the E.L.E the Bible calls the Flood. It is quite probable that this same event also caused the Ice Age, the current tilt of the earth and the initial fractures that later separated (divided) the world (Pangaea) during the time of Peleg, all at the same time. If this is true, it might explain why the planet rocked so violently, why the "fountains of the great deep were broken up" and why the "windows of heaven were opened," eventually (7 days later from Noah's perspective) causing the water canopy to disintegrate and rain down for 40 days and 40 nights. Whether my theory is true or not is irrelevant. One way or another, the ancient record testifies that *something* rocked the Earth seven days before the Flood waters completely destroyed everything on the planet, and that explains why Genesis says that the "fountains of the deep were broken up" first and then the rains came down later as the "windows of heaven were opened."

13 And at the end of seven days, in the six hundredth year of the life of Noah, the waters of the flood were upon the earth.

14 And all the fountains of the deep were broken up, and the windows of heaven were opened, and the rain was upon the earth forty days and forty nights.

15 And Noah and his household, and all the living creatures that were with him, came into the ark on account of the waters of the flood, and the Lord shut him in.

16 And all the sons of men that were left upon the earth, became exhausted through evil on account of the rain, for the waters were coming more violently upon the earth, and the animals and beasts were still surrounding the ark.

17 And the sons of men assembled together, about seven hundred thousand men and women, and they came unto Noah to the ark.

18 And they called to Noah, saying, Open for us that we may come to thee in the ark--and wherefore shall we die?

19 And Noah, with a loud voice, answered them from the ark, saying, Have you not all rebelled against the Lord, and said that he does not exist? and therefore the Lord brought upon you this evil, to destroy and cut you off from the face of the earth.

20 Is not this the thing that I spoke to you of one hundred and twenty years back, and you would not hearken to the voice of the Lord, and now do you desire to live upon earth?

21 And they said to Noah, We are ready to return to the Lord; only open for us that we may live and not die.

22 And Noah answered them, saying, Behold now that you see the trouble of your souls, you wish to return to the Lord; why did you not return during these hundred and twenty years, which the Lord granted you as the determined period?

23 But now you come and tell me this on account of the troubles of your souls, now also the Lord will not listen to you, neither will he give ear to you on this day, so that you will not now succeed in your wishes.

24 And the sons of men approached in order to break into the ark, to come in on account of the rain, for they could not bear the rain upon them.

25 And the Lord sent all the beasts and animals that stood round the ark. And the beasts overpowered them and drove them from that place, and every man went his way and they again scattered themselves upon the face of the earth.

26 And the rain was still descending upon the earth, and it descended forty days and forty nights, and the waters prevailed greatly upon the earth; and all flesh that was upon the earth or in the waters died, whether men, animals, beasts, creeping things or birds of the air, and there only remained Noah and those that were with him in the ark.

GENESIS 7

11 In the six hundredth year of Noah's life, in the second month, the seventeenth day of the month, the same day were all the fountains of the great deep broken up, and the windows of heaven were opened.

12 And the rain was upon the earth forty days and forty nights.

13 In the selfsame day entered Noah, and Shem, and Ham, and Japheth, the sons of Noah, and Noah's wife, and the three wives of his sons with them, into the ark;

14 They, and every beast after his kind, and all the cattle after their kind, and every creeping thing that creepeth upon the earth after his kind, and every fowl after his kind, every bird of every sort.[28]

15 And they went in unto Noah into the ark, two and two of all flesh, wherein is the breath of life.

16 And they that went in, went in male and female of all flesh, as God had commanded him: and the Lord shut him in.

28. Here again, we see the repetitive phrase, "after their/his kind" being brought to our attention. But notice that it only specifies "after their kind" in reference to the animals. It does not say the same thing concerning the humans onboard. It simply says "They" followed by a description of all the animals after their kind.

17 And the flood was forty days upon the earth; and the waters increased, and bare up the ark, and it was lift up above the earth.

18 And the waters prevailed, and were increased greatly upon the earth; and the ark went upon the face of the waters.

19 And the waters prevailed exceedingly upon the earth; and all the high hills, that were under the whole heaven, were covered.

20 Fifteen cubits upward did the waters prevail; and the mountains were covered.

21 And all flesh died that moved upon the earth, both of fowl, and of cattle, and of beast, and of every creeping thing that creepeth upon the earth, and every man:[29]

22 All in whose nostrils was the breath of life, of all that was in the dry land, died.

23 And every living substance was destroyed which was upon the face of the ground, both man, and cattle, and the creeping things, and the fowl of the heaven; and they were destroyed from the earth: and Noah only remained alive, and they that were with him in the ark.

24 And the waters prevailed upon the earth an hundred and fifty days.

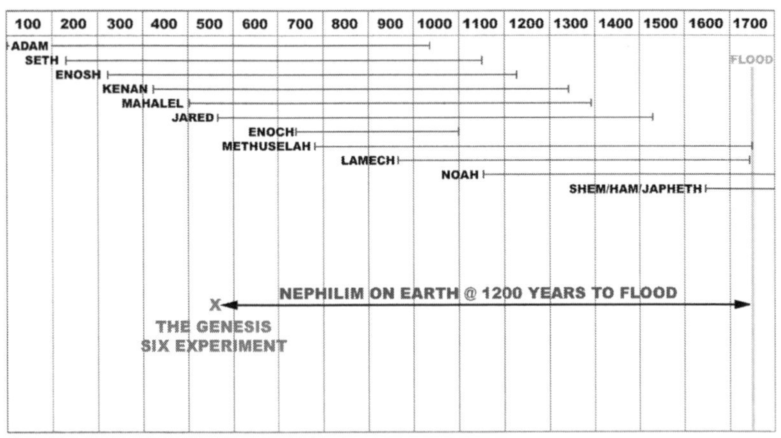

Figure 11

29. Note that the phrase *"after their/his kind"* is curiously missing here.

In this chapter, we have seen how the ancient Hebrew texts synchronized beautifully, telling a very detailed story, with each text filling in more of the gaps not covered in the other. We saw how the whole thing began on Mount Hermon in the days of Jared and how it ended with the Great Flood of Noah nearly 1,200 years later (**Figure 11**). In between, we saw the first generation Nephilim rise and fall. Then, we saw how something altogether different brought about the corruption of all flesh in a ***pre***-Flood context. Now, let's take a closer look at the return of the Nephilim *before* the Flood.[30]

30. For more interesting details concerning the antediluvian and post-Flood worlds, see also ***Appendix A*** for Enoch's prophetic "Animal Apocalypse Dream."

Chapter Five

RETURN OF THE NEPHILIM BEFORE THE FLOOD

And after this they sinned against the beasts and birds, and all that moveth and walketh on the earth: and much blood was shed on the earth, and every imagination and desire of men imagined vanity and evil continually. (Jubilees 7:24)

Genesis 6:4 makes it clear that the sons of God came in unto the daughters of men and produced offspring. The synchronized, biblically endorsed, extra-biblical texts elaborate on who these beings were, where they landed, when they came, what they did and what happened to them as a result. Thus we learn that 200 Watcher-class fallen angels landed on Mount Hermon in the days of Jared. They participated in what I call *The Genesis Six Experiment*, mating with women to produce angel-human-hybrids known as the Nephilim.

Those first generation hybrid offspring lived no longer than 500 years and killed each other off while their fathers were made to

"watch" before they were themselves severely judged and sentenced to everlasting chains of darkness, buried under the sands of the earth for 70 generations.[1]

> *And when their sons have slain one another, and they have seen the destruction of their beloved ones,* ***bind them*** [the 200 Watchers] ***fast for seventy generations in the valleys of the earth****, till the day of their judgment and of their consummation, till the judgment that is for ever and ever is consummated.* (1 Enoch 10:12)

There were 200 Watchers, some of whom went down to Tartarus and others who were buried under the valleys of the earth (where rivers flow). The book of Revelation just so happens to record a release of four such angels who are bound under the Euphrates River:

> *Then the sixth angel sounded, and I heard a voice from the four horns of the golden altar which is before God, one saying to the sixth angel who had the trumpet, "Release the four angels who are bound at the great river Euphrates." And* ***the four angels, who had been prepared for the hour and day and month and year, were released,*** *so that they would kill a third of mankind.* ***The number of the armies of the horsemen was two hundred million****; I heard the number of them.* (Revelation 9:13-16 NASB)

These four fallen angels are released at some point in the Last Days, and along with king Nimrod (a.k.a. Apollyon),[2] they will lead an army of 200 million horsemen. If we are to believe that we are getting close to the time when these events are to unfold, we must be careful to note that these 200 million *horsemen* are not the Russians, the Chinese, the Muslims nor any other people group on this planet. The text clearly tells us a few verses prior that this is a

---

1 1 Enoch 10:11,12; 1 Peter 3:19; 2 Peter 2:4; Jude 1:6

2. See Chapter Two of Book 1, *Babylon Rising: And The First Shall Be Last* for more on *"The Man of Many Names."*

Nephilim army that comes up out of the bottomless pit!

> *And* ***the shapes of the locusts were like unto horses prepared unto battle****; and on their heads were as it were crowns like gold, and their faces were as the faces of men. And they had hair as the hair of women, and their teeth were as the teeth of lions. And they had breastplates, as it were breastplates of iron; and the sound of their wings was as the sound of chariots of many horses running to battle. And they had tails like unto scorpions, and there were stings in their tails: and their power was to hurt men five months. And they had a king over them, which is the angel of the bottomless pit, whose name in the Hebrew tongue is Abaddon, but in the Greek tongue hath his name Apollyon.* (Revelation 9:7-11)

Some would say that the locust-like horses written about above are separate from the horses of verse 16. I can see justification for that view, but still, even if they are different, consider the description given below:

> ***The number of the armies of the horsemen was two hundred million****; I heard the number of them. And* ***this is how I saw in the vision the horses*** *and those who sat on them: the riders had breastplates the color of fire and of hyacinth and of brimstone; and* ***the heads of the horses are like the heads of lions; and out of their mouths proceed fire and smoke and brimstone****. A third of mankind was killed by these three plagues, by the fire and the smoke and the brimstone which proceeded out of their mouths. For the power of the horses is in their mouths and in their tails; for* ***their tails are like serpents and have heads****, and with them they do harm.*
> (Revelation 9:16-19 NASB)

No matter how you look at it (if you subscribe to a literal interpretation of Scripture), the text is describing a chimeric creature. It is not describing a massive army riding on horseback! To further elaborate, there are only 60 to 70 million horses on the planet.[3] So, how can there be 200 million mounted troops on only 70 million horses? Besides all that, what army in the world today (that would be of any real threat) uses horses anyway? It may be time to seriously re-evaluate most standard models of eschatology. Once you insert the Nephilim into the equation everything changes! But I'm getting way ahead of myself. We'll come back to these "horsemen" later. For now, I want you to see that what started back in Genesis will indeed come full circle in Revelation.

A variety of different types of Nephilim were on the earth for nearly 1,200 years prior to the Flood. A lot of strange and wild things happened in that time-frame. One thing is certain: it was definitely a scary time to live on this planet! Let's look at the pre-Flood time-line once again:

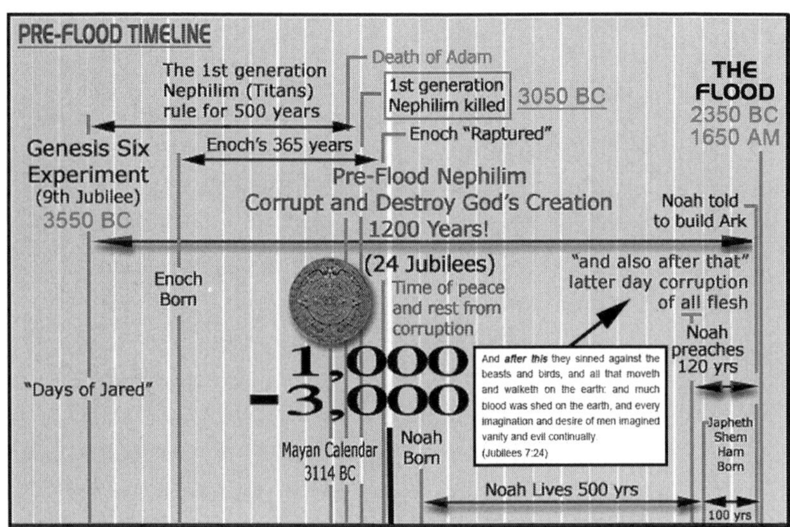

Figure 12

3. According to The Ultimate Horse Site, as of 2006, there were only 58,372,106 horses in the world. See: http://www.ultimatehorsesite.com/info/horsequestions/hq_numberofhorses.htm

Here we see that the Watchers first showed up around 3550 BC. They landed on Mount Hermon in the days of Jared. We know this not only because of what is written in 1 Enoch, but also because the canon of Scripture records a child being born and named due to this significant event.

Many times in the Scriptures, we see that children are often named "so and so" because "such and such" had happened or because of some emotion felt by the parents or some physical characteristic of the child stood out to them at birth. I certainly would not discount the idea that God had a hand in "inspiring the parents" to name their children either. In fact, Dr. Chuck Missler makes an interesting observation concerning the names of the pre-Flood patriarchs and the hidden meaning contained therein:

NAME	HEBREW MEANING
Adam	man
Seth	appointed
Enosh	mortal
Kenan	sorrow
Mahalalel	blessed God
Jared shall	shall come down
Enoch	teaching
Methusaleh	his death shall bring
Lamech	despairing
Noah	rest

Table 2

Putting it all together, Dr. Missler reasons that the names of these ten Pre-Flood men spell out a sentence revealing God's Master Plan:

> ***Man (is) appointed mortal sorrow; (but) the Blessed God shall come down teaching (that) His death shall bring (the) despairing rest.***

Mahalaleel named his son Jared because his name means "shall come down," "descended" or "to descend." Thus, according to Scripture, we can know exactly when the Watchers "descended," and as already stated, this is confirmed by 1 Enoch as well.

> *And they were in all two hundred **who descended** in the days of Jared in the summit of Mount Hermon...* (1 Enoch 6:6)

According to 1 Enoch 10:9,10, their offspring only lived for 500 years and they killed each other off by around 3050 BC (about 24 years after the death of Adam). Enoch then goes on to record in some detail about how the Watchers were judged and sentenced after that and the canon of Scripture gives us a brief snapshot concerning their fate:

> *For if God didn't spare the angels who sinned, but threw them down into Tartarus and delivered them to be kept in chains of darkness until judgment;* (2 Peter 2:4 HCSB)

> *And the angels which kept not their first estate, but left their own habitation, he hath reserved in everlasting chains under darkness unto the judgment of the great day.* (Jude 6)

What I find interesting about the combination of Genesis with 1 Enoch, Jasher and Jubilees is the way they each fill in the blanks of the story. Genesis is like the *Cliff Notes* version—giving us just the basics of what we need to know for God's bigger picture. 1 Enoch focuses in on a specific event (recorded in just a few verses of Genesis 6) and the resulting consequences. Regarding that event, the book of Jasher is silent. Instead, Jasher focuses on the character, personality and righteous deeds of Enoch, which led him into becoming one so highly favored of God. After the birth of Jared (which is represented by only one verse, 2:37), Jasher spends all of its third chapter discussing the life and activities of Enoch.

It records the funeral of Adam in verses 14-16. The following verses state that it was at that time that Enoch resolved to separate himself from the sons of men in order to serve the Lord. He would spend more and more time alone with Him as the narrative and the years progressed, until it got to the point where he was spending 364 out of 365 days alone with God and only one day with men. This clearly had a profound effect on him!

> *...the sons of men were greatly afraid of Enoch, and they feared to approach him on account of the Godlike awe that was seated on his countenance; therefore no man could look at him, fearing he might be punished and die.* (Jasher 3:20b)

Since the first generation Nephilim offspring were killed off about two decades after Adam's death, and the Watchers were judged and sentenced shortly thereafter, I would place the events of 1 Enoch happening by about this time in Jasher's account. Enoch continued to minister to men for a short time after, then eventually, he got a call from Heaven:

> *Some time after, when the kings and princes and the sons of men were speaking with Enoch, and Enoch was teaching them the ways of God, an angel of the Lord then called to Enoch from Heaven, and wished to bring him up to heaven* ***to make him reign there over the sons of God****, as he had reigned over the sons of men on earth.* (Jasher 3:23)

Apparently, after all the hubbub was over with the Watchers and their (immediate) offspring, Enoch had a chance to share some final words of wisdom from God to the sons of men and as a result, there was a time of peace.

> *He taught them wisdom and knowledge, and gave them instruction, and he rebuked them, and he placed before them statutes and judgments to do on earth, and* ***he made peace among them****, and taught them everlasting life,*

> *and lived with them some time teaching them all these things.*(Jasher 3:26)

Not long after that, Enoch got "raptured" up into Heaven.

> *And all the days of Enoch were three hundred sixty and five years: And Enoch walked with God: and he was not; for God took him.* (Genesis 5:23,24)

That event happened around 3015 BC—about 65 years prior to Noah's birth (circa 2950 BC). This time of peace actually seems to be reflected in the name of Noah.

NOAH'S NAME MEANS REST

One of the things that I have learned about reading the Bible is that whenever an author of Scripture takes a moment to insert some extra details in the text, we probably should take notice. There is a reason why the Holy Spirit had them do it. Apart from the quick remark concerning Enoch's unusual departure, there are no other added details given for anyone else in the lineage of Seth until we get to Noah. Concerning the birth of this child, Moses pauses to give us the following additional information:

> *And Lamech lived an hundred eighty and two years, and begat a son: And he called his name Noah, saying, This same shall comfort us concerning our work and toil of our hands, because of the ground which the LORD hath cursed.* (Genesis 5:28, 29)

That may sound a bit vague in terms of this thesis, but once again, the synchronized, biblically-endorsed, extra-biblical texts give us a little bit more detail about this story. Remember, after the initial incursion, God commanded that the first generation Nephilim would kill each other off within 500 years and that the good archangels would bind and bury the Watchers. This all happened about 65 years before Noah was born.

> *And destroy all the spirits of the reprobate and the children of the Watchers, because they have wronged mankind.* ***Destroy all wrong from the face of the earth and let every evil work come to an end****: and let the plant of righteousness and truth appear: and it shall prove a blessing; the works of righteousness and truth shall be planted in truth and joy for evermore.* (1 Enoch 10:15)

> *And Methuselah called his name Noah, saying, "The earth was in his days* ***at rest and free from corruption****." And Lamech his father named him Menachem, saying, "This one shall comfort us in our works and miserable toil in the earth, which God had cursed.* (Jasher 4:14)

It is as if Methuselah and Lamech feel like things are somewhat back to normal and so they name the baby, "rest and comfort." Now, Genesis tells us that Lamech named his son Noah. Jasher appears to tell a different story, stating his name as Menachem. So, was it Lamech or Methuselah who named him Noah? I suspect it was a little of both. The ancient texts say that Methusaleh was not only Lamech's father, but he was also the king who reigned in the land after Enoch's departure.

> *And when Enoch had ascended into heaven, all the kings of the earth rose and took Methuselah his son and anointed him, and they caused him to reign over them in the place of his father.* (Jasher 4:2)

Therefore, if Methuselah were to insist on the name, "Noah" I'm quite sure Lamech would have deferred to his father/the king's wishes. Besides that, we see in Genesis that Lamech died early.

> *And all the days of Lamech were seven hundred seventy and seven years: and he died.* (Genesis 5:31)

Jasher takes the story a step further and explains that Lamech died having not gone in the ways of his father.

> *And Lamech the father of Noah, died in those days; yet verily he did not go with all his heart in the ways of his father, and he died in the hundred and ninety-fifth year of the life of Noah.* (Jasher 5:19)

Thus, we see Noah coming under the guidance of his grandfather Methuselah. Though Genesis states that Lamech called his name Noah, it should be noted that in Hebrew, Menachem means "comforter"[4] which is not all that different from "rest" anyway. Ginzberg's *The Legends of the Jews* puts it this way:

> *By the name Noah he was called only by his grandfather Methuselah; his father and all others called him Menahem. His generation was addicted to sorcery, and Methuselah apprehended that his grandson might be bewitched if his true name were known, wherefore he kept it a secret. Menahem, Comforter, suited him as well as Noah; it indicated that he would be a consoler, if but the evil-doers of his time would repent of their misdeeds. At his very birth it was felt that he would bring consolation and deliverance.*[5]

THE LATTER DAY CORRUPTION

Noah lived for 600 years before the Flood waters came. In that time, a "new breed" of evil emerged and grew to corrupt the entire planet. Who were these new breed and where did they come from?

> *There were giants* [Nephilim] *in the earth in those days;* ***and also after that****, when the sons of God came in unto the daughters of men, and they bare* ***children*** *to them, the same* ***became*** *mighty men which were of old, men of renown.* (Genesis 6:4)

4. See definition in ***A Dictionary of Scripture Proper Names*** by J.B. Jackson (© 1909, Seventh Printing 1980, Loizeaux Brothers, Neptune, NJ), page 64
5. ***The Legends of the Jews*** by Louis Ginzberg Chapter 4.

We learned in the previous chapters exactly what the "*and also after that*" really means. Most ***assume*** it means after the Flood, but we have learned that it really means after *The Genesis Six Experiment* and yet *before* the Flood. Jasher seems to confirm that notion:

> *But in the* ***latter days of Methuselah****, the sons of men turned from the Lord; they corrupted the earth, they robbed and plundered each other, and they rebelled against God; they went contrary to,* ***they corrupted their ways****, and would not listen to the voice of Methuselah, but rebelled against him.* (Jasher 4:4)

This evil continued to escalate in those *latter* days to the point where Moses wrote:

> *And God saw that the wickedness of man was great in the earth, and that* ***every imagination of the thoughts of his heart was only evil continually****.* (Genesis 6:5)

Even the worst of the Nazis probably had a kind moment or two with those they loved. So, what could cause men's hearts to imagine ***only evil continually***? That's pretty hardcore! What could cause such a radical thing to happen? Again, Jasher offers us a clue:

> *And their judges and rulers went to the daughters of men and took their wives by force from their husbands according to their choice,* ***and the sons of men in those days took from the cattle of the earth, the beasts of the field and the fowls of the air, and taught the mixture of animals of one species with the other****, in order therewith to provoke the Lord; and God saw the whole earth and it was corrupt, for* ***all flesh had corrupted its ways on the earth, all men and all animals****.*
> (Jasher 4:18)

This is a direct parallel to the *Genesis* account:

> *And God looked upon the earth, and, behold, it was corrupt; for **all flesh had corrupted his way upon the earth**. And God said unto Noah, The end of all flesh is come before me; for the earth is filled with violence through them; and, behold, I will destroy them with the earth.* (Genesis 6:12,13)

The only thing I can think of that would make men's hearts imagine "***only*** *evil continually*" would be Nephilim, demonic seed. Notice that the book of Jubiliees gives us a second confirming witness:

> *And* ***after this they sinned against the beasts and birds, and all that moveth and walketh on the earth: and much blood was shed on the earth, and every imagination and desire of men imagined vanity and evil continually****. And the Lord destroyed everything from off the face of the earth; because of the wickedness of their deeds, and because of the blood which they had shed in the midst of the earth He destroyed everything.* (Jubilees 7:24,25)

I believe the "latter days" of Jasher and the "after this" of Jubilees are direct parallels to the "and also after that" of Genesis 6:4 (see **Table 3**). The text is referring to the genetic tampering that took place several hundred years after the destruction of the first generation Nephilim. Therefore, I propose that since Genesis 6 is giving us the exact play-by-play account of what caused God to wipe out the world with a Flood—***following the same exact linear progression of events*** recorded in 1 Enoch, Jasher and Jubilees—we should keep the entire chapter in that context. By that context, I am referring to the time period that began in 3550 BC in the days of Jared and extended for 1,200 years until the Flood waters came. There is no reason—*apart from making assumptions*—to ascribe the "and also after that" of Genesis 6:4 to post-Flood events (even though there were indeed giants in the land after the Flood, just as there were before it).

The phrase perfectly fits as it is in the context of the pre-Flood world.

GENESIS 6:4	JUBILEES 7:24	JASHER 4:4
There were giants in the earth in those days; **and also after that**, when the sons of God came in unto the daughters of men, and they bare children to them, the same became mighty men which were of old, men of renown.	And **after this** they sinned against the beasts and birds, and all that moveth and walketh on the earth: and much blood was shed on the earth, and every imagination and desire of men imagined vanity and evil continually.	But **in the latter days of Methuselah**, the sons of men turned from the Lord; they corrupted the earth, they robbed and plundered each other, and they rebelled against God; they went contrary to, **they corrupted their ways**, and would not listen to the voice of Methuselah, but rebelled against him.

Table 3

If we keep it all in that context, then we can see something pretty amazing taking place concerning the return of the Nephilim ***before*** the Flood that may actually be directly related to their return ***after*** the Flood... and in the days ahead!

In the 2009 movie *Splice*, the scientists decide to blend humans with animals. The result was an animal-human hybrid, female they called "Dren." But by the end of the movie, this female creature turned/evolved into a *male* demon! Is that just a coincidence? Or is it yet another case of what may soon become life imitating art? Is that movie showing us why the pre-Flood "judges and rulers" mixed species in order to bring back the Nephilim? Is this showing us how the Nephilim may return in the near future? Or worse... is this showing us how they may have *already* returned?

According to the Bible, the Nephilim originally appeared as a result of the sons of God (Watchers) mating with women. According to 1 Enoch, those offspring were destroyed 500 years later. But what about *their* offspring? Were there second, third, fourth... generations of Nephilim offspring continuing to walk the earth, beginning in the days of Jared and going all the way up until the time of the Flood? Could be. In fact, based on the testimony of the Greek version of 1 Enoch and also that of Jubilees, I strongly suspect that there were. Whether we are talking about that possibility or the idea of other pre-Flood "incursions," the commonly accepted canon of Scripture is silent. However, based on what we *can* see in the available information given to us in the Biblical account — and without making *any* assumptions — I think the return of the Nephilim in the pre/post-Flood world has more to do with the *scientific* mixture of species, just like in the movie, *Splice*.

In the previous chapter we saw that there were waves of evil that came and went and progressively got worse "in the latter days of Methuselah." Essentially, this is the order of events that we can derive from the parallel stories of Genesis and the synchronized, biblically-endorsed, extra-biblical texts:

1. ***200 Fallen Angels known as the Watchers came down in the days of Jared, and after landing on Mt. Hermon they took and mated with the daughters of men.***
2. ***Their offspring were massive giants (450 footers).***
3. ***God judged the children of the Watchers - the first generation Nephilim - by having them kill each other off within 500 years while their parents were made to watch.***
4. ***God then judged the Watchers and had them bound in Tartarus and under the sands of the earth in chains of darkness where they are to remain for 70 generations.***
5. ***There was a time of peace when Noah was born.***
6. ***Then after that, there was another wave of evil that***

took place as a result of the mixture of species that began in the latter days of Methuselah and resulted in all flesh being corrupted.

7. ***The Flood came and washed everything away except those who made it onto Noah's Ark.***

When exactly was this "and also after that" on the timeline? It is my strong suspicion that it was in the last 120 years of Methuselah's life. Coincidentally, it was during the 120 years before the Flood that the Apostle Peter says Noah preached and begged the pre-Flood people to stop what they were doing, repent from their evil ways and turn back to God.

REPENTING FOR DOING WHAT?

> *For if God spared not the angels that sinned, but cast them down to hell [Tartarus], and delivered them into chains of darkness, to be reserved unto judgment; And spared not the old world, but saved Noah the eighth person,* ***a preacher of righteousness****, bringing in the flood upon the world of the ungodly;* (2 Peter 2:4,5)

We know this is what Noah was doing for that 120 years because of the testimony of Peter as well as that of his disciple, Clement of Rome:

> *Let us turn to every age that has passed, and learn that, from generation to generation, the Lord has granted a place of repentance to all such as would be converted unto Him.* ***Noah preached repentance****, and as many as listened to him were saved.* (1 Clement 7:5,6)

> *The Lord is not slack concerning his promise, as some men count slackness; but is longsuffering to us-ward,* ***not willing that any should perish, but that all should come to repentance****.* (2 Peter 3:9)

I am so thankful that God is "longsuffering" toward us, not willing that any should perish! Contrary to what some may think, the Bible makes it clear that YHVH does not delight in the destruction of the wicked:

> *Say unto them, As I live, saith the Lord GOD,* ***I have no pleasure in the death of the wicked; but that the wicked turn from his way and live:*** *turn ye, turn ye from your evil ways; for why will ye die, O house of Israel?* (Ezekiel 33:11)

God does not want to punish sinners. He wants to save them! That's why He sent His only begotten Son, in the first place:

> *For God so loved the world, that he gave his only begotten Son, that whosoever believeth in him should not perish, but have everlasting life.* ***For God sent not his Son into the world to condemn the world; but that the world through him might be saved.*** (John 3:16,17)

God's desire has always been to seek and save that which is lost (Luke 19:10). I like the way the First Fruits of Zion Torah Club study guide describes the process of repentance:

> *God does not want to punish sinners. He wants them to turn from their evil ways so they will not need to be punished. Turning away from evil is called "repentance." In Hebrew, the word for "repent" is "**shuv**." It means "to turn around." Repentance ("teshuvah" in the noun form) is a foundational concept in the Bible. It means "to return." Unlike the Greek equivalent, which implies a change of mind, "teshuvah" means "to turn around and go back in the other direction." To repent means "to quit sinning, turn around and start doing good." It is more than just a change of mind; "teshuvah" demands a change of behavior. It's about starting over fresh and trying to do better.*[6]

6. First Fruits of Zion: ***Torah Club, Volume 1***, page 26

The way of escape from the judgement of the coming Deluge was to repent and get on the Ark. But what exactly were the pre-Flood men supposed to repent of? You cannot repent of being born a Nephilim. You don't have any choice in that. Therefore, it had to have been something else that brought about the wrath of God. Genesis gives us several clues:

> *And God said, Let the earth bring forth grass, the herb yielding seed, and the fruit tree yielding fruit* ***after his kind****, whose seed is in itself, upon the earth: and it was so. And the earth brought forth grass, and herb yielding seed* ***after his kind****, and the tree yielding fruit, whose seed was in itself,* ***after his kind****: and God saw that it was good.* (Genesis 1:11,12)

> *And God created great whales, and every living creature that moveth, which the waters brought forth abundantly,* ***after their kind****, and every winged fowl* ***after his kind****: and* ***God saw that it was good****.* (Genesis 1:21)

> *And God said, Let the earth bring forth the living creature after his kind, cattle, and creeping thing, and beast of the earth* ***after his kind****: and it was so. And God made the beast of the earth* ***after his kind****, and cattle* ***after their kind****, and every thing that creepeth upon the earth* ***after his kind****: and* ***God saw that it was good****.* (Genesis 1:24,25)

What do those verses all have in common? Obviously, God's emphasis on everything reproducing "after its kind."

> *So* ***God created man in his own image****, in the image of God created he him; male and female created he them. And God blessed them, and God said unto them, Be fruitful, and multiply, and replenish the earth, and subdue it: and have dominion over the fish of the sea, and over the fowl*

> *of the air, and over every living thing that moveth upon the earth. And God said, Behold, I have given you every herb bearing seed, which is upon the face of all the earth, and every tree, in the which is the fruit of a tree yielding seed; to you it shall be for meat. And to every beast of the earth, and to every fowl of the air, and to every thing that creepeth upon the earth, wherein there is life, I have given every green herb for meat: and it was so. And* ***God saw every thing that he had made, and, behold, it was very good****. And the evening and the morning were the sixth day.*(Genesis 1:27-31)

God created everything exactly the way He wanted it and in the end of the Creation process, He looked at it and called it "very good." But fallen angels inserted their evil seed into that creation, corrupting both animals and humans. God severely judged those angels for this and killed off their first generation offspring. Then we find in the ancient text that there was a *further* corruption of genetic material. Jasher and Jubilees both tell us **exactly** what pre-Flood men were doing in the latter days of Methuselah, that God was desperately trying to get them to repent of and stop doing: It was the practice of transhuman, genetic engineering, which resulted in all flesh becoming corrupted. Notice what Moses wrote concerning that which survived the Flood:

> *And of every living thing of all flesh, two of* ***every sort*** *shalt thou bring into the ark, to keep them alive with thee; they shall be male and female. Of fowls* ***after their kind****, and of cattle* ***after their kind,*** *of every creeping thing of the earth* ***after his kind****, two of every sort shall come unto thee, to keep them alive.* (Genesis 6:19,20)

> *And the rain was upon the earth forty days and forty nights. In the selfsame day entered Noah, and Shem, and Ham, and Japheth, the sons of Noah, and Noah's wife, and the three wives of his sons with them, into the ark; They, and*

> *every beast* ***after his kind****, and all the cattle* ***after their kind****, and every creeping thing that creepeth upon the earth* ***after his kind****, and every fowl* ***after his kind****, every bird of* ***every sort****. And they went in unto Noah into the ark, two and two of all flesh, wherein is the breath of life. And they that went in, went in male and female of all flesh, as God had commanded him: and the LORD shut him in.* (Genesis 7:12-16)

Now observe what *did not* make it on the Ark, and thus perished in the Flood:

> *And all flesh died that moved upon the earth, both of fowl, and of cattle, and of beast, and of every creeping thing that creepeth upon the earth, and every man: All in whose nostrils was the breath of life, of all that was in the dry land, died. And every living substance was destroyed which was upon the face of the ground, both man, and cattle, and the creeping things, and the fowl of the heaven; and they were destroyed from the earth: and Noah only remained alive, and they that were with him in the ark.* (Genesis 7:21-23)

Did you notice that the phrase "after his kind" does not appear in reference to that which perished in the Flood? Could it be that those were all genetically modified organisms that were no longer after the original "kind" that God created them to be at the beginning, and which He pronounced "very good?" I strongly suspect this to be the case.

Now concerning the *people* that were on the Ark, you might be tempted to say that they were all genetically pure and qualified for each being "after his kind" just like the animals. But we must acknowledge that this is an *assumption*. Nowhere does the text does say that *they* were. It only says that Noah was! Still, could verse 14 lead us to believe that all of the people were "after his kind" too?

> ***They***, *and* ***every beast after his kind***, *and all the cattle* ***after their kind***, *and every creeping thing that creepeth upon the earth* ***after his kind***, *and every fowl* ***after his kind***, *every bird of* ***every sort***. (Genesis 7:14)

The word "They" is a bit vague and hardly strong enough to build a case for genetic purity in all of the people on board. As we will see in the next chapter, apparently they weren't all pure. Believe it or not, the truth of Noah's singular purity may actually serve as a foreshadowing of salvation through *one* pure man named Yeshua (Jesus). Note how Noah is described in Genesis:

> *These are the generations of Noah: Noah was a just man and* ***perfect in his generations***, *and Noah walked with God.* (Genesis 6:9)

The phrase, "perfect in his generations" comes from the Hebrew word, *tamim* which means without defect — in other words, he was genetically pure. This is the same word used in Numbers 19:2 when describing the pure red heifer that has no blemish. So, Noah was both genetically pure and morally righteous and these were the attributes that may have saved his family.

> *The Torah does not say that Noah's family was also righteous and deserved to be saved. They were spared because of their association with the righteous Noah. This illustrates how salvation works. Yeshua of Nazareth, the Son of God, lived a life of perfect righteousness. He did not share in the sins of other human beings. He did not merit the punishment of other human beings. Therefore, God raised Him from the dead. Others can join Him. Simply by virtue of being associated with Him and His righteousness we are spared from the final judgment.*[7]

This of course is confirmed by the writing of the Apostle Paul in the book of Romans:

---

7. First Fruits of Zion: ***Torah Club, Volume 1***, page 26

> *(...And not as it was by one* [Adam] *that sinned, so is the gift: for the judgment was by one to condemnation, but the free gift is of many offences unto justification. For if by one man's offence death reigned by one; much more they which receive abundance of grace and of the gift of righteousness shall reign in life by one, Jesus Christ.) Therefore as by the offence of one judgment came upon all men to condemnation; even so* ***by the righteousness of one*** [Yeshua] ***the free gift came upon all men unto justification of life. For as by one man's disobedience many were made sinners, so by the obedience of one shall many be made righteous.*** (Romans 5:16-19)

What a wonderful word picture concerning righteousness! But what about *genetic* purity?

> ***These are the generations of Noah****: Noah was a just man and perfect* [tamim] *in his generations, and Noah walked with God.* ***And Noah begat three sons, Shem, Ham, and Japheth.*** (Genesis 6:9,10)

The structure of these two sentences leads us to believe that Shem, Ham and Japheth were just as "*tamim*" as Noah was. And if Noah and his three sons were pure, it stands to reason that Noah's wife must have been as well. So, that *blood* family was pure, but there's a problem concerning the three wives of Noah's sons: they are not mentioned until after the Scripture that specifically says ***all*** flesh had become corrupted and *after* Noah was instructed to build the Ark.

Again, you cannot repent for being born as the Nephilim offspring of angels who had mated with humans. You can't help who your parents are, so there's no way anyone could have repented for that. There had to have been something else going on that people *could* have repented and turned away from doing. I believe God essentially gave mankind 115 years to repent of the practice of corrupting all flesh through genetic engineering—mixing species and creating hybrids that were never meant to exist.

CORRUPTING THE IMAGE

What possible reason could there have been for wanting to blend different terrestrial species together in the first place?

> *And God looked upon the earth, and, behold, it was corrupt; for* ***all flesh had corrupted his way upon the earth.***(Genesis 6:12)

> *And* ***their judges and rulers went to the daughters of men and took their wives by force from their husbands according to their choice, and the sons of men in those days took from the cattle of the earth, the beasts of the field and the fowls of the air, and taught the mixture of animals of one species with the other****, in order therewith to provoke the Lord; and God saw the whole earth and it was corrupt, for* ***<u>all flesh</u> had corrupted it's ways on the earth****, all men and all animals.* (Jasher 4:18)

> *And* ***after this they sinned against the beasts and birds, and all that moveth and walketh on the earth****: and much blood was shed on the earth, and every imagination and desire of men imagined vanity and evil continually.* (Jubilees 7:24)

The book of Jasher gives us the most detail. It tells us that the "judges and rulers" of the people forcefully took women from their fathers and husbands. Note this passage says ***<u>absolutely nothing</u>*** about anyone having sex with angels in that context. Rather, the text goes on to describe men doing scientific experiments with animals (and presumably the abducted women) creating trans-genetic species.

Why were they doing that? Why are scientists doing the exact same thing today? Are our "rulers" really the ones behind the so-called "alien abduction phenomena"—just like the primary plot of *The X-Files* TV series suggests? There certainly appears to be mounting evidence to suggest that they are. Why? Could this be a way to bring back the Fallen Ones? Is that how the Nephilim giants returned "after that"—that being the initial First Cause Incursion? Is that how they will return again? Were people mixing their seed with the offspring of the first generation Nephilim? Does mixing human seed with animal seed open up "portals" for demons to enter?

If nothing else, this should give us serious pause to consider the implications of genetically cross-breeding species and modifying the "kinds" that God previously called "very good" as He originally created them. We may be opening *Forbidden Gates*[8] and thus *Corrupting the Image*[9] of God, and if so, the results will not be good. Be assured, God won't like it in our day anymore than He did in the days of Noah, during the latter days of Methuselah!

Indeed, there is a further danger in all of this. God's Spirit dwells in that which ***He*** created. But when man intervenes and starts creating his own "kinds" of beings, will His Spirit be in it, or will it contain the spirit of something else? The Septuagint version of Genesis 6:3 seems to indicate the latter:

> *And the Lord God said,* ***My Spirit shall certainly not remain among these men for ever****, because they are flesh, but their days shall be an hundred and twenty years.* (Genesis 6:3 LXX)

This would be a very odd Scripture if not for that interpretation. Man was flesh the moment God formed him out of clay and made Adam in His image. So what's the difference here? Is this passage saying that the hybridization process is causing humans to exist that do not have (or can not have) the Spirit of God within them?

8. ***Forbidden Gates*** is the title of a book by Tom and Nita Horn dealing with the issue of transhumanism.
9. ***Corrupting the Image*** is the title of a book by Doug Hamp that deals with similar issues. concerning transhumanism.

> *And the Lord God said,* ***My Spirit shall certainly not remain among these men for ever****, because they are flesh, but their days shall be an hundred and twenty years.* (Genesis 6:3 Douay-Rheims Bible)

Since that Scripture is sandwiched between Genesis 6:2 and Genesis 6:4, I'd have to say yes. Perhaps that was the Devil's plan: to corrupt the image of God so that the Spirit of God could no longer dwell within it.

Paul wrote that our bodies are the temple of the Holy Spirit.

> *What? know ye not that* ***your body is the temple of the Holy Ghost*** *which is in you, which ye have of God, and ye are not your own?* (1 Corinthians 6:19)

The hybridization process would seem to destroy that temple, causing either the Holy Spirit to withdraw from it or preventing the Holy Spirit from even entering it at all. That being the case, is it any wonder that the ancient texts say that every imagination of their heart was ***only evil*** continually?

> *And after this they sinned against the beasts and birds, and all that moveth and walketh on the earth: and much blood was shed on the earth, and* ***every imagination and desire of men imagined vanity and evil continually.*** (Jubilees 7:24)

From that verse we learn that every imagination and desire of men became only evil continually as the result of blending animals with humans. The absence of light causes darkness. Therefore, the absence of God's Spirit can only result in pure evil.

CREATED IN WHOSE IMAGE?

In his book, *Interview With The Giant*, Dr. Judd Burton had something very interesting to say concerning the fate of the Nephilim giants that may shed more light on this subject:

> *Despite the loss of their physical bodies* [from dying in the Flood], *there is reason to believe that the giants' spirits continued to exist. In this state, they were (and are) demonic entities. Like other sentient creatures, they have an eternal spirit at their essence. Therefore, the Nephilim and related tribes of giants never really ceased to exist, only their physicality was lost.*[10]

This fact caused me to wonder if there wasn't another purpose and plan regarding the blending of terrestrial species. We've already learned that corrupting the images of the "kinds" which God had originally created causes Him to remove (or not implant) His Spirit into such a body, but could there be more to this story?

> *So God created man in his own image, in the image of God created he him; male and female created he them.* (Genesis 1:27)

The Bible tells us that original man was created in God's own image and likeness. Lucifer cannot create anything from scratch. He can only manipulate that which the Creator had already created.

> *Also out of the midst thereof came the likeness of four living creatures. And this was their appearance; they had the likeness of a man. And every one had four faces, and every one had four wings. And their feet were straight feet; and the sole of their feet was like the sole of a calf's foot: and they sparkled like the color of burnished brass. And they had the hands of a man under their wings on their four sides; and they four had their faces and their wings. Their wings were joined one to another; they turned not when they went; they went every one straight forward. As for the likeness of their faces, they four had the face of a man, and the face of a lion, on the right side: and they four had the face of an ox on the left side; they four also had the face of an eagle.* (Ezekiel 1:5-10)

10. ***Interview With The Giant: Ethnohistorical Notes on the Nephilim*** by Judd H. Burton (© 2009 Burtom Beyond Press), Chapter 2, page 14.

Could it be that the angels were trying to create a being in *their* likeness? Was this Plan B? Were they trying to create host bodies that were fit for their angel-human-hybrid Nephilim children's disembodied, demonic spirits to enter? I believe so, and if this is true, imagine the implications! Indeed, the creators of *Splice* seemed to imagine it. Note what the director had in mind concerning the creation of Dren:

> *I always felt that Dren, the roots of Dren, lay in this: that she is in some ways a kind of genetically engineered angel.*
>
> — Vincenzo Natali[11]

You have many characteristics about you, which came from your parents. You may have blue eyes, or dark hair, fair skin, dark skin, a large or small nose, attached or detached earlobes, and any number of other physical characteristics that you share with your mom and dad. After all, it was their combined genetic information that made you. In that genetic make-up, certain personality traits were likely passed along to you as well. There can be no denying the fact that we are the offspring of our parents and we share much in common with them.

Now imagine an entity who had one parent that was a fallen angel and the other a human female. Such a creature would have the physical characteristics of its mother as well as some from its angelic father. It would also have some of their personality traits too. It would be a hybrid of the two, with a spirit that did not come from God dwelling inside. When such a creature dies, 1 Enoch says that spirit leaves the body and becomes an evil, wandering spirit we call a demon. Presuming spirits retain the personality traits of the host it once inhabited, that demon spirit would go out as a former Nephilim, bearing all of the traits of its father and mother.

When we consider how big and powerful the Nephilim were,

11. See: http://www.firstshowing.net/2010/interview-cube-and-splice-directorwriter-vincenzo-natali/

it becomes very easy for us to then understand how a little girl possessed with a demon can tear off metal chains with her bare hands and throw 200 pound, grown men across the room. Such things are possible because there is a big *thing* inside a small package exercising some of its former attributes!

Azazel was known as having many characteristics in common with goats. Imagine his offspring's disembodied spirit being able to inhabit a goat-man hybrid (satyr) body. As Dr. Burton pointed out, it had only lost its physicality when its original body died. So, in a new body of "like kind" (in this case a goat-man), that spirit would once again have physicality.

Figure 13

This is exactly why I believe genetic manipulation took place: to bring back a return of the original Nephilim (before the Flood), which were killed off just prior to the birth of Noah. If this theory is true, it explains much about the hybrids of the post-Flood world; especially characters like Pan, the goat-demon-god of mythology.

Could it be that the spirit of Azazel's original offspring just kept inhabiting satyr bodies over and over again until the last one was destroyed and man had forgotten the mechanism by which such hybrids could be produced? What if through the current trend of creating animal-human chimeras we create just the right host body that would be a "fit extension" for Pan to return once again in our day?

What if the centaurs, minotaurs, and satyrs were specific, genetically engineered "like kinds" which were naturally fit extensions for the disembodied spirits of dead Nephilim? What if we're creating those kinds again? What if... ?

And I looked and turned to another part of the earth, and saw there a deep valley with burning fire. And they brought the kings and the mighty, and began to cast them into this deep valley. And there mine eyes saw how they made these their instruments, iron chains of immeasurable weight. And I asked the angel of peace who went with me, saying: 'For whom are these chains being prepared?'

And he said unto me: 'These are being prepared for the hosts of Azâzêl, so that they may take them and cast them into the abyss of complete condemnation, and they shall cover their jaws with rough stones as the Lord of Spirits commanded.

And Michael, and Gabriel, and Raphael, and Phanuel shall take hold of them on that great day, and cast them on that day into the burning furnace, that the Lord of Spirits may take vengeance on them for their unrighteousness in becoming subject to Satan and leading astray those who dwell on the earth.'

And in those days shall punishment come from the Lord of Spirits, and he will open all the chambers of waters which are above the heavens, and of the fountains which are beneath the earth. And all the waters shall be joined with the waters: that which is above the heavens is the masculine, and the water which is beneath the earth is the feminine. And they shall destroy all who dwell on the earth and those who dwell under the ends of the heaven. And when they have recognized their unrighteousness which they have wrought on the earth, then by these shall they perish.

(1 Enoch 54)

SECTION II

THE POST-FLOOD NEPHILIM HYBRIDS

—— Chapter Six ——

SUSPICIOUS WOMEN AND THE RISE OF THE X-MEN

And we took all his cities at that time, and utterly destroyed the men, and the women, and the little ones, of every city, we left none to remain:
(Deuteronomy 2:34)

So far, we have eliminated the notion of multiple incursions as a likely explanation for the return of the Nephilim before and after the Flood. In the last chapter, we learned about the cause of the corruption of all flesh which led to God having to destroy the whole world with the Flood. According to the synchronized, biblically-endorsed, extra-biblical texts, this corruption came about as a result of transhuman, genetic engineering. So what's left? I believe the return of the Nephilim in the post-Flood world is directly related to their return in the pre-Flood world. In fact, they are *genetically* related. These genetics appear to have been passed along via three suspicious women, who I believe represent the best explanation for the presence of the post-Flood Nephilim. In my opinion, this belief requires the fewest new assumptions and has the most evidence going for it.

TIMING IS EVERYTHING

I know many believe that it took Noah 120 years to build the ark, but I would like to point out that it was just a big box. Granted, it had three decks and lots of compartments within it, but do you really think it took Noah and sons that long to do build such a relatively simple structure? Jasher tells us it actually only took them five years.

> *And Noah rose up, and he made the ark, in the place where God had commanded him, and Noah did as God had ordered him. In his five hundred and ninety-fifth year Noah commenced to make the ark, and* ***he made the ark in five years****, as the Lord had commanded.*
> (Jasher 5:33,34)

In Genesis 6:3, God announced that there would be 120 years left for men to repent. Thus, Noah preached for at least 115 of those years before God finally told him that it was time to start building the ark. Such a construction project likely drew a lot of attention, so naturally, Noah would have continued to preach as he worked.

With only five more years left to save those who were still *tamim*, Noah and his sons got busy and as we saw, according to Jasher it took them exactly five years to complete the project. After the work was done, one thing remained: Noah had to pick three wives for his three sons.

> *Then Noah took the three daughters of Eliakim, son of Methuselah, for wives for his sons, as the Lord had commanded Noah. And it was at that time Methuselah the son of Enoch died, nine hundred and sixty years old was he, at his death.*
> (Jasher 5:35,36)

Here we see that the three wives were not chosen until ***after*** the ark was completed, roughly seven days before the Flood. Some may resist this as being unbiblical since Genesis doesn't say that, so for the sake of argument, let's look at what Genesis *does* say:

> *And God looked upon the earth, and, behold, it was corrupt;* ***for all flesh had corrupted his way upon the earth****. And God said unto Noah, The end of all flesh is come before me; for the earth is filled with violence through them; and, behold, I will destroy them with the earth.*
>
> *Make thee an ark of gopher wood; rooms shalt thou make in the ark, and shalt pitch it within and without with pitch. And this is the fashion which thou shalt make it of: The length of the ark shall be three hundred cubits, the breadth of it fifty cubits, and the height of it thirty cubits. A window shalt thou make to the ark, and in a cubit shalt thou finish it above; and the door of the ark shalt thou set in the side thereof; with lower, second, and third stories shalt thou make it.*
>
> *And, behold, I, even I, do bring a flood of waters upon the earth, to destroy all flesh, wherein is the breath of life, from under heaven; and every thing that is in the earth shall die. But with thee will I establish my covenant; and thou shalt come into the ark, thou, and thy sons, and thy wife,* ***and thy sons' wives with thee****.*
> (Genesis 6:12-18)

Without making any assumptions, we see that there is a progression of events given in a specific order in Genesis, which is confirmed and elaborated on in the synchronized, biblically-endorsed, extra-biblical texts. If we are to assume Genesis is written in chronological order, following a linear progression of events, we see the same thing: Earth and ***all flesh*** becomes corrupted, violence fills the earth, God decides to destroy it, He gives the instructions for how to build the ark and finally, for the first time, the wives of Noah's sons are mentioned. There is no mention of them prior and verse 18 follows verse 12, therefore the chronology given in Genesis is exactly the same as that given in Jasher. In the latter, there is no contradiction, only elaboration.

In showing how Genesis syncs up with the books of 1 Enoch, Jasher and Jubilees, it may be summarized as follows:

1. **Genesis 6:1-4 –> Angels mating with humans.**
   Syncs with: 1 Enoch 6:1 – 7:2 and Jubilees 5:1 (see also recap of 7:21-23)
2. **Genesis 6:5-7 –> Shows how God feels about the resulting violence.**
   Syncs with: 1 Enoch 7:3-6 and Jubilees 5:2-4
3. **Genesis 6:8-10 –> Reveal how Noah and his sons were genetically pure.**
   Syncs with: Jasher 4:12-15 (see also Jasher 5:13-17) and Jubilees 5:5
4. **Genesis 6:11,12 –> Earth and <u>all</u> flesh becomes corrupted.**
   Syncs with: Jasher 4:16-18 and Jubilees 5:19
5. **Genesis 6:13-17 –> God grows increasingly angry and tells Noah to build the ark and how to do it.**
   Syncs with: Jasher 4:19-21 & 5:25-29 and Jubilees 5:21,22
6. **Genesis 6:18 –> First mention of the wives of Noah's three sons.**
   Syncs with: Jasher 5:32-36 (Noah chose the three wives just 7 days before the Flood!)

The text seems to show quite plainly that the wives were a late addition in the chronology and since they came after the corruption of "***<u>all</u> flesh***," we have to acknowledge that Noah's choices for wives must have been rather limited indeed. All things considered, I'd say he did a pretty good job.

How long of a time period are we talking about between Genesis 6:1 and verse 18? Well, let's look at the pre-Flood timeline chart again. In **Figure 14**, we see that the Watchers came down in the days of Jared, which was at about 3550 BC. Then, 500 years later, the first-generation Nephilim hybrids were destroyed and the Watchers were judged shortly thereafter. Enoch continued to preach for a short time and then he was raptured around 3015 BC—about 65 years prior to Noah's birth, which was around 2950 BC.

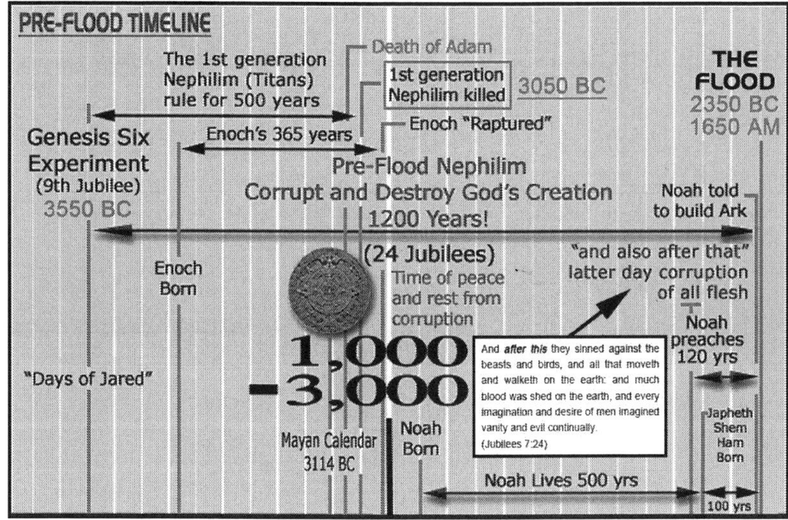

Figure 14

Since the ancient Hebrew (extra-biblical) texts referred to a corruption of flesh beginning "in the latter days of Methusaleh" and Genesis says that Noah preached for 120 years, we'd probably be safe in saying that the following represents a pretty accurate timeline:

1. **Noah was found to be genetically pure** (vs 8,9) - at least 120 years before the Flood.
2. **Noah had three genetically pure sons** (vs 10) - 100 years before the Flood (Jasher 5:13-18 says that Noah took a wife when he was 498 years old and they had his sons a few years later when he was 500 - 502 years old - see also Genesis 5:32 for confirmation of that age).
3. **Violence and corruption erupts in the earth** (vs 11) - sometime within the 100 years prior to the Flood.
4. **ALL flesh becomes corrupted** (vs 12) - sometime within the 100 years prior to the Flood.
5. **God announces that He is going to destroy the world by Flood** (vs 13) - sometime between 120 to 5

years prior to the Flood.

6. **God instructs Noah on how to build the Ark** (vs 14-16) -Jasher 5:34 says that Noah commenced to make the Ark five years before the Flood and that it took him that long to build it. Presumably his now 95 year old (young) sons helped him with the building and thus would have had very little time for marriage. Jasher 5:35,36 confirms this when it says that Noah picked the three wives for his sons literally right around the same time that Methusaleh died — which was just seven days prior to the Flood. So it appears that there was both a funeral and a wedding at the same time![1]
7. **God says He is going to destroy the whole earth, but will preserve Noah, his wife, his sons and his son's wives** (vs 17-18) — God's promise right before the Flood waters came (when Noah was 600 yrs old).

Based on the above, easily verifiable timeline, there is little need for assumptions. The texts say what they say. ***All flesh*** had become corrupted and Noah didn't pick the three wives for his three sons until the very end, during the last few days before the Flood waters came. So, could it be that those three women might have fallen into the category of those whose flesh had been corrupted? Genesis, Jasher and Jubilees would lead us to believe that they were. Naturally, that means God allowed corrupted DNA onto the ark.

THAT'S ABSURD!

My detractors say that my position regarding Nephilim genetics possibly surviving in any member of Noah's crew is absurd and makes no sense. They ask, *"If God had to wipe out the whole world with a Flood, why would He allow any Nephilim genetics to survive on the ark?"*

1. This may have significant prophetic meaning when we look at the events of the Last Days (that Jesus said would be just like the days of Noah).

They are focusing on the symptom not the root cause. Why they can't see that their position is even ***more absurd***, I will never know. God had to *destroy the whole world* because of what the Watchers and their offspring did. His entire Creation had become completely corrupted. That was the reason for the Flood! So, if that's the case, why would God simply allow the *same thing* to happen again? What? Was the Flood just a half-time show that the Watchers watched as the playing field was washed clean? Was God just wiping everything out so they could simply pick up where they left off and start all over again almost immediately after the ground was dry? No. That makes absolutely no sense at all.

Whereas, it makes perfect sense why God may have allowed ***microscopic genetic codes*** (i.e. a remnant of genetic **information**) to survive—just long enough for His people to wipe them out. Why? Because as we will soon see, it was through the heroic acts of the Hebrew people that the whole post-Flood world came to fear them and YHVH, their God—the one true God of Abraham, Isaac and Jacob. God got the glory through His chosen people and this new nation of "giant slayers" stood as a testimony to all other nations of the awesome power and truth of the living Creator of heaven and earth.

> *Now before they lay down, she came up to them on the roof, and said to the men, " I know that the Lord has given you the land, and that* ***the terror of you has fallen on us, and that all the inhabitants of the land have melted away before you.*** *For we have heard how the Lord dried up the water of the Red Sea before you when you came out of Egypt, and what you did to the two kings of the Amorites who were beyond the Jordan, to Sihon and Og, whom you utterly destroyed.* ***When we heard it, our hearts melted and no courage remained in any man any longer because of you; for the Lord your God, He is God in heaven above and on earth beneath.*** (Joshua 2:8-11)

When you consider what this tiny nation did to entire cultures of massive post-Flood giants, it is very easy to see why God "allowed" Nephilim genetic **information** to survive—long enough to be wiped out by His people. In so doing, God demonstrated to the world and to the fallen angels what *people* in right relationship with Him can do.

X AND Y CHROMOSOMES

We know from Genesis that God created man in His own image and *likeness*. This is most interesting if we take that notion down to the genetic level. I began to wonder, does God have chromosomes? Considering the fact that Adam was created in His *likeness,* it would seem so. Chromosomes are information packages.

A man has both X and Y chromosomes. Women lack the Y chromosome and instead have two X chromosomes. So when God took Eve "out of Adam" it would appear that God replicated the X chromosome. When the Holy Spirit "overshadowed" Mary and impregnated her with the "seed" that would germinate her egg, thus producing the promised Messiah, He must have added His Y to her X in order to produce the male child.

> *Now the birth of Jesus Christ was on this wise: When as his mother Mary was espoused to Joseph, before they came together,* ***she was found with child of the Holy Ghost****.* (Matthew 1:18)

> *Then said Mary unto the angel, How shall this be, seeing I know not a man? And the angel answered and said unto her,* ***The Holy Ghost shall come upon thee, and the power of the Highest shall overshadow thee****: therefore also that holy thing which shall be born of thee shall be called the Son of God.* (Luke 1:34,35)

In both cases, the first Adam and the "Second Adam" were given their Y chromosome from God Himself. I believe this is absolutely critical in understanding the value of all of the *men* on Noah's ark being pure and why "tainted genes" in the women are far less of a problem than what you can expect from the notion of multiple incursions, where male angels are reintroducing bad Y chromosomes into the gene pool.

We know from Scripture that Eve's sin did not cause the downfall of the human race. It was only when Adam took a bite of the "forbidden fruit" that sin entered the world.

> *Wherefore, as* ***by one man sin entered into the world,*** *and death by sin; and so death passed upon all men, for that all have sinned:* (Romans 5:12)

When Adam sinned, the human race fell. Sin entered the world through a man, therefore sin had to be paid for by a man. This is why God didn't have an "only begotten daughter" to save mankind, but rather a son.

> *But the free gift is not like the transgression.* ***For if by the transgression of the one the many died, much more did the grace of God and the gift by the grace of the one Man, Jesus Christ, abound to the many.*** *The gift is not like that which came through the one who sinned; for on the one hand the judgment arose from one transgression resulting in condemnation, but on the other hand the free gift arose from many transgressions resulting in justification. For if* ***by the transgression of the one, death reigned through the one, much more those who receive the abundance of grace and of the gift of righteousness will reign in life through the One, Jesus Christ.*** (Romans 5:15-17 NASB)

The interesting thing about the Y chromosome, is it can only come from a father. Thus, every Y chromosome in existence today had to have come from fathers, which can be traced all the way back to Noah; the one *genetically pure* male whose untainted Y chromosome could be traced all the way back to Adam; the man who received the first Y chromosome directly from God Himself.

In order for mankind to eventually be saved, there would have to be a pure Y chromosome genetic line going all the way back to Adam. To achieve this, God made absolutely certain that the first generation Nephilim offspring who received their Y chromosomes from *angels* would be killed off within 500 years of their birth.

> *And to Gabriel said the Lord: 'Proceed against the bastards and the reprobates, and against the children of fornication: and destroy [the children of fornication and] the children of the Watchers from amongst men [and cause them to go forth]: send them one against the other that they may destroy each other in battle:* ***for length of days shall they not have****. And no request that they (i.e. their fathers) make of thee shall be granted unto their fathers on their behalf; for they hope to live an eternal life, and that* ***each one of them will live five hundred years****.'*
> (1 Enoch 10:9,10)

This same story is given in the book of Jubilees as well:

> *And against their sons went forth a command from before His mouth that they should be killed with the sword, and be removed from under heaven. And He said "My spirit will not always abide on man; for they also are flesh and their days shall be one hundred and twenty years."*[2] *And He sent His sword into their midst that each should slay his neighbor, and* ***they began to slay each other till they all fell by the sword and were destroyed from the earth****. And their fathers were witnesses (of their destruction), and after this they were bound in the depths of the earth for ever, until the day of the great condemnation when judgment is executed on all those who have corrupted their ways and their works before the Lord.*[3] *And* ***He destroyed all from their places, and there was not left***

2. This is a parallel text to Genesis 6:3
3. See also 1 Enoch 10:12, 2 Peter 2:4 and Jude 6

> ***one of them whom He judged not according to all their wickedness.*** (Jubilees 5:7-11)

Figure 14 shows the pre-Flood timeline, illustrating the time period wherein the first-generation offspring of the Watchers lived and died. I would liken that first group to the Titans of Greek mythology. If that is an accurate assumption, let's look at the possibilities concerning other generations of Nephilim.

MULTIPLE GENERATIONS OF NEPHILIM

I think it is a reasonable assumption to say that the first-generation offspring of the Watchers may have had offspring themselves during the 500 year timeframe that they lived. Some disagree with that notion altogether, suggesting that the Nephilim were sterile. However, I must reject that idea based on numerous Scriptures that talk about giants who were sons of other giants. Take Numbers 13:33 for instance. This text clearly states that the sons of Anak were Nephilim who came of (or from) other Nephilim:

> *And there we saw the giants* [Nephilim], *the sons of Anak, which come of the giants* [Nephilim]*: and we were in our own sight as grasshoppers, and so we were in their sight.* (Numbers 13:33)

The giants the Hebrew spies saw are here described as being the offspring of Anak, who was himself the son of a giant named Arba.[4] For Nephilim to be producing other Nephilim, clearly they could not have been sterile! 2 Samuel 21:16-22 also mentions Ishbibenob and Saph who were described as *"sons of the giant."* Another man of great stature, with six fingers and toes was likewise described as one who *"also was born to the giant."* In all, we read about four giants (some say these were all the brothers of Goliath) who were killed by David and his mighty men.

4. See Joshua 15:13 and 21:11

> ***These four were born to the giant in Gath****, and fell by the hand of David, and by the hand of his servants.* (2 Samuel 12:22)

How can giants be born to other giants if the Nephilim are supposedly sterile? I don't know where that line of thinking got started, but clearly it is not supported by the biblical text.

We also see evidence of a variety of Nephilim *types* both in the Hebrew as well as pagan extra-Biblical texts. For instance, the book of Jubilees talks about Nephilim offspring known as the Elioud (or Eljo):

> *And they begat sons the Nâphîdîm, and they were all unlike, and they devoured one another: and the Giants slew the Nâphîl, and the Nâphîl slew the Eljô, and the Eljô mankind, and one man another.* (Jubilees 7:22)

Remember what I showed you in Chapter Three concerning the Greek version of 1 Enoch? There we learned that the Greek manuscripts vary considerably from the Ethiopic text, especially in 1 Enoch 7:1-3 where we find the following added to that section:

> *"And they* [the women] *bore to them* [the Watchers] *three races-first, the great giants. The giants brought forth the Naphilim, and the Naphilim brought forth the Elioud. And they existed, increasing in power according to their greatness."* [5]

In the above account, it appears that the first-generation offspring of angels and humans were simply called the "great giants" (which I believe were the Greek Titans)[6] and that it was their offspring who were called the Nephilim (possibly the Olympians) from whom came the Elioud (these could be the demigods of Greek mythology,

5. See footnote #3 of Chapter Three
6. Dr.I.D.E. Thomas agrees. See ***The Omega Conspiracy*** Chapter 5, page 68

such as Hercules). Whatever the case may be, we see both in Jubilees as well as in 1 Enoch that there were generations of offspring that came from the original children of the Watchers. I believe this same idea is reflected in the Sumerian myths as the difference between the Anunnaki and the Igigi,[7] and as stated above, in the Greek myths as the difference between Titans, Olympians and the demigods. This then raises another question:

WERE THERE FEMALE NEPHILIM TOO?

We've already addressed a number of misconceptions concerning Nephilim, but I want to tackle another one here. Many not only say that the Nephilim were all sterile, but also that they were all male. Is that true? We don't see any *direct* evidence for female giants, Nephilim or Elioud/Eljo in Scripture (as in a description of any female giants interacting with the Israelites). We do however find *indirect* references from which we may infer that female offspring of "like kind" may have existed. Indeed, I believe they did. Why else would God order the "utter destruction" of men, *women* and children in some of Israel's military campaigns to conquer the land of Canaan?

> *All these cities were fenced with high walls, gates, and bars; beside unwalled towns a great many. And we utterly destroyed them, as we did unto Sihon king of Heshbon,* ***utterly destroying the men, women, and children****, of every city.* (Deuteronomy 3:5-7)

> *When the Lord thy God shall bring thee into the land whither thou goest to possess it, and hath cast out many nations before thee, the Hittites, and the Girgashites, and the Amorites, and the Canaanites, and the Perizzites, and the Hivites, and the Jebusites, seven nations greater and mightier than thou; And when the Lord thy God shall deliver them before thee;* ***thou shalt smite them, and***

7. See the Original Babylonian Version (OBV) of ***Atrahasis*** Tablet I

> ***utterly destroy them;*** *thou shalt make no covenant with them, nor shew mercy unto them:* ***Neither shalt thou make marriages with them;*** *thy daughter thou shalt not give unto his son,* ***nor his daughter shalt thou take unto thy son.*** (Deuteronomy 7:1-3)

Either God is quite prejudice and into random acts of genocide, or He has a legitimate reason for wanting even the women and children (which were usually taken as "spoils of war") to be ***utterly destroyed*** along with the men.

If we compare the Hebrew narratives to that of the Greeks, we see that there certainly were female "goddesses" that were every bit as famous as their male counterparts. At least one of these even found her way into canonized Scriptures:

> *And when the town clerk had appeased the people, he said, Ye men of Ephesus, what man is there that knoweth not how that the city of the Ephesians is a worshipper of* ***the great goddess Diana****, and of the image which fell down from Jupiter?* (Acts 19:35)

Diana was the Roman equivalent of the Greek goddess Artemis, who, according to the mythology was the sister of Apollo and daughter of Zeus. We've already discussed who Apollo really was/is in *Babylon Rising* Book 1, so I won't spend time on him here. But since Artemis/Diana was his sister and also associated with the hunt, the moon and birthing (among other attributes), it is easy to see that her Assyrian equivalent was in reality Nimrod's sister Semiramis, who was known as Ishtar to the Mesopotamians, Isis to the Egyptians, Astarte in the Northwestern Semetic regions, and Inanna to the Sumerians.

She had temples at Sidon and Tyre, and the Philistines of Askelon apparently venerated her as well.[8] She was everywhere! In North Africa, she was known as Tanith, which means the

8. See 1 Samuel 31:1-10 and Herodotus i. 105

"Face of Baal" signifying that she was his consort.[9] And in the land of Canaan, she was known as Ashtoreth and even King Solomon went after her:

> *For it came to pass, when Solomon was old, that his wives turned away his heart after other gods: and his heart was not perfect with the Lord his God, as was the heart of David his father. For* ***Solomon went after Ashtoreth the goddess of the Zidonians****, and after Milcom the abomination of the Ammonites. And Solomon did evil in the sight of the Lord, and went not fully after the Lord, as did David his father.* (1 Kings 11:4,5)

Solomon built a high-place for her near Jerusalem which lasted until the time of King Josiah, who finally tore it down.[10] The extent of her cult among the Israelites is proven by numerous biblical references and frequent representations (such as Asherah poles) of the deity in various forms and names all related to the same individual.

The Encyclopedia Britannica has the following to say concerning this individual under the name Ishtar:

> *"As the great nature-goddess, the attributes of fertility and reproduction are characteristically hers, as also the accompanying immorality which originally, perhaps, was often nothing more than primitive magic.* ***As patroness of the hunt,***

Figure 15

9. See Barton, ***Semetic Origins*** page 253, note 6
10. See 2 Kings 23:1-14

> ***later identification with Artemis was inevitable. Hence the consequent fusion with Aphrodite, Artemis, Diana, Juno and Venus,*** *and the action and reaction of one upon the other in myth and legend. Her star was the planet Venus, and* ***classical writers give her the epithet Caelestis and Urania.***[11]

The link to Urania is particularly interesting to me. Remember the nine Muses I mentioned in the Introduction? She was one of them and was associated with Astronomy. There is book known as the *Urantia Book*, that I consider to be perhaps one of the most dangerous books on the planet. It claims to be of "extra-terrestrial origin" and is sometimes simply called the "Blue Book."[12] It is over 2,000 pages thick and contains a lot of details concerning the layout, structure and function of the Orvonton universe (supposedly the Milky Way)[13] and of earth in particular (known in this book as Urantia). Could this book have been "channeled" by an entity (Muse) known as Urania?

Figure 16

In the United States, this same goddess has been propped up as Columbia and is thus perched on top of our Capitol Building

11. ***Encyclopedia Britannica***, 14th Edition, Vol. 2, pages. 570-571
12. According to some, there is reason to believe that the U.S. government UFO think-tank known as "Project Blue Book" may be directly linked to the ***Urantia Book***.
13. See: http://www.urantiawiki.org/wiki/index.php?title=Orvonton/en

(**Figure 16**), which is referred to as the "Temple of Liberty" (another name for Columbia, Ishtar, Isis, Diana, etc.).

To many cultures, the entity described above was simply known as the "Queen of Heaven." She is the one that the prophet Jeremiah wrote about, quoting YHVH, the one true God of Heaven who clearly was not happy that the Israelites (Judah) were worshipping her.

> *"Therefore do not pray for this people, nor lift up a cry or prayer for them, nor make intercession to Me; for I will not hear you. Do you not see what they do in the cities of Judah and in the streets of Jerusalem? The children gather wood, the fathers kindle the fire, and the women knead dough, to make cakes* ***for the queen of heaven****; and they pour out drink offerings to other gods, that they may provoke Me to anger. Do they provoke Me to anger?" says the Lord. "Do they not provoke themselves, to the shame of their own faces?"*
>
> *Therefore thus says the Lord God: "Behold, My anger and My fury will be poured out on this place—on man and on beast, on the trees of the field and on the fruit of the ground. And it will burn and not be quenched."*
> (Jeremiah 7:16-20)

There certainly is no real "Queen of Heaven" sitting beside our King YHVH. And since we find absolutely no evidence in Scripture for the notion of female angels,[14] we must therefore conclude that these so-called "goddesses" were in fact giants, Nephilim, and/or Elioud.

14. Some will try to use Zachariah 5:9 as an example of female angels, but the Hebrew words used to describe these individuals do not indicate this to be true. They are simply described as women (Hebrew: *ishshah* - Strong's # 802) with wings. This could either be allegorical or we could be looking at hybrids, but one thing is certain, there is no supporting evidence in Scripture that would indicate they are female angels.

We've heard stories of giant female Amazon warriors. If we are to accept the ancient myths of other cultures as having originated from some measure of truth, then we are forced to acknowledge the fact that these gods and goddesses mated with one another as much as they did with normal humans. In the Greek myths for example, we know that the Titans were paired off as follows:[15]

- Cronus and Rea
- Coeus and Phoebe
- Hyperion and Theia
- Oceanus and Tethys

In the Greek myths, some of the children of the first-generation Titans are also referred to as Titans and they were both male and female:

- Asteria
- Astraea (Dike)
- Astraeus
- Atlas
- Eos (Dawn)
- Eosphorus (or Hesperus)
- Epimetheus
- Helius
- Leto (mother of Apollo and Artemis/Diana)
- Menoetius
- Pallas
- Perses
- Prometheus
- Selene

15. See: http://www.greek-gods.info/titans/ for a good breakdown of these gods.

The Titans Cronus and Rea were said to have been the parents of the Olympian gods Hera, Demeter, Hestia, Poseidon, Hades and Zeus. The female Titan, Leto was the daughter of Coesus and Phoebe and she was herself the mother of Apollo and Artemis/Diana (the so-called "Queen of Heaven") through her union with Zeus.

Some would argue that Zeus was in fact an angel because he was known as a "sky-god" who would come down and mate with women. Yet, where do we see precedence anywhere in Scripture for angels being born, growing up and dying? Nowhere. Zeus was no angel.We get all of our stories about Zeus from the Greek mythology/history, and in those writings we find that this so-called "king of the gods" was born and then later hidden away on the island of Crete by his mother Rhea who didn't want her son to be eaten by his father Cronus.[16] From there, young Zeus grew up and as Genesis 6:4 states, became a "great man of renown," but then he died and was buried at Knossos, Crete.

> *"From the terrace of my rooms in the inn at Knossos I can see Mount Dicta where Jupiter* [Zeus] *was born, Mount Ida where he was brought up, and Mount Joukta where tradition locates his tomb. There is a depth of philosophical thought in this landscape which overcomes me, and every evening I return to gaze again on the violet coloured heights of Mount Joukta. The great dome of the mountain above the ruins of Knossos is truly worthy to be the tomb of a god."*
>
> —Angelo Mosso[17]

Dr. Ken Johnson agrees:

> *Jupiter's* [Zeus'] *tomb is in Crete, on the north side of the city of Knossos. Knossos was supposed to have been*

16. NOTE: Cannibalism is a common trait of the Nephilim, thus it would appear that Cronus was likely one of the "great giants" - a first generation offspring of the Watchers.
17. ***The Palaces of Crete and Their Builders*** by Angelo Mosso,page 202

> *founded by Vesta* [Rhea], *his mother. The inscription over the tomb of Jupiter says in Greek, "Zan Kronou," which means "Zeus, son of Kronos."*
>
> — Ken Johnson, Th.D.[18]

If we are prepared to accept that Zeus was indeed a real individual that lived sometime in the ancient past, and we can acknowledge that he is nowhere described as an angel, nor does he even fit any description of one, then we must conclude that he was some sort of powerful man; most likely a later generation Nephilim. If we can accept this as truth, then his sister goddesses would also therefore have to fit that same description. If we can safely come to that conclusion, then it is very easy to see why God would want to wipe out all the men, ***women*** and children in known Nephilim villages within the land of Canaan.

CONFIRMATION?

Shortly after I began writing this chapter, I got a call from an old friend. His name is Jeff Randle. Jeff and I met back in 2003. We lost contact shortly after that when he moved from Dallas to New York and as a result we had not spoken or written to each other in over seven years. Recently, while doing a Google search on the Nephilim, he found my name popping up all over the place on news articles, blogs, images, books, DVDs and radio shows. He couldn't believe his eyes, so he called me out of the blue and inquired about my involvement with the subject of the Nephilim and how it was that I got into that research. I told him my story and he shared his with me. Turns out, God has had us both on a very similar path.[19] A couple of weeks later, I got a voicemail from him, stating that he was back in town and wanted to meet.

Sheila and I met Jeff for lunch at a local Cracker Barrel restaurant. After catching up on our lives, he pulled out a high-quality, first

18. ***Ancient Post Flood History*** by Dr. Ken Johnson, page 84
19. See Jeff's website: http://www.nephilimskulls.com

generation replica of one of the cone-head skulls from Paracus, Peru and laid it out on the table. It was the skull of a female!

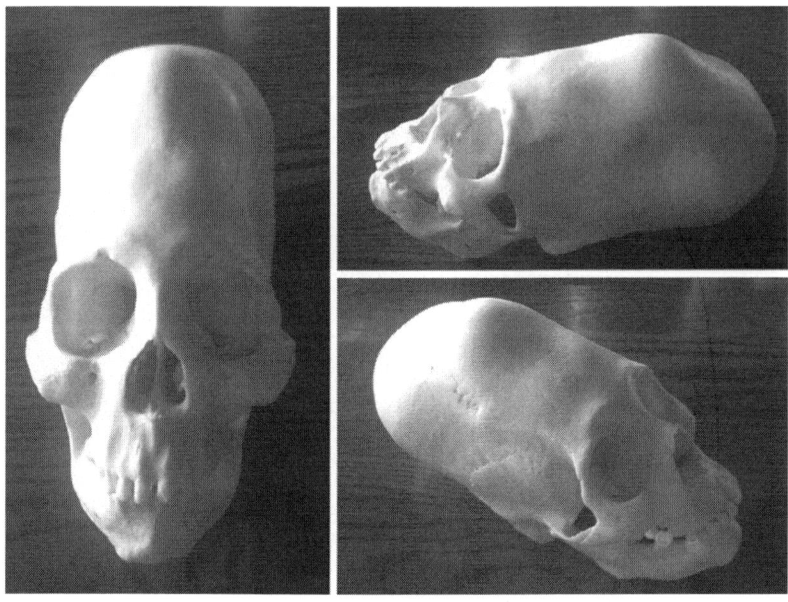

Figure 17

Needless to say it quickly became the center of attention! In fact, it actually turned out to be great bait for witnessing to the lost. Our waitress came over to the table and we had a lengthy conversation about the topic of the Nephilim, the Bible and God's plan for mankind (explaining why God did all those "bad things" to people in the Old Testament). It was a very enjoyable meeting. After it was over, Jeff gave me the skull! He said, *"Maybe this will help you with your research."* Indeed it has!

Figure 18

This is an extraordinary skull. The more you look at it, the more you see it is something beyond human. It is not the result of "cranial deformation" due to dolichocephalism[20] While skull binding does change the shape of a skull, there is strong debate as to whether or not it can produce a larger brain cavity. In their book, *The Enigma of Cranial Deformation*, David Hatcher Childress and Brien Foerster explain:

> *While it is assumed that headbinding will allow the cranium to enlarge and stretch, creating a larger volume in a skull than would be in a normal person, not all researchers believe that this is possible.* ***Some researchers maintain that headbinding would not enlarge the volume in a person's skull as the amount of skeletal material would not increase, only the shape of the skull would change.*** *Until more research is done on this subject, we will not have a definitive answer on whether headbinding can double to volume of a crania.*[21]

A normal human skull has between 1,100 and 1,900 cc of brain cavity. According to my friend Jeff, the skull he gave me has about a 40% larger brain capacity than any comparable size skull, whether shaped by head-binding or not. It has a number of other odd attributes as well. Please take a moment to watch the following videos by Brien Foerster concerning some of the strange differences in the elongated skulls of Paracus, Peru:

babylonrisingbooks.com/book2/videosC103.html

The skull of which I now have a replica was determined to have been of a female that stood about 5 feet, 4 inches tall. Some say it is shaped the way it is due to having been stretched through the

---

20. The practice of strapping boards to a baby's head in order to stretch and shape the skull into a conehead.
21. ***The Enigma of Cranial Deformation: Elongated Skulls of the Ancients*** (© 2012 Adventures Unlimited Press), by David Hatcher Childress and Brien Foerster, page 28

practice of head-binding. Others point out that, due to the many oddities found in its makeup, the person appears to have been born that way. In support of that thesis, a number of baby skeletons have been found that already had elongated skulls. In fact, Childress and Foerster even describe an occasion where an unborn *foetus* with an elongated skull was found inside a mummy!

> *Even at that time scientists were proclaiming that the skulls had been artificially elongated by head binding, a claim currently in favor for the Australian Kow Swamp skeletons. However, Dr. Tschudi commented, "Two crania (both of children scarcely a year old), had in all respects, the same form as those of adults. We ourselves have observed the same fact in many mummies of children of tender age..* ***The same formation of the head presents itself in children yet unborn****, and of this truth we have had convincing proof in sight of a foetus enclosed in the womb of a mummy of a pregnant woman... aged 7 months!"*[22]

If babies were being *born* with elongated skulls, that shows evidence of an entirely different race from that of normal humans. If not normal humans, then what are they? Only DNA testing would definitely determine that, but in this layperson's opinion, I would say these very well could be the remains of Nephilim (including females).

Figure 19

Consider also the example of Nefertiti of Egypt. That's not just a fancy headdress she's wearing in **Figure 19**.

22. ***The Enigma of Cranial Deformation: Elongated Skulls of the Ancients*** (© 2012 Adventures Unlimited Press), by David Hatcher Childress and Brien Foerster, page 19. See also the picture of this foetus on page 102, depicted as a drawing done by Johan Jacob von Tschudi, MD and presented in hjs book, co-authored by Mariano E. Rivero published in 1851 called, ***Peruvian Antiquities***.

Figure 20

This person, like her husband Akhenaten, had an elongated head! So also did their children! Check out their three ***daughters*** below:

Figure 21

Figure 22

In **Figure 21**, we see three young females with elongated skulls, sitting on the laps of their parents who both have elongated skulls themselves. Although the one on the queen's lap appears to have a headdress on, the one on her shoulder and the one in the king's arms do not. They appear to be very young, with already cone-head shaped skulls.

Assuming this is an accurate likeness of the queen, **Figure 22** shows a profile of Nefertiti revealing just how incredibly large and elongated her head was. Was she born that way? Were her daughters (like the one below) born that way too?

Figure 23

It wasn't just the Egyptians and Peruvians who demonstrated these traits. Many cultures from all around the world (including

Figure 24

those of Malta, Turkey, Iraq, Iran, Korea, Bolivia, Mexico, Siberia, Easter Island, China, ancient Sumer, Mesopotamia and elsewhere), who never interacted with one another either had beings walking among them with these naturally manifested traits or else they were independently all engaging in the practice of cranial deformation. The question is, why? If they were not born this way, why did they want to do this to themselves? Indeed, that is a question Childress and Foerster asked and spent a lot of time trying to answer, as they explored the possibilities in their book, but ultimately they concluded:

> *As for the fascinating concept that some skeletons with elongated skulls are of a different race from Homo sapiens, or that they are from another planet altogether, we have to wait for some daring and specialized DNA analysis to prove the matter one way or the other. Until then, no doubt there will be plenty of speculation; hopefully, more research will be done, and more books and articles will be written on the enigma of cranial deformation and the proliferation of coneheads in our past.* [23]

23. ***The Enigma of Cranial Deformation: Elongated Skulls of the Ancients*** (© 2012 Adventures Unlimited Press), by David Hatcher Childress and Brien Foerster, page 217

Though there is some disagreement and a lot of speculation, the general consensus is that if these individuals (often of the royal classes) did not have skulls naturally shaped like this to begin with, they were intentionally modifying themselves and their children to look like beings who did.

Since it wasn't just the males doing this, it stands to reason that the females who were desirous of this particular look, were subjecting themselves to such modification in order to look like the female "goddesses" who naturally *did* have that appearance. Thus, even if the above are not examples of actual female Nephilim, the historical and Biblical records clearly show, at the very least, circumstantial evidence that there were indeed Nephilim of the female variety who walked this earth at one time in the distant past that normal human women desired to emulate their appearance. As such, I believe this may be confirmation of my thesis concerning the possibility that the three wives of Noah's sons could have had corrupted, Nephilim DNA running through their veins.

NEPHILIM PUNNETT SQUARES

The Punnett Square is a powerful tool in genetic analysis. It is a diagram that is used to predict the outcome of a breeding experiment. I've been building a case for why I believe the women on the ark may have had "tainted genes." Assuming all three of Noah's sons were as genetically pure as he and his wife were, if we were to do some simple Punnett square-like examples, we would see that the "bad" X chromosomes (I'll depict them as NX) would be passed along to the offspring of the post-Flood population as follows:

X-Y Normal Male + NX-X Tainted Female = Four possibilities:

- NX-X = Nephilim female
- NX-Y = Nephilim male
- XX = Normal female
- YX = Normal male

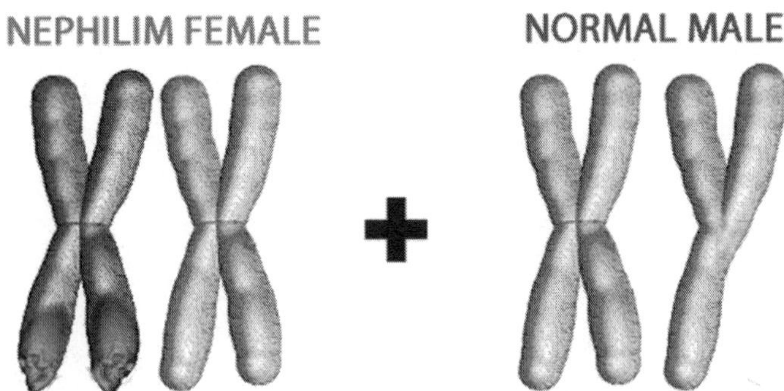
NEPHILIM FEMALE
NORMAL MALE

FOUR POSSIBLE OFFSPRING:

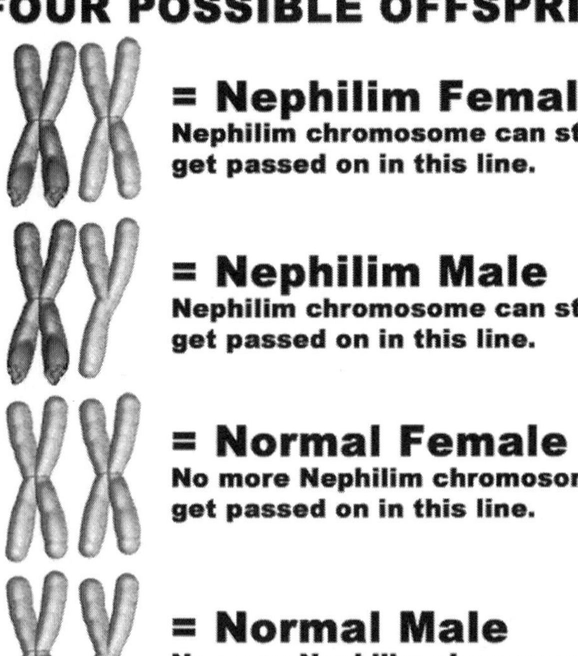
= Nephilim Female
Nephilim chromosome can still get passed on in this line.
= Nephilim Male
Nephilim chromosome can still get passed on in this line.
= Normal Female
No more Nephilim chromosomes get passed on in this line.
= Normal Male
No more Nephilim chromosomes get passed on in this line.

Figure 25

Here we see a 50/50 ratio of possible outcomes, both male and female. In **Figure 25**, I am assuming we are dealing with essentially a 50/50 hybrid female. However, it is my personal belief that the percentage of "Nephilim genes" contained within what (for the sake of this discussion) I will call *Nephilosomes* would be significantly lower due to the length of time from the last of the first generation Nephilim being killed off and the time that the three wives were born. Assuming they were roughly the same age as Noah's sons, that would mean there was about 500 years for the original Nephilosomes to become watered down through repeated interbreeding with normal humans. At least, that's one possible scenario, which assumes their genes were passed down from successive generations descended from the first-generation Nephilim.

Another possibility would involve corruption of their genetics via the hybridization process of being genetically mixed with animals as discussed in Chapter Five. For the sake of argument, and to keep the example simple, let's imagine the results are the same: she is 50% part normal human female and 50% part corrupted flesh.

What you see depicted in this Nephilim Punnett Square is the likelihood that a normal male, paired with a 50% hybrid, would have four possible outcomes: Nephilim male/female children or normal male/female children. If the odds worked in favor of the latter, there is no problem. All future offspring would be 100% normal. If the former, well, you keep plotting out the Punnett Squares as you see here and you find a variety of similar results. The key is there is only one X-Nephilosome being passed around — and that's a good thing! Why? Because if there were Y-Nephilosome*s* being passed around, the problem and the odds are significantly worse.

RISE OF THE X-MEN

I can already hear my detractors asking, *"But Rob, how do we know it works this way?"* To which I would respond, *"Of course we don't know for certain, but then how do we know that it doesn't work this way?"* Naturally, this is all speculation, but we do know that God put laws in motion that cannot be violated. If He created man in His own image and *likeness*, then there has to be some form of X-Y chromosome-like information packages at work in the spirit

NORMAL FEMALE
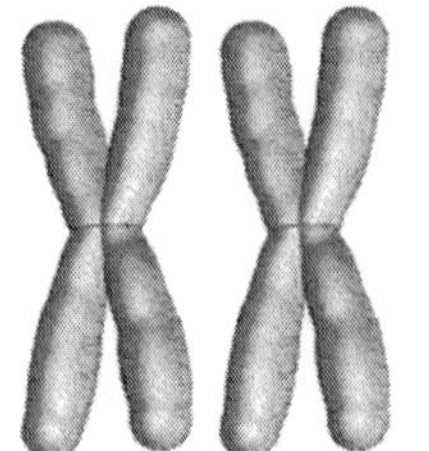

FALLEN MALE ANGEL
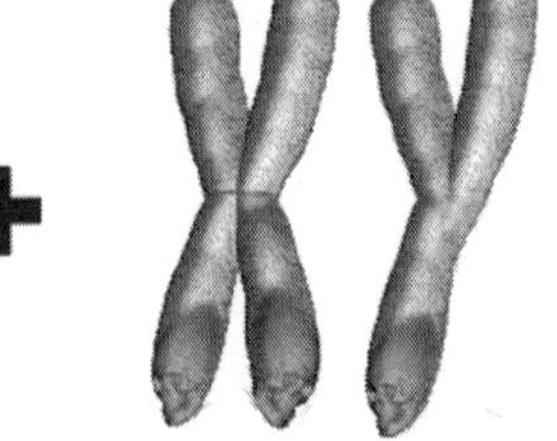

TWO POSSIBLE OFFSPRING:

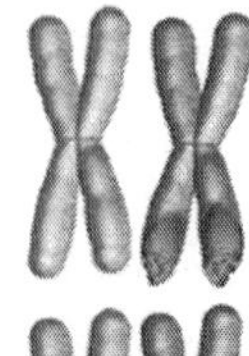
= Nephilim Female
Nephilim chromosome can still get passed on in this line.

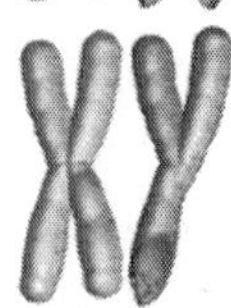
= Nephilim Male
Nephilim chromosome can still get passed on in this line.

WHICH LEADS TO A WIDE RANGE OF CONTINUING PROBLEMS:

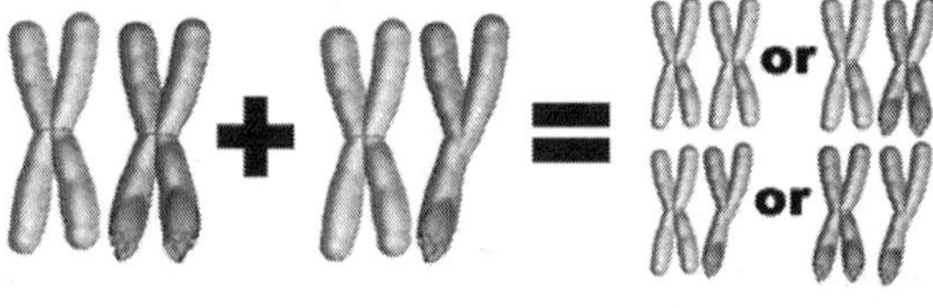
or
or
or
or

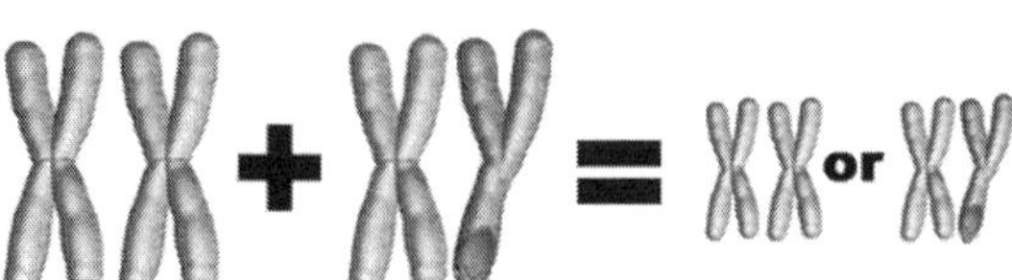
or

Figure 26

realm too. Assuming this also applies to angels who leave their first estate and appear in human form, capable of procreation, they must have *something* akin to X and Y chromosomes to pass along to their offspring. When the Holy Spirit "overshadowed" Mary, she conceived and bore a Son, Who's Y chromosome could have only come from YHVH since women are incapable of passing along a Y chromosome.

I wrote earlier that it was a good thing that only X-Nephilosomes were being passed along because the notion of multiple incursions significantly complicates the issue when you do a Nephilim Punnett Square. This is because the fallen angel is not a hybrid of one pure chromosome and one bad as would be the case with a female Nephilim. Instead, you would have two bad Nephilosomes to deal with: an X and a Y.

Figure 26 illustrates the problem, which only compounds as you play out the scenarios. Every time you introduce potent, fallen Y-Nephilosomes into the gene-pool of humanity, it results in pure and never ending chaos! This is why I believe God put a quick end to it, more than 650 years before the Flood.

No matter what theory you subscribe to: mine or that of the Multiple Incursion Theory, you have genetic issues to deal with. My contention is that the Multiple Incursion Theory introduces a ***far greater*** genetic threat than does the idea that female Nephilim hybrids entered the ark. At least in **Figure 25** we can see that there is a 50/50 chance you could have offspring who were completely normal. Whereas **Figure 26** shows percentages that are not so good, which if perpetuated only become compounded, posing a far greater threat to humanity.

Figure 27 takes it to the next level. If we are to believe that angels just continued to copulate with women again and again in *multiple* incursions, then watch what happens with the Nephilim Punnett Squares in such a scenario:

ANOTHER INCURSION POSSIBILITY:

NEPHILIM FEMALE

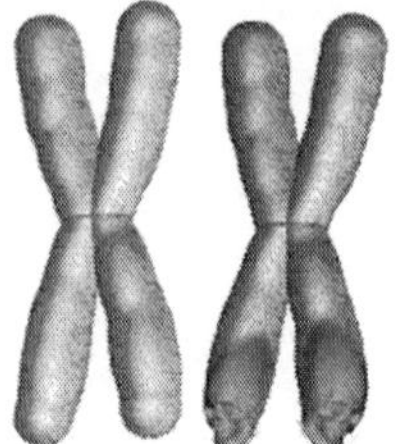

FALLEN MALE ANGEL

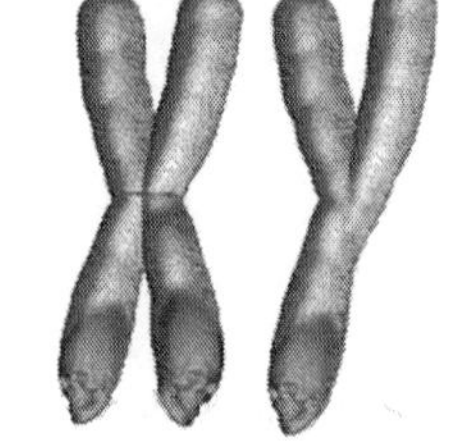

+

FOUR POSSIBLE OFFSPRING:

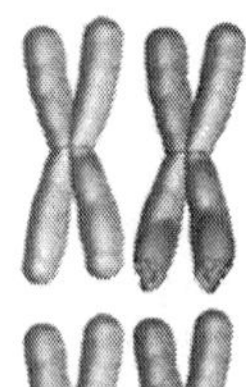

= Nephilim Female
Nephilim chromosome can still get passed on in this line.

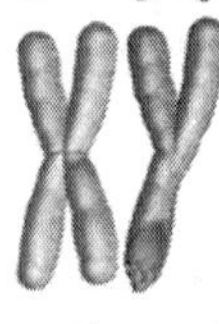

= Nephilim Male
Nephilim chromosome can still get passed on in this line.

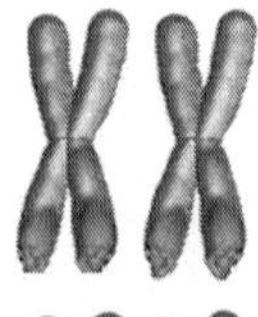

= Female Nephilim-Angel
This combination is most interesting and disturbing as it is doubly potent.

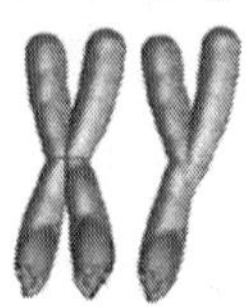

= Male Nephilim-Angel
This combination is most interesting and disturbing as it is doubly potent.

THE POTENTIAL OFFSPRING OF THIS LAST GROUP WOULD BE EXCEPTIONALLY PROBLEMATIC EPECIALLY IF ANGELS KEPT MATING WITH THIS GROUP.

Figure 27

Figure 27 shows what happens if fallen angels were to mate with already tainted Nephilim females. In this scenario, which would be akin to believing that Zeus was a fallen angel (as some do believe) mating with one of the demigod females. In that case, you'd have two X-Nephilosomes and one bad Y-Nephilosome producing four very bad possible outcomes. If you continue playing out the Nephilim Punnett Squares in this scenario, the results are truly catastrophic.

No. I believe **Figure 25** illustrates the most likely scenario, which is one mankind could easily survive. Any other scenario would spell certain doom for the human race, which only reinforces my belief that the Multiple Incursions Theory is the most absurd of possibilities in terms of what we may think God allowed to happen during and after the Flood. Thinking He allowed fallen angel seed to be continually reintroduced into the human gene-pool is infinitely more absurd than allowing a remnant of tainted genetics to pass through the female line, which could still lead to a 50/50 chance that normal children would still be produced in the wake of ***all flesh*** having previously become corrupted.

The ones that were born not-so-normal, I will now refer to as the first "X-Men." These were men who received a fallen X-Nephilosome from their mother and a good Y chromosome from their normal father. Thus, whatever super-human attribute they received — be it enormous height, strength, double rows of teeth, polydactylism or other unnatural abilities — it would have come from their mother.

I believe the first X-Man to arrive on the Biblical scene may have been Canaan, son of Ham. He had a variety of additional X-Men children who had some very interesting names, which are given in Genesis 10:

> *15 And Canaan begat Sidon his first born, and Heth,*
> *16 And the Jebusite, and the Amorite, and the Girgasite,*
> *17 And the Hivite, and the Arkite, and the Sinite,*

> *18 And the Arvadite, and the Zemarite, and the Hamathite: and afterward were the families of the Canaanites spread abroad.*
> *19 And the border of the Canaanites was from Sidon, as thou comest to Gerar, unto Gaza; as thou goest, unto Sodom, and Gomorrah, and Admah, and Zeboim, even unto Lasha.*
> *20 These are the sons of Ham, after their families, after their tongues, in their countries, and in their nations.*
> (Genesis 10:15-20)

These were all the "ites" that the Israelites were told to utterly destroy (including the women and children and even in some cases, the animals too).

RH NEGATIVE BLOOD

As I dove deeper into this research and started doing seminars on the subject matter contained in this book, the issue of Rh negative, "blue bloods" kept coming up. So, I will do my best to address it here.

There are four basic blood types: A, B, AB and O. Blood types are determined by the types of antigens on the blood cells and antibodies in the plasma.[24]

- **Type A** has A antigens on the red cells and anti B antibodies in the plasma.
- **Type B** has B antigens on the red cells and anti A antibodies in the plasma.
- **Type AB** has both A and B antigens on the red cells and no blood type antibodies in the plasma.
- **Type O** has no antigens on the red cells and both anti A and anti B antibodies in the plasma

24. See: http://bioweb.wku.edu/courses/biol115/wyatt/genetics/blood_type.htm

In addition to the designation of either A,B, AB and/or O, we often hear the word "positive" or "negative" when referring to blood types. This comes from an inherited protein of the red blood cells known as the Rh factor, or "antigen D." Antigens are proteins that trigger a response from the immune system to create antibodies, which fight off foreign invaders.[25] A person who is Rh-negative lacks the "D antigen" (the Rh factor) on the surface of their red blood cells. Those who do have it are considered to be Rh-positive.

The Rhesus antigen or "Rh factor" is actually named after the Rhesus Macaque, a monkey variety that has been used extensively for scientific testing based on the belief that this particular primate apparently shares about 93% of their DNA with that of humans.[26] Some of the scientific breakthroughs associated with this work include:

- Development of the rabies, smallpox and polio vaccines.
- Creation of drugs to manage HIV/AIDS
- Understanding of the female reproductive cycle and development of the embryo and the propagation of embryonic stem cells.
- Both the U.S. and Soviet space programs launched Rhesus monkeys into space, making them the first living "earthlings" to travel out of the Earth's atmosphere and return alive.

Take the above for whatever you think it is worth, but it is interesting to note that the vast majority of the world's population are considered Rh-positive. Supposedly, only about 7% of the world's population (and 15% of the U.S.) are considered to have Rh-negative blood. While I do not subscribe to the Theory of Evolution, I do find it interesting that both humans and primates contain the Rh factor. If that's supposed to be the default, the obvious question then is, where did this inherited Rh negative trait come from?

---

25. See: http://americanpregnancy.org/pregnancycomplications/rhfactor.html and http://medical-dictionary.thefreedictionary.com/antigen
26. See: http://en.wikipedia.org/wiki/Rhesus_macaque

Some claim that it may have been introduced as a result of the sons of God mating with women and producing angel-human hybrids. Of course this is pure speculation, but I actually think that makes sense. Unlike humans, an angel would have no need of the D antigen.

People with Rh positive blood, have an antigen that produces antibodies, which ward off disease. Rh negative people don't have this particular antigen. Yet, isn't it interesting that when an Rh negative woman marries someone with Rh positive blood, their offspring is in danger of being terminated in the womb? Consider what americanpregnancy.org has to say about this:

> ***What may happen if I am Rh-negative and pregnant?***
>
> *If you are Rh-negative, you may develop antibodies to an Rh-positive baby. If a small amount of the baby's blood mixes with your blood, which often happens, your body may respond as if it were allergic to the baby.* ***Your body may make antibodies to the Rh antigens in the baby's blood.*** *This means you have become sensitized and your antibodies can cross the placenta and attack your baby's blood. They break down the fetus's red blood cells and produce anemia (the blood has a low number of red blood cells). This condition is called hemolytic disease or hemolytic anemia.* ***It can become severe enough to cause serious illness, brain damage, or even death in the fetus or newborn.***[27]

Another website called rhogam.com puts it this way:

> *WHEN NEGATIVE AND POSITIVE MEET AND MATE*
>
> *If you're Rh-negative and carrying a baby who is Rh-positive (like the baby's father), your baby may be at*

27. See: http://americanpregnancy.org/pregnancycomplications/rhfactor.html

> *risk for a serious disease.* ***When your immune system (which fights off invaders to keep you healthy) is exposed to your baby's Rh-positive blood, it will begin producing antibodies that are sensitized (designed specifically) to destroy these "foreign" blood cells.***[28]

How interesting that a person who lacks the D antigen would now suddenly create other antibodies specifically for the purpose of destroying an Rh positive fetus!

The website justmommies.com states:

> ***So how is being Rh negative a problem?***
>
> *When Rh negative blood is exposed to Rh positive blood the Rh negative person begins producing antibodies to fight the invading blood. Antigens trigger your body to produce antibodies. Antibodies are usually a good thing and serve to protect a person from foreign invaders.*
>
> *Now the problem lies when a pregnant woman is carrying a baby that is Rh positive.* ***If the mother has antibodies to the Rh antigen, those antibodies can attack the baby's red blood cells.*** *This can lead to complications to the baby including anemia, jaundice, and other blood related problems.*[29]

All of these pregnancy websites go on to give the "good news" that these complications can be avoided with a drug called RhoGam. My question is, what if these complications are there for a reason?

I recently came across an article called *"BLOOD OF THE GODS"* that had some interesting observations about this issue:

---

28. See: http://www.rhogam.com/Patient/WhatRhNegativeMeans/Pages/Whatdoseit-meantoRhNegative.aspx
29. See: http://www.justmommies.com/articles/rh_negative.shtml

> *All animals and other living creatures known to man can breed with any other of their species. Relative size and color makes no difference. Why does infant's haemolytic disease occur in humans if all humans are the same species? Haemolytic disease is the allergic reaction that occurs when an Rh negative mother is carrying a Rh positive child. Her blood builds up antibodies to destroy an ALIEN substance (the same way it would a virus), thereby destroying the infant. Why would a mother's body reject her own offspring? Nowhere else in nature does this occur naturally. This same problem does occur in mules - a cross between a horse and donkey. This fact alone points to the distinct possibility of a cross-breeding between two similar but genetically different species.*
>
> *No one has tried to explain where the Rh negative people came from. Most, familiar with blood factors, admit that these people must at least be a mutation if not descendants of a different ancestor. If we are a mutation, what caused the mutation? Why does it continue with the exact characteristics? Why does it so violently reject the Rh factor, if it was in their own ancestry? Who was this ancestor?* [30]

This article, like many others that I've read, goes on to reveal the fact that for some reason the highest percentage of Rh negative bloodlines are among the Basque people of Spain and France. Another on-line source says:

> *This group possesses the highest percentage of such blood compared to other populations. It is hypothesized the Basque themselves count Neanderthals as their predominant ancestors. This means that Neanderthals may be the true originators of this blood antigen.* [31]

30. From ***UFO'S ANCIENT ASTRONAUT MAGAZINE***, October 176, page 46 according to: http://www.greatdreams.com/reptlan/rhneg.htm
31. From: http://www.originopedia.com/origin-of-rh-negative-blood/

There are those who say that the so-called "blue bloods" of European royalty and other members of the "elite" are Rh negative and imply that they are descendants of the gods. While I do subscribe to the idea that there is a ruling elite whose bloodlines can be traced all the way back to Nimrod, and who are quite evil, I want to be careful here. This whole issue of Rh negative blood — what it is, where it came from, who has it, etc. — can lead you down many rabbit trails full of all kinds of wild conspiracy theories and speculation. I do not intend to go there nor drag you down that path either. Suffice it to say, I do find this stuff interesting on many levels, especially as it pertains to these questions: *"What if Rh negative blood is a remnant of Nephilim seed still woven into the fabric of humanity? Is there any spiritual significance that we should be concerned about?"*

Let me clearly state that **I do _not_ believe anyone who has Rh negative blood is condemned**. Contrary to what some researchers teach, even if there is a connection to fallen angel/ Nephilim genetics involved, I do not believe this has any bearing on whether or not Rh negative people can be saved. God looks at a person's heart, not their blood antigens.

> ***He that believeth and is baptized shall be saved;*** *but he that believeth not shall be damned.* (Mark 16:16)

> *I am the door: by me* ***if any man enter in, he shall be saved,*** *and shall go in and out, and find pasture.* (John 10:9)

> *But what does it say? "The word is near you, in your mouth and in your heart"— that is, the word of faith which we are preaching, that* ***if you confess with your mouth Jesus as Lord, and believe in your heart that God raised Him from the dead, you will be saved;*** *for with the heart a person believes, resulting in righteousness, and with the mouth he confesses, resulting in salvation. For the Scripture says, "Whoever believes in Him will not be disappointed." For there is no distinction between Jew*

> *and Greek; for the same Lord is Lord of all, abounding in riches for all who call on Him; for **"Whoever will call on the name of the Lord will be saved."*** (Romans 10:8-13 NASB)

Again, I am not here to condemn anyone. I do not believe Rh negative people are any more good or evil than Rh positive people. So please hear me: If you are someone who has Rh negative blood, please do not get into fear. God loves you and sent His Son to pay the price for your sins just as He did for mine. The Scriptures state:

> *The Lord is not slack concerning his promise, as some men count slackness; but is longsuffering to us-ward, **not willing that any should perish, but that all should come to repentance**.* (2 Peter 3:9)

Don't go away from reading this thinking Rh negative people are Nephilim and thus cannot be saved. That is not for us to judge. A true, full blown Nephilim (at least in the Biblical sense) does not appear *capable* of repentance:

> *And God saw that the wickedness of man was great in the earth, and that **every imagination of the thoughts of his heart was only evil continually**.* (Genesis 6:5)

Unless that fits you, I would not worry about it. Any person who acknowledges that they are a sinner and who makes a conscious and deliberate effort to repent and receive Christ as their savior will obtain salvation.

> *I tell you, Nay: but, except ye repent, ye shall all likewise perish.* (Luke 13:3)

> *Likewise, I say unto you, there is joy in the presence of the angels of God over one sinner that repenteth.* (Luke 15:10)

> *Then Peter said unto them, Repent, and be baptized every one of you in the name of Jesus Christ for the remission of sins, and ye shall receive the gift of the Holy Ghost.* (Acts 2:38)

> *Repent ye therefore, and be converted, that your sins may be blotted out, when the times of refreshing shall come from the presence of the Lord.* (Acts 3:19)

Thus, Spiritually speaking, it doesn't matter whether or not you have Rh positive/negative blood. Salvation comes as the result of repentance, faith and belief, not genetics.

According to any number of on-line sources, other intriguing "facts" concerning Rh negatives (supposedly) include, but are not limited to:

- Hitler was obsessed with this group
- The Nazis believed that Rh negative was proof of their ET origin from their ancient Nordic gods they believed came from the Aldebaran system
- Rh negatives are more copper based than iron
- More women are Rh negative than men
- More homosexuals in this group
- Rh negative cells cannot be cloned
- High resistance to the AIDS virus
- The blood on the Shroud of Turin is Rh negative
- A feeling of not belonging
- Truth seekers
- Sense of a "mission" in life
- Empathy and compassion for mankind
- An extra rib or vertebra

- Higher than average IQ
- Love of space and science
- More sensitive vision and other senses
- Increased of psychic/intuitive abilities
- Lower body temperature
- Higher blood pressure (some say lower)
- Predominantly blue, green, or Hazel eyes
- Red or reddish tint to hair color
- Increased sensitivity to heat & sunlight
- Unexplained scars
- Piercing eyes
- Tend to be healers
- Empathetic illnesses
- Ability to disrupt electrical devices
- Prone to alien abductions
- Experience unexplained phenomenon
- Physic dreams, ESP and/or other such abilities

The list goes on and on. How much of that is true and how much is just tabloid nonsense? I don't know. I only offer this information here to challenge you to do your own research into the strange issues surrounding Rh negative blood. I suspect there's much more here to discover and consider.

Could it be that Rh negative blood is a remnant of inherited genetics passed down to us from the original fallen angels,[32] or from the later-generation X-Men? Is that why some say the Bilderberg's and

32. Angels are angels. The state of the Fallen Ones came about as the result of their rebellion not genetics. Therefore, anything such as an Rh factor, which may have been introduced into the human race by them would not necessarily have to be inheriently evil.

governments of the world have supposedly been cataloging and tracking people who have it?[33] Right after I wrote the footnote below concerning this, I got the following message from one of my Facebook friends regarding the issue of cataloging:

> *When I went to donate for the first time after the Aurora [Colorado] theatre shooting, they had all my info on file in their system and none of the nurses could explain why. Also, this is the first I have heard of any if this....so when I entered my name and email through the bonfils website, it automatically pulled up whole blood donor and my personal info. But I've never donated... little paranoid now.*

As Arsenio Hall would say, *"Things that make you go, hmm."*

THE ARCHON X-PRIZE

Speaking of genetics, there is another little piece of trivia that recently caught my attention, and that is The Archon X-Prize. In fact, it's what got me thinking about the whole idea of X-Men in the first place.

The title of this book is, *Archon Invasion: The Rise, Fall and Return of the Nephilim.* "Archon" is a Greek word (Strong's # 758) that means, *"a ruler, prince, leader."* We have an example of this word in book of Ephesians:

> *Wherein in time past ye walked according to the course of this world, according to the* ***prince*** *of the power of the air, the spirit that now worketh in the children of disobedience:* (Ephesians 2:2)

The book of 1 Enoch names 20 archons of the 200 Watcher-class

33. I have not been able to substantiate this claim, but it shows up all over the "conspiracy websites" and you often hear people like David Icke talking about such things. It certainly is worth further investigation. I did see that there is a website for Rh-negative people to register: http://www.rhnegativeregistry.com

angels who came down from the sky (air) and sinned with the daughters of men.

> *And they were in all two hundred; who descended in the days of Jared on the summit of Mount Hermon, and they called it Mount Hermon, because they had sworn and bound themselves by mutual imprecations upon it. And these are the names of their leaders: Sêmîazâz, their leader, Arâkîba, Râmêêl, Kôkabîêl, Tâmîêl, Râmîêl, Dânêl, Êzêqêêl, Barâqîjâl, Asâêl, Armârôs, Batârêl, Anânêl, Zaqîêl, Samsâpêêl, Satarêl, Tûrêl, Jômjâêl, Sariêl. These are their chiefs of tens.* (1 Enoch 7:6-8)

Later we read about another one named, *Azazel.* These evil angels taught men lots of things.

> *And Azâzêl taught men to make swords, and knives, and shields, and breastplates, and made known to them the metals of the earth and the art of working them, and bracelets, and ornaments, and the use of antimony, and the beautifying of the eyelids, and all kinds of costly stones, and all colouring tinctures. And there arose much godlessness, and they committed fornication, and they were led astray, and became corrupt in all their ways. Semjâzâ taught enchantments, and root-cuttings, Armârôs the resolving of enchantments, Barâqîjâl, (taught) astrology, Kôkabêl the constellations, Ezêqêêl the knowledge of the clouds, Araqiêl the signs of the earth, Shamsiêl the signs of the sun, and Sariêl the course of the moon. And as men perished, they cried, and their cry went up to heaven . . .* (1 Enoch 8)

Others are listed in 1 Enoch 69, including Kâsdejâ:

> *this is he who showed the children of men all the wicked smitings of spirits and demons, and* ***the smitings of the embryo in the womb****, that it may pass away, and*

> *[the smitings of the soul] the bites of the serpent, and the smitings which befall through the noontide heat, the son of the serpent named Tabââ't.*

It would seem that every bad thing from abortion to warfare and the (false) reading of the stars was taught to us by the Archons. So, how interesting is it that there should be a genetics competition called, *The Archon Genomics X-Prize*? According to their website, this is their objective:

> *This global, incentivized competition will inspire breakthrough genome sequencing innovations and technologies with the potential* ***to create a new era of personalized medicine****. $10 million will be awarded to the first team to rapidly, accurately and economically sequence 100 whole human genomes to an unprecedented level of accuracy.*
>
> ***The 100 human genomes to be sequenced in this competition will be donated by 100 centenarians (ages 100 or older) from all over the world, known as there*** [sic] ***100 Over 100.*** *Sequencing the genomes of the 100 Over 100 presents a unique opportunity to identify those "rare genes" that protect against disease, while giving researchers valuable clues to health and longevity.*[34]

Sounds innocent enough… if it weren't for the name. Hmm.

34. See: http://genomics.xprize.org/competition-details/prize-overview

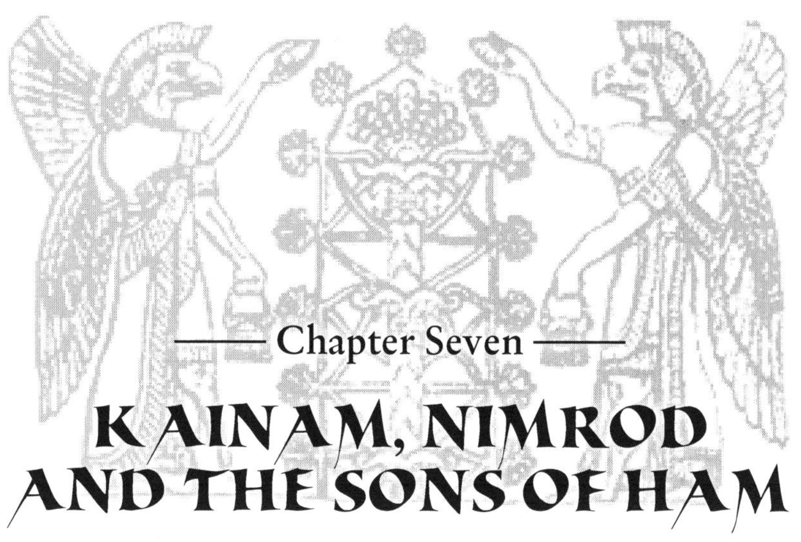

—— Chapter Seven ——

KAINAM, NIMROD AND THE SONS OF HAM

Occam's Razor: a principle that generally recommends, when faced with competing hypotheses that are equal in other respects, selecting the one that makes the fewest new assumptions.

When looking at the ancient Hebrew record, the first suspicious post-Flood clue concerning the activity of the Watchers may exist in this strange passage of Jubilees 8:

> *In the twenty-ninth jubilee, in the first week, in the beginning thereof Arpachshad took to himself a wife and her name was Rasu'eja, the daughter of Susan, the daughter of* [Shem's son] *Elam, and she bare him a son in the third year in this week, and he called his name Kainam. And the son grew, and his father* [Arphaxad] *taught him writing, and he went to seek for himself a place where he might seize for himself a city. And* ***he found a writing which former (generations) had carved on the rock, and he read what was thereon, and he transcribed it and***

> ***<u>sinned owing to it</u>; for it contained the teaching of the Watchers in accordance with which they used to observe the omens of the sun and moon and stars in all the signs of heaven.*** *And he wrote it down and said nothing regarding it; for he was afraid to speak to Noah about it lest he should be angry with him on account of it.* (Jubilees 8:1-5)

What did Kainam find that caused him to have "sinned owing to it?" The text does not say, stating only that it was something written down by the Watchers from a time before the Flood. Did this rock contain instructions for creating hybrids? Some suggest it might have. However, I tend to think it likely had more to do with astrology/astronomy due to the description given in the text itself, "*for it contained the teaching of the Watchers in accordance with which they used to observe the omens of the sun and moon and stars in all the signs of heaven.*"

Figure 28

Could it be that perhaps Kainam may have found a version of the Aztec Calendar Stone? It is said to have been created in 3114 BC (according to the Gregorian calendar).[1] If true, that places its origin in a pre-Flood context (see **Figure 6**). As such, it very well could have been created by the Watchers just prior to their judgment and the death of their beloved ones (the first generation Nephilim), which all happened about 100 years *after* 3114 BC. This calendar, of course, gives measurements of time. Genesis 1 tells us that the sun, moon and starts are there for us to calculate times, signs and seasons.

1. See: https://smithsonianassociates.org/ticketing/tickets/reserve.aspx?performanceNumber=224607 and http://www.webexhibits.org/calendars/calendar-mayan.html http://en.wikipedia.org/wiki/Mesoamerican_Long_Count_calendar

> *And God said, Let there be lights in the firmament of the heaven to divide the day from the night; and* ***let them be for signs, and for seasons, and for days, and years****: And let them be for lights in the firmament of the heaven to give light upon the earth: and it was so. And God made two great lights; the greater light to rule the day, and the lesser light to rule the night: he made the stars also.* (Genesis 1:14-16)

It seems clear to me that whatever Kainam found had more to do with reading the stars than any notion of creating Nephilim hybrids.

The other problem I have with this account is that Kainam is not listed in the Table of Nations of Genesis 10 as an offspring of Arpachsad (or Arphaxad). In fact, he's not mentioned at all. So, either we disregard this account altogether, or perhaps Jubilees is explaining *why* he is excluded from the lineage of Genesis 10. Then again, perhaps Genesis 10 is not giving us an exhaustive list of offspring. Women are rarely mentioned in biblical genealogies, but we know that there must have been female children as men cannot have babies. So if we wanted to get dogmatic about Genesis 10 as being a complete and exhaustive list of *all* the offspring of Noah's sons, our argument would quickly fall apart. Also, we must acknowledge that Arphaxad was of the generation that lived to be over 400 years of age. Yet, Genesis 10 lists him as having only one son.

> *And Arphaxad begat Salah; and Salah begat Eber.* (Genesis 10:24)

Only one son in 438 years? I doubt it. It appears this son Salah and his offspring Eber are listed in the narrative because they are the direct ancestors of those who would ultimately lead to the birth of Yeshua, and are thus highlighted for us. Still, I think a *reasonable assumption* can be made that Arphaxad may have had plenty more children than that in his four century-long lifetime. So, it wouldn't be out of the question to suppose that Kainam was in fact an offspring of Arphaxad even though he does not appear in the Table of Nations in Genesis 10. In either case, this story does not do much for us in terms of providing solid evidence for the return of the Nephilim in the Biblical, post-Flood world.

STICKING WITH THE CANON OF SCRIPTURE

In the *Multiple Incursions*? chapter, I gave a number of reasons for why I do not subscribe to the idea that there were any more sexual encounters between fallen angels and women. Some have challenged my position and asked, "*Who are you to say what angels can and cannot do*?" It is not what I say that matters, it is what the Bible says — or even what it does *not* say — that matters.

For starters, you will *never again see any other reference in the canon of Scripture* to angels mating with humans apart from what I consider to be a faulty reading/interpretation of Genesis 6:4. Scripture will always self-authenticate, confirm (with multiple witnesses) and interpret itself. This is one of the things that makes the Bible so unique among all other ancient (and even modern) texts. Those who hold to the Multiple Incursions Theory, sadly, have no further confirming Scriptures to support their thesis and must therefore rely on pure speculation and assumption as they move forward in the text.

We, on the other hand, are going with the Occam's Razor approach, and as such, are trying to limit the number of additional assumptions necessary to solve the problem of how the Nephilim returned after the Flood. With no other Scriptures to support the usual "sons of God mating with women again and again" view of Genesis 6:4, we concluded in the previous chapter that the most likely candidates for perpetuating the Nephilim genetics were the wives of Noah's three sons.

Now let's use the canon (66 books) of Scripture to see for ourselves whether or not this idea rings true. We will do so, moving forward with the premise that Genesis 6:4 is talking about a "first cause" that had lasting effects in the Scriptures that follow. That is not an assumption, but rather a concept based on an equally valid interpretation of the same Scripture:

> *Now giants were upon the earth in those days.* ***For after the sons of God went in to the daughters of men*** *and they brought forth children, these are the mighty men of old, men of renown.* (Genesis 6:4 Douay-Rheims Bible)

After the Flood, we see that Noah's sons began to have offspring. Remember, if the Holy Spirit inspired the authors to give added details about an individual, there's a reason for it. These details are there in order to help us clearly see what is really going on, and they appear rather often — especially in reference to the children of Ham. Take note of this text in Genesis 9 for instance:

> *And the sons of Noah, that went forth of the ark, were Shem, and Ham, and Japheth:* ***and Ham is the father of Canaan.*** (Genesis 9:18)

Why does the Holy Spirit inspire Moses to give that added detail — especially when we consider that the Table of Nations is about to be given to us in the next chapter? One could argue that this is done as a set up for the next few verses, which deal with the strange incident in Noah's tent. I call it a "strange incident" because the culprit in the story appears to be Ham, and yet whatever happened there was somehow directly linked to *Canaan*!

> *And Ham,* ***the father of Canaan,*** *saw the nakedness of his father, and told his two brethren without. And Shem and Japheth took a garment, and laid it upon both their shoulders, and went backward, and covered the nakedness of their father; and their faces were backward, and they saw not their father's nakedness. And Noah awoke from his wine, and knew what his younger son had done unto him.*

> *And he said,* ***Cursed be Canaan****; a servant of servants shall he be unto his brethren.*
>
> *And he said, Blessed be the LORD God of Shem; and* ***Canaan shall be his servant****.*
>
> *God shall enlarge Japheth, and he shall dwell in the tents of Shem; and* ***Canaan shall be his servant****.* (Genesis 9:22-27)

CURSED BE CANAAN

Many have offered up all sorts of speculation concerning what may have taken place there in Noah's tent. Everything from homosexuality to incest has been suggested. I believe the Bible itself provides at least three witnesses that help us to understand what may have happened. Note what Leviticus has to say concerning the phrase "nakedness of his father."

> *The nakedness of thy father, or the nakedness of thy mother, shalt thou not uncover: she is thy mother; thou shalt not uncover her nakedness.* ***The nakedness of thy father's wife shalt thou not uncover: it is thy father's nakedness.*** (Leviticus 18:7,8)

> *And* ***the man that lieth with his father's wife hath uncovered his father's nakedness****: both of them shall surely be put to death; their blood shall be upon them.* (Leviticus 20:11)

The "nakedness of his father" in Genesis 9:22 *could* be an idiom in reference to Noah's wife just as much as it could simply mean that Noah alone was found naked. In either case, Genesis only says Ham *saw* this. It does not say he "knew" her/him (in the sexual sense), nor does it imply that anything took place at all. The text simply says that Ham saw nakedness. Perhaps the book of Habakkuk provides more detail for us to consider:

> *Woe unto him that gives his neighbor drink, that presses your wineskin to him, and makes him drunk also, that you may look on his nakedness!* (Habakkuk 2:15)

That seems to sum it up for me, but I did find some interesting commentary by John Gill in his *Exposition of the Bible* concerning this matter that might also be worth considering:

> *Ham is represented by many writers as a very wicked, immodest, and profligate creature: Berosus makes him a magician, and to be the same with Zoroast or Zoroastres, and speaks of him as the public corrupter of mankind; and says that he taught men to live as before the flood, to lie with mothers, sisters, daughters, males and brutes, and creatures of all sorts; and that he actually did so himself, and therefore was cast out by his father Janus, or Noah, and got the name of "Chem", the infamous and immodest:*
>
> *...some of the Jewish Rabbins, as Jarchi relates, say that Canaan first saw it, and told his father of it; and some say, that he or Ham committed an unnatural crime with him; and others, that he castrated him; and hence, it is supposed, came the stories of Jupiter castrating his father Saturn, and Chronus his father Uranus: and* ***Berosus says, that Ham taking hold of his father's genitals, and muttering some words, by a magic charm rendered him impotent****: and some will have it that he committed incest with his father's wife; but these things are said without foundation: what Noah's younger son did unto him, besides looking on him, we are not told, yet it was such as brought a curse on Canaan; and one would think it would be more than bare sight, nay, it is expressly said there was something done, but what is not said.*
>
> —John Gill[2]

2. ***Gill's Exposition of the Entire Bible***, commenting on Genesis 9:22. See: http://gill.biblecommenter.com/genesis/9.htm

What I find most intriguing about this commentary is the fact that we find no record of Noah having any more children after the Flood—even though he lived another 350 years. Could that be why Noah cursed Ham's offspring? Or could there be something more to the story?

All outside commentary aside, Biblically speaking, we know that whatever Ham did it, displeased Noah such that he cursed his grandson Canaan. This of course seems to imply that Canaan was present, which means he was either born on the ark or shortly after it had finally come to rest on dry ground. When looking at Canaan's offspring, they appear to be loaded with Nephilim characteristics. This is *pure speculation* on my part, but I believe Canaan might have been born polydactyl (having six fingers and six toes). Why? Because we know that some of the Biblical giants had this characteristic and they had to have inherited it from someone.

> *And it came to pass after this, that there was again a battle with the Philistines at Gob: then Sibbechai the Hushathite slew Saph, which was of the sons of the giant. And there was again a battle in Gob with the Philistines, where Elhanan the son of Jaareoregim, a Bethlehemite, slew the brother of Goliath the Gittite, the staff of whose spear was like a weaver's beam. And there was yet a battle in Gath,* ***where was a man of great stature, that had on every hand six fingers, and on every foot six toes, four and twenty in number****; and he also was born to the giant. And when he defied Israel, Jonathan the son of Shimeah the brother of David slew him. These four were born to the giant in Gath, and fell by the hand of David, and by the hand of his servants.* (2 Samuel 21:18-22)

Granted, the Philistines were not members of Canaan's offspring (they descended from Caphtor, son of Mitzraim)[3] and perhaps not every giant had twenty-four digits, but there seems to be

3. Genesis 10:14; Jeremiah 47:4; Amos 9:7

quite a bit of evidence suggesting that many of them did, as well as double rows of teeth, elongated heads and a host of other abnormal traits.[4]

WHAT'S IN A NAME?

The Bible gives us a *lot* of detail worth considering in the Genesis 10 Table of Nations. There we are given a comprehensive list of the offspring of Noah's sons. Of particular note are the meanings of the names. For the most part, the sons of Shem and Japheth have very complimentary names. However, here are the meanings of Ham and his offspring's names:

Ham [tumult: he raged] begat:

- Cush [black: terror]
- Mizraim [double straightness]
- Phut [afflicted]
- Canaan [a trafficker]

Cush's sons:

- Seba [drink thou]
- Havilah [anguish]
- Sabtah [compassed the chamber]
- Raamah [thunder]
- Sabtechah [compassed the smiting]
- Nimrod [we shall rebel]

Mizraim's sons:

- Ludim [firebrand: travailing]
- Anamim [affliction of water]
- Lehabim [flames: blades]

4. For an in depth look at giants past and present, be sure to check out Steve Quayle's book, ***Genesis 6 GIANTS***.

- Naphtuhim [openings]
- Pathrusim [moistened morsel]
- Casluhim [forgiven ones]
- Caphtorim [bowing to spy] (from whom the Philistines came-see Jeremiah 47:4 and Amos 9:7)

Canaan's sons:

- Sidon [hunting]
- Heth [terror]
- the Jebusite [trodden down]
- the Amorite [sayers]
- the Girgasite [stranger draw near]
- the Hivite [showers of life]
- the Arkite [my gnawing]
- the Sinite [thorn, clay, mire]
- the Arvadite [shall break loose]
- the Zemarite [double woolens]
- the Hamathite [enclosure of wrath].

Putting them together in a (Chuck Missler-like) possible paragraph rendering, we end up with a very interesting little story:

> *He raged (a) black terror, double straight, afflicted trafficker.*
>
> *Black terror drink thou anguish. Compass the chamber. Thunder compassed the smiting. He who is coming, their love: we shall rebel.*
>
> *(A) double straight firebrand: travailing, affliction of water - blades opening the moistened morsel - forgiven ones bowing to spy.*
>
> *(A) trafficker hunting terrors, trodden(ed) down sayers, (the) strangers draw near. Showers of life, gnawing (like) thorns, (they) shall break loose, double woolen enclosure(s) of wrath.*

We know from numerous examples in Scripture that people and places were named such-and-such because of some characteristic related to that name. For instance:

> *Now the first came forth red, all over like a hairy garment; and they named him Esau.*[5] *Afterward his brother came forth with his hand holding on to Esau's heel, so his name was called Jacob;*[6] *and Isaac was sixty years old when she gave birth to them.* (Genesis 25:25,26 NASB)

With this fact in mind, the names given for Ham's offspring should certainly give us pause to think about the nature and character of these individuals — especially the Canaanites. I mean what would cause a parent to name their kid "terror" or "enclosure of wrath" anyway? Clearly, something was not right about these offspring! Genesis 10:15-19 gives us the details concerning Canaan and his children:

> *Canaan's oldest son was Sidon, the ancestor of the Sidonians. Canaan was also the ancestor of the Hittites, Jebusites, Amorites, Girgashites, Hivites, Arkites, Sinites, Arvadites, Zemarites, and Hamathites. The Canaanite clans eventually spread out, and the territory of Canaan extended from Sidon in the north to Gerar and Gaza in the south, and east as far as Sodom, Gomorrah, Admah, and Zeboiim, near Lasha.* (Genesis 10:15-19 NLT)

Pay attention to this section of the Table of Nations. The names given there will show up again and again later in the canon of Scripture — especially the Canaanites, Hittites, Jebusites, Hivites and Amorites. These "X-Men" tribes were apparently loaded with Nephilim genes that God (working through His people) would later wipe out. They are the people groups God constantly commanded the Israelites to "utterly destroy."

---

5. Esau means "hairy" or "shaggy."
6. Jacob means "one who takes by the heel"

> *But **you shall utterly destroy them**, the Hittite and the Amorite, the Canaanite and the Perizzite, the Hivite and the Jebusite, as the Lord your God has commanded you,* (Deuteronomy 20:17 NASB)

Again, either God is quite prejudice and into random acts of genocide, or He has other reasons for wiping out the same people groups who were first mentioned in Genesis 10:6-20.

NEPHILIM FROM NEPHILIM

In his book, *The Cosmic Chessmatch*, L.A. Marzulli echoes the same belief shared by *many* other scholars concerning the notion of a second incursion, based on Numbers 13. Regarding the spotting of the Nephilim by the Hebrew spies when they first entered the Promised Land, he writes:

> *You may remember that these are the same creatures we see in the Genesis 6 passage. In other words, it would seem that there is, in fact, a second incursion of the unthinkable; the fallen angels have once again procreated with the women of the earth and the result is a demonic/human hybrid known as the Nephilim. There are those who tell us that this could not have happened; however, we have the written word of the Torah (the first five books of the Hebrew and Christian Bibles) that tells us that the Nephilim were in the land. We also have the writing of the first century Jewish historian, Flavius Josephus, who tells us that the bones of these creatures were openly on display in Jerusalem at the time of his writing, which was thousands of years later!*
>
> *Is it a coincidence that when the spies are sent to the land they encounter the same entities that we see in Genesis 6? I think not, and would submit to you that the presence of the fallen angels creating these unholy hybrids, or Nephilim,*

> *is once again a deliberate attempt by the Fallen One to thwart the plans of the Most High God. I want you to examine the text for yourself:*
>
> — L.A. Marzulli[7]

Taking his advice, I did examine the text for myself, but with all due respect to my friend, I have to admit, I came to an entirely different conclusion. In his book, L.A. quotes Numbers 13:25-33, but I think the key is in verses 28 and 33:

> *Nevertheless the people be strong that dwell in the land, and the cities are walled, and very great: and moreover we saw* ***the children of Anak*** *there.* (Numbers 13:28)

> *And there we saw the giants* [Nephilim], ***the sons of Anak, which come of the giants*** [Nephilim]*: and we were in our own sight as grasshoppers, and so we were in their sight.* (Numbers 13:33)

Looking at Numbers 13:25-33, we do ***not*** see any mention of fallen angels. Instead, we see that these Nephilim came from other Nephilim! Specifically, we discover they were the sons of Anak. Anak was a son of Arba. As we will later discover, Arba was an Amorite. The Amorites came from Amorreus, son of Canaan, son of Ham. There are no angels mentioned anywhere. Next to the Amorites (who are mentioned 82 times in Scripture), the most popular giants in the Bible were the Philistines (who are mentioned 224 times). They came from Caphtor, son of Mizraim, son of Ham. Again, no angels are mentioned anywhere in the post-Flood, biblical accounts of giants.

Occam's razor demands that when faced with competing hypotheses that are equal in other respects, we must select the one that makes the fewest new assumptions. With no mention of angels ever again

7. ***The Cosmic Chessmatch***, by L.A. Marzulli (©2011 Spiral of Life) page 92.

mating with women anywhere in the Scriptures, and repeated statements directly linking the giants to offspring of those who stepped off the ark, the only logical conclusion, without making any assumptions is therefore, that the post-Flood Nephilim are giants who (as Numbers 13:33 clearly states) came from other Nephilim, who apparently were passengers on the ark. Since Noah and his wife were pure, it stands to reason that their sons were as well. The only option we have left are the three wives.

According to Genesis 6:18, the wives were not chosen until after the corruption of all flesh (Gen. 6:12). I have chosen to use only Scripture thus far, however, if we were to broaden our search parameters to include 1 Enoch, Jasher and Jubilees, we clearly see what happened. 1 Enoch 10:10 says the first generation Nephilim were killed off within 500 years. Jubilees 7:24 tells us that the "after that" of Genesis 6:4 involved the mixture of animals with humans and is in a pre-Flood context. Jasher 4:18 confirms this and states that the "corruption of all flesh," which took place in the days of Noah had more to do with the forbidden activity of mixing animals and humans than it did angels mating with humans. Jasher 5 also confirms the chronology of Genesis 6:12-18 by stating that the three wives of Noah's sons were not chosen until just 7 days before the Flood. These are all multiple, confirming witnesses that I believe clearly state how the Nephilim returned.

WERE ALL OF NOAH'S SON'S OFFSPRING NEPHILIM?

Of course, when considering what I have written thus far, it may be tempting to think that ***all*** of Noah's son's offspring had Nephilim genetics, which, by implication, would seem to mean you and I do too. Not so. As seen in **Figure 25**, there was a 50/50 chance that offspring could have been born completely normal, even if all three of Noah's son's wives had corrupted genetics. For forty years in a row leading up to the destruction of the Temple in Jerusalem, on the Day of Atonement, the lot fell to Azazel. According to one on-line source, the odds of that happening are about 5.5 billion to one![8] Only God could do that, so clearly we have evidence of Him affecting random chance. In the case of Shem's offspring, it would appear that the "genetics lot" always fell on the 50% normal side. In the case of Japheth, I see no *biblical* proof of giants in his lineage, however we do find evidence in the historical record and we will discuss this further in Chapter Eleven. Apparently the odds varied in his line, but landed predominantly on the normal side. Of course, in Ham's lineage, we find that the lot fell on both sides, but more often on the 50% Nephilim side. We don't see evidence of giants in Phut's lineage or Cush's (with the possible exception of Nimrod, who apparently affected his own change through defilement). Thus, I really find no biblical grounds to say that ***all*** of Noah's son's offspring — or even all of Ham's lineage for that matter — were carriers of Nephilim seed. That said, Canaan's offspring and possibly some of Mizraim's (e.g., Caphtor) appear to have contained the majority of post-Flood Nephilim genetics.

Assuming this theory is true, we don't know how "strong" those Nephilim genes were. A married couple who both have blue eyes can give birth to a child that has brown eyes, thus passing on a genetic trait neither of them have, but which came from an ancestor. The same is true for hair color and other attributes. It all depends on the dominant combinations of genes that get passed through. Therefore, it is possible and reasonable to assume that every now and then, Ham's ***pure*** genetics could override the impurities in his wife's genetics and thus produce a child that is free of Nephilim genes (see also **Figure 25**).

Another possibility (admittedly arguing from a position of silence in the text) is that Ham could have had other wives after the Flood. Women often died in child birth. Men often had more than one wife. So, there are any number of factors that could lead to Ham's other children being pure and free of Nephilim genetics.

---

8. See: http://www.jewishencyclopedia.com/articles/2203-azazel and http://www3.telus.net/public/kstam/en/temple/details/evidence.htm

In any case, for the record, let me state in no uncertain terms, that this thesis does not in any way have to imply that all of Ham's seed — usually (wrongly) assumed to be "people of color" — would be of Nephilim descent! I feel the need to emphasize this point because I don't want anyone to think for a minute that I am implying black people (those generally assumed to be exclusively from Ham's lineage) are of Nephilim seed — the way some would like to interpret my thesis. I've already taken heat for this. So, let's put that rumor to rest here and now.

ISSUES OF SKIN COLOR AND RACE

We are creatures created in the image and likeness of God. Whatever differences we may find in outward appearances are only due to very minor variants in size, shapes and colors. Some have a small nose, and some have a big nose. Some have high cheekbones. Others have a dimple on their chin. Some have slanted eyes, while others have more rounded eyes. Some have light colored skin. Others have dark skin. Who cares? People are people. There is one race and it is the human race. Regardless of our outward appearances, inside we are all made up of the same materials. It is for these reasons and more that I reject all forms of racism and bigotry!

Still, for whatever reason, many are prejudice. They think one color is better than another and persecute those who are different than they are. Some of those prejudice attitudes go back to misconceptions concerning the origins of the so-called races that supposedly sprung up out of Noah's three sons. I wish to destroy such misconceptions and set the record straight as far as where I am coming from with this thesis concerning the wives of Noah's sons and their offspring,

First of all, we must understand that skin tone is determined by the amount of melanin found in a person's skin, which itself is largely determined by the amount of exposure an individual has to the sun over extended periods of time. Melanin protects the body by absorbing solar radiation. Excessive solar radiation causes direct and indirect damage to the skin and the body naturally combats and seeks to repair the damage and protect the skin by creating and releasing more melanin into the skin's cells. With the increased production of melanin, the skin color darkens.

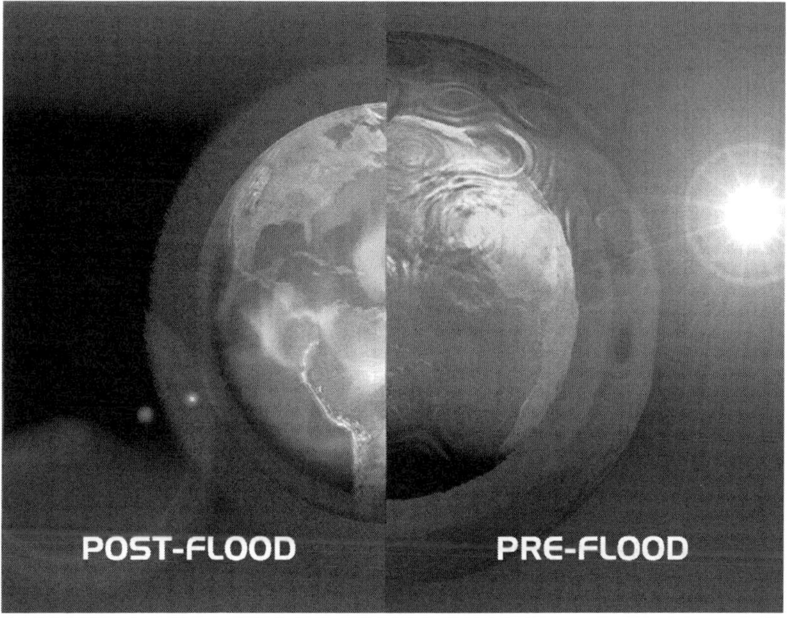

Figure 29

Before the Flood a protective canopy surrounded the earth,[9] which means little to no harmful radiation would have penetrated the atmosphere. Thus, there would have been little need for any excessive production of melanin to protect the skin of pre-Flood man. Therefore, it is my belief that all men, at one point were the same color. What color? Well, Adam's name means both "man" and "red." This would seem to indicate that Adam was a "red-man" or a man of lighter color; probably more pink than anything else (as there would be very little need for the darker pigment-causing melanin). If all humans descended from him, they would be of

9. See Genesis 1:6-10 and 2 Peter 3:5. Note that one of Jupiter's moons, Europa (which has a protective ice canopy) also serves as a witness within our solar system to this idea.

the same color. Assuming Noah and his wife were of one color, it stands to reason that *all three* of their children would have been the same color too.

After the Flood, the environment changed. Depending on where you lived, you would have ended up with darker or lighter skin due to the intensity of sun exposure in that region and the resulting production of skin-protecting melonin—or the lack thereof. It's as simple as that and it does not matter which son of Noah you came from.

Some of Shem's descendents settled in Ethiopia. Guess what? There are black Shemites there to this day. The descendants of Ham settled in the Middle East and in parts of Southern Europe as well as throughout North and East Africa. Not all descendants of Ham are black. The people who's skin darkened were those who settled in the equatorial regions—whether they came from Shem, Ham or Japheth is irrelevant. Those who moved to the northern regions, developed different traits (such as metabolizing fats differently to survive the cold). This is merely the body's natural way of adapting to its environment.[10]

Racism originates from Darwinian evolutionary thinking and is faulty at best and detrimental at worse. So, forget all that. As we see in Genesis 11, all of Noah's descendents were together in the plain of Shinar at one point, which meant the offspring of Shem, Ham and Japheth mingled and intermarried. They were all living together in one location until the dispersing of the languages into people groups and nations.

There are hundreds of different breeds of dog, which all descended from one "kind" of the canine-class of creature that was originally created by God. Man took and blended dominant characteristics from different litters to breed dogs for different purposes. Today, we have dogs that have a wide variety of seemingly specialized characteristics,

10. Adaptation within a species does not constitute evolution. The species does not "morph" into something new, it merely takes on variant attributes and characteristics common to the "kinds" God created.

which have produced everything from the tiny Chihuahua to the elongated Dachshund, the fuzzy, curly haired Poodle, the cute Maltese, the loyal German Shepherd, the long-haired Collie and smart, herding Boarder Collie, the speedy Greyhound, the feisty Terriers, the massive Great Dane and everything in-between. Yet, all of these descended from a wolf-like creature, bred by man for specific purposes and characteristics within confined parameters.

What we *call* races are simply people groups with different outward characteristics. I do not attribute those characteristics to Nephilim (though it is possible that *some* Nephilim genetics may have contributed to certain features). With this in mind, it is not unreasonable to assume that at the Tower of Babel, people dispersed into language groups as well as into groups, which not only had the same speech, but also similar physical traits. Over time, these traits became accentuated due to inter-breeding within confined, control group-like settings.

Most scholars believe that Japheth became the father of the European nations. Supposedly, Shem became the father of the Semitic Middle Eastern and Asian nations and Ham was the father of the African nations. While this may be *generally* true, it is not something we can be overly dogmatic about as clearly the offspring of all three sons mixed within each other's territories.

Josephus records the regions of Japheth's lineage in *Antiquities of the Jews,* Book 1, Chapter 6, Section 1. Jubilees 9:24-30 also establishes what land was occupied by Japheth, making note that his land *"is cold, and the land of Ham is hot, and the land of Shem is neither hot nor cold, but it is of blended cold and heat."* Josephus records the regions of Shem in *Antiquities of the Jews*, Book 1, Chapter 6, Section 4. Jubilees does the same in Jubilies 8:12-17. Josephus spends a fair amount of effort dealing with Ham's lineage in *Antiquities of the Jews*, Book 1, Chapter 6, Section 2, showing how they went all over the map.

In the book, *Ancient Post Flood History*, by Ken Johnson, Th.D., on page 56, the author notes:

> *Ham's land is described as the continent of Africa. But it is noted that the descendants of Ham invaded and occupied the territory of Shem from the Mediterranean Sea to the Euphrates River.*

We simply cannot make a blanket statement saying that all of Japheth's descendents are white Europeans, all of Shem's are Asian or Middle Easterners and all of Ham's are black Africans. That argument simply does not work. Some of Ham's descendents (Caphtor) went to Crete and later expanded into Europe. One of Shem's descendants (Ophir) apparently settled in the African continent and another (Lud) settled way up in Japheth's territory. Several of Ham's descendants settled the Middle East. We also know that later, Shemites settled in Ethiopia and other parts of Africa as well. Furthermore, Dr. Johnson makes note of Ham's seed occupying the five islands of Balearic, Sicily, Sardinia, Crete and Cypress — which were also occupied by Japheth's lineage (page 53, Ibid). Thus, I believe it is wholly in error to assume that all of Ham's children were black and that only those who lived in Africa were his descendants. History, science, and the Bible would all disagree with that notion.

In short, people went everywhere and you can't just lump them all into three happy categories as so many try to do. The world is a melting pot and we are all descended from three brothers who came from one couple, Noah and his wife, who themselves ultimately descended from one man, Adam, who was created in the image and likeness of God. Therefore, I submit to you that all forms of racism are ungodly, ludicrous, and just plain unjustified.

Still, some have tried to use the Genesis 9:18-27 passage to justify slavery of Africans. In similar fashion, some have read my thesis and accused me of being a racist. Let me again state in no uncertain terms that I am not. This has absolutely ***nothing*** to do with red, yellow, black or white men. It has everything to do with Nephilim seed! Noah was not cursing the black man, but rather he cursed the offspring of the Nephilim, revealing that they are to remain under the subjugation of man. He said that the Canaanites would serve all the others. Well, considering what we know about where the Canaanites settled, we can see how they felt about that idea. They went and set up shop right in the middle of Shem's territory and ruled that land for quite some time.

NIMROD AND HIS GIANT COUSINS

Genesis 10 starts off with a statement about the generations of the sons of Noah. Moses goes on to list the sons of Japheth with no elaboration on any of them. By the time we get to verse 6, we are told about Ham's children. The sons of Cush are listed in verse 7. Verse 8 goes on to mention one of Cush's sons in particular: Nimrod. The text then pauses for a moment to give us more—five verses worth of details—about this individual, thus drawing our attention specifically to him as someone clearly important for us to remember:

> *And Cush begat Nimrod:* ***he began to be a mighty one in the earth****. He was a mighty hunter before the LORD: wherefore it is said, Even as Nimrod the mighty hunter before the LORD.*
>
> *And the beginning of his kingdom was Babel, and Erech, and Accad, and Calneh, in the land of Shinar. Out of that land went forth Asshur, and builded Nineveh, and the city Rehoboth, and Calah, And Resen between Nineveh and Calah: the same is a great city.* (Genesis 10:8-12)

We could argue that this detail is given as a set up for the next chapter, which will focus on this individual's activity in the plains of Shinar. So, essentially the added detail given here sets the stage for understanding future events. That is precisely why I believe we are given added detail all through the Scriptures. In this particular section, we have learned some interesting facts concerning Nimrod. By way of review:

Based on the various meanings for the Hebrew word *"chalal"* that is translated as "began" in the above text, it appears that through some sort of profane (sexual?) defilement Nimrod began to become a "gibbor." Previously, we learned that there are at least three ways to look at this:

1. Nimrod simply became a strong and powerful man.
2. Nimrod began to become a giant himself (through some sort of defilement).
3. Nimrod began to become a hunter of giants.

In Chapter Three, I showed you how that word "*chalal*" is very interesting concerning the idea of profaning, defiling, and prostituting. Observe how it is used elsewhere:

> *And thou shalt not let any of thy seed pass through the fire to Molech, neither shalt thou* ***profane*** *the name of thy God: I am the LORD.* (Leviticus 18:21)

> *Uncontrolled as water, you shall not have preeminence, Because you went up to your father's bed; Then you* ***defiled*** *it -- he went up to my couch.* (Genesis 49:4 NASB)

> *Do not* ***prostitute*** *thy daughter, to cause her to be a whore; lest the land fall to whoredom, and the land become full of wickedness.* (Leviticus 19:29)

With these definitions in mind, I stated my suspicion that all three of the above bullet-point possibilities concerning Nimrod may be true. Remember, the Septuagint plainly states that he was a giant:

> *And Chus begot Nebrod:* ***he began to be a giant*** *upon the earth. He was a giant hunter before the Lord God; therefore they say, As Nebrod the giant hunter before the Lord.* (Genesis 10:8,9 LXX)

Additionally, according to many ancient cultures, Nimrod was often depicted as a mighty warrior, giant and possibly a hunter and subduer of giants as well. In fact, giants are even said to have helped him build the Tower of Babel. An Arabic manuscript found at Baalbek says:

> *After the flood, when Nimrod reigned over Lebanon, he sent giants to rebuild the fortress of Baalbek, which was so named in honour of Baal, the god of the Moabites and worshippers of the Sun.*[11]

Figure 30

11 ***History of Baalbek*** by Michael Alouf, pg. 41

Considering the massive foundation stones and structures (**Figure 30**) found at Baalbek, the most logical conclusion is that giants must have cut, moved and built them.

Figure 31

For the sake of illustration, I have created **Figure 31** in Photoshop to show how big two 36 foot giants would be as compared to a 6 foot man standing in front of one of those massive blocks of stone. I personally believe the giants of that day were even bigger, but even at *just* 36 feet tall,[12] we can see how easily those stones could have been cut and moved into place by such massive people. If true, the Biblical and historical evidence appears to suggest that Nimrod may have been their task master!

We move on from the introduction of Nimrod in Genesis 10 to learn about Mitzraim's sons. Again, the author pauses to give us added detail about one son: Caphtor. This one is a bit tricky though — depending on the English translation you use. The *King James* and a number of other translations render verse 14 as:

> *And Pathrusim, and Casluhim (out of whom came the Philistines,) and Caphtorim.* (Genesis 10:14)

12. Amos 2:9 tells us that the Amorites were as tall as cedar trees and as strong as the oaks. Cedar tress grow from between 35ft and 150ft (the cedars of Lebanon) in height.

The *New Living Translation* renders it as:

> *And Pathrusim and Casluhim and Caphtorim, from whom came the Philistines.* (Genesis 10:14 NLT)

Why the discrepancy? Who is right? How should we interpret this verse correctly? Using the premise that Scripture will always interpret itself, we can ask, "*Why does that text include an elaboration in the first place*?" The author is drawing our attention for a reason. Strangely enough, the King James translators got it right elsewhere, so I don't understand why they missed it in Genesis 10:

> *Because of the day that cometh to spoil all the Philistines, and to cut off from Tyrus and Zidon every helper that remaineth: for the LORD will spoil the Philistines,* ***the remnant of the country of Caphtor***. (Jeremiah 47:4)

> *Are ye not as children of the Ethiopians unto me, O children of Israel? saith the LORD. Have not I brought up Israel out of the land of Egypt? and the* ***Philistines from Caphtor****, and the Syrians from Kir?* (Amos 9:7)

In this case, the NLT seems to me to be the better translation, as it is the most consistent with other confirming Scriptures. Caphtor was the father of the Philistines — a group of people we later learn had giants within their midst. Note also that many commentators and Bible translators associate the land of Caphtor with the island of Crete. I find it quite interesting that much of Greek mythology originates in Crete. Could it be that the giant "gods" of the Greek myths were really just the ancestors of gibborim such as Goliath?

Something else worth noting is the fact that Mizraim and his offspring's names all end in the suffix "im" which generally represents a plurality.

> *And Mizraim begat Ludim, and Anamim, and Lehabim, and Naphtuhim, And Pathrusim, and Casluhim, (out of whom came Philistim,) and Caphtorim.*
> (Genesis 10:13,14)

Figure 32

Although it is true that the "im" suffix usually represents a plural form of the word, I can't help but wonder if it may also represent a qualitative connotation as much as a quantitative. In other words, in this case, could it be saying that Mizraim and his offspring were not so much great in number, but rather great in size? His name means, "double straightness." Could that mean, twice as long? I don't know, but it is interesting to note the number of ancient depictions of giants in the land of Mizraim (Egypt).

Were they just making colossal statues to match giant egos or were they accurately depicting the scale (or size comparison) of those being represented? Note the size of a mature woman depicted in **Figure 33** compared to this Egyptian giant. There are many such depictions.

As I was writing this chapter, someone posted an article on my Facebook page about the Bir Hooker artifact: a 15 inch mummified human finger that was apparently found in Egypt. It is a very interesting story that you can read at unexplainedmysteriesoftheworld.com.[13] If this story is true and the pictures are real, a finger of this size would have belonged to a giant (Egyptian) that was nearly 20 feet tall! Proportionately speaking, that would be pretty close to the scale depicted in **Figures 32** and **33**.

---

13. Read the entire article and see pictures taken by Gregor Spörri in Egypt in 1988: unexplainedmysteriesoftheworld.com/archives/finger-of-a-giant-found-in-egypt

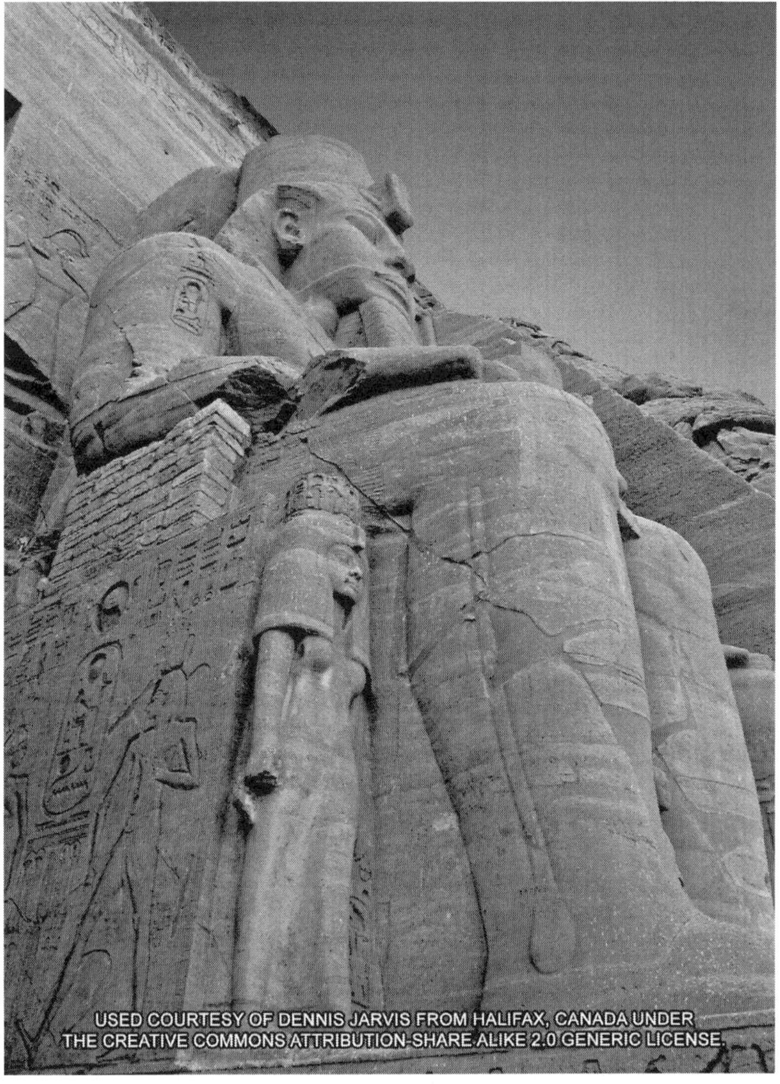

Figure 33

The Caphtorim-born Philistines are mentioned most often in the Scriptures as an enemy of Israel that consisted of giants; second only in size to the Amorites. One of the first Amorites we meet by name is found as early as Genesis 13:

> *Then Abram moved his tent and came and dwelt by the oaks of Mamre, which are in Hebron, and there he built an altar to the LORD.* (Genesis 13:18 NASB)

Mamre is a very interesting character in the Bible. In Genesis 14:13, we learn that he has two other brothers, Eshcol and Aner. These three were Abram's allies in the land of the Canaanites. According to J.B. Jackson's, *A Dictionary of Scripture Proper Names*,[14] their names mean:

- **Mamre**: "causing fatness
- **Eshcol**: "a cluster"
- **Aner**: "a lamp swept away"

These three are early descendants of Canaan's son Amorreus,[15] from whom came all of the Amorites. We'll see much more of the sons of Amorreus as we move forward in the text. Since, of all the sons of Canaan, the Amorites are so prominent in the Scriptures, we will use them to construct a post-Flood timeline showing very clearly that the Bible gives us a direct lineage of giants going straight back to the Flood and progressing forward all the way to the time of David.

Moving on in the Table of Nations, we find that the sons of Shem are given in Genesis 10:21-31, with added detail given only for the sons of Eber:

> *And unto Eber were born two sons: the name of one was* ***Peleg; for in his days was the earth divided;*** *and his*

14. On-line at: biblecentre.org/ebooks/jbj_dictionary_of_bible_names.htm
15. In ***Antiquities*** 1.6.2, Josephus records the sons of Canaan as: The sons of Canaan were these: Sidonius, who also built a city of the same name; it is called by the Greeks Sidon Amathus inhabited in Amathine, which is even now called Amathe by the inhabitants, although the Macedonians named it Epiphania, from one of his posterity: Arudeus possessed the island Aradus: Arucas possessed Arce, which is in Libanus. But for the seven others, [Eueus,] Chetteus, Jebuseus, **Amorreus**, Gergesus, Eudeus, Sineus, Samareus, we have nothing in the sacred books but their names, for the Hebrews overthrew their cities; and their calamities came upon them on the occasion following. - The Works of Flavius Josephus.

> *brother's name was Joktan.* (Genesis 10:25)

This verse is interesting for a number of reasons. First of all, it tells us when the "division of languages" took place, which gives us a time marker for the Tower of Babel. Based on the ages of the patriarchs given in Genesis 11 and the timelines that can be drawn using those ages, most scholars place the time of the Tower of Babel and the division of languages at approximately 100 to 150 years after the Flood.

Second, the name Peleg is the same as the Hebrew word *"peleg"* which means "*earthquake*" or "*violent separation*" and caries with it the concept of water (rivers, streams, canals, channels, etc). So, there appears to have been more going on in his days than a simple split up of people groups. I believe there was some sort of massive continental plate shifting which took place in his days. Why? Well, because you don't name your kid, "*violent separation by earthquake and water*" unless something major happened to make you want to do so! And his brother's name was Joktan, which comes from the word "qaton," which means "*to be made small*" or "*to diminish from something larger.*" Based on the meanings of those two names, we can conclude that in the days of Eber's offspring, the world was indeed divided—and that division happened not long after the Flood.

Genesis 11 is a powerhouse of information! It tells us about the building of the Tower of Babel and how the "whole earth" (as in all of the generations of Noah's offspring) were together in one place. Whatever they were planning to do did not please God, so He divided the languages (and apparently the continents too). Moses then lays out the lineage from Shem to Abram, giving us an easy to track timeline. I want to explore that timeline a bit more here. To aide us in doing so, I have prepared a chart, (**Figure 34**) showing the ages from Adam to Abraham, extended to include the Exodus and the Israelite's entry into the Promised Land.

Looking at this chart, we can see that the Nephilim were on the earth for about 1,200 years leading up to the Flood and they were on the earth for about the same amount of time after the flood as well. Contrary to the views of some who adhere to the Multiple Incursions Theory and suppose the giants just seem to "pop up out of nowhere" in the Biblical text, I believe the canon of Scripture reveals a steady lineage of giants on the earth right from the end of the Flood to the time of David and I intend to prove that fact here.

Nimrod is connected to many other characters in history, and quite a few of them were depicted as giants. Let's look again at his introduction in Scripture:

> *And Cush begat Nimrod: he began to be a* ***mighty one*** *in the earth. He was a* ***mighty hunter*** *before the LORD: wherefore it is said, Even as*

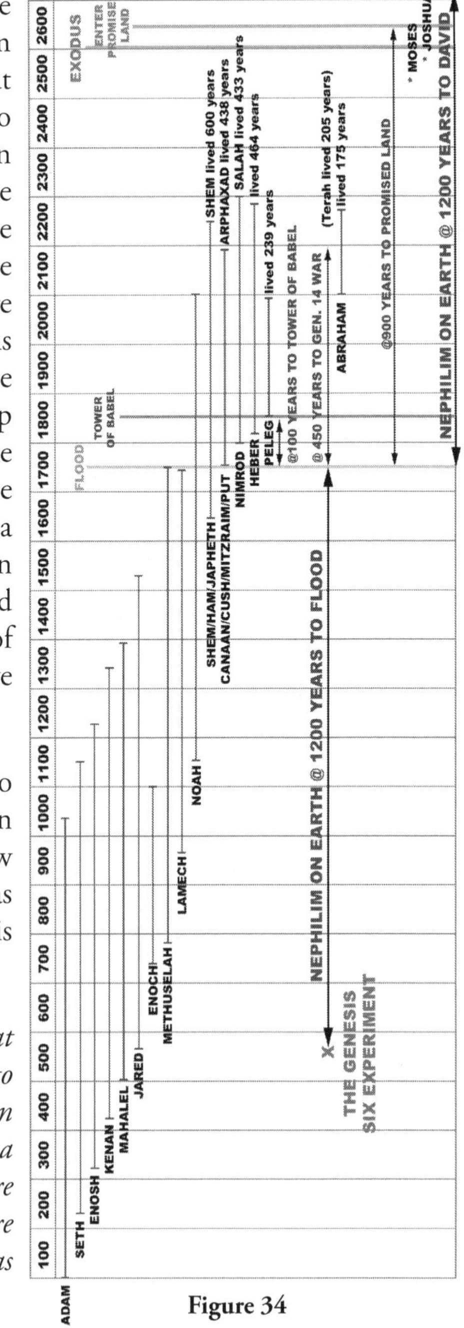

Figure 34

> *Nimrod the* ***mighty hunter*** *before the LORD.*
> (Genesis 10:8,9)

I believe the correct interpretation of "gibbor" in his case is to be thought of as "giant" for the same reason it is in Genesis 6:4, Job 16:14 and 1 Samuel 17:51 and by virtue of the fact that Moses uses the word *three times* in those two verses. He certainly seems to be stressing the point!

I believe there is something else going on here concerning Cush. Remember, parents name their children what they name them for a reason. Though the text does not explicitly say so, it appears that Cush named his son, Nimrod. If this is true, then essentially what we have here is Cush being the one who declared through the naming of his son, that "*We shall rebel.*"

If the Tower of Babel incident took place less than 150 years after the Flood, presumably Nimrod had to have been old enough to have orchestrated the whole affair. The Bible does not record the time of his birth, but it appears to me that he was probably born 30 to 50 years prior to the construction of that tower (and city). At some point approximately 50 years or so after the Flood, Nimrod was born and soon began to become a giant. If the other stories that we learned about earlier concerning Baalbek are true, the other giants had to have been born about the same time. I believe the Biblical texts show that they were. In fact, as a son of Canaan, Amorreus (the father of the Amorite giants) would have been a direct, contemporary cousin to Nimrod.

Back in Genesis 10, Moses drew our attention to Nimrod's uncle Mitzraim, which would make Caphtorim a first cousin. He is the father of a group of people we later discover had giants within their midst, namely Goliath and his Philistine brothers who were "the sons of a giant in Gath."

> *And it came to pass after this, that there arose war at Gezer with the Philistines; at which time Sibbechai the*

> *Hushathite slew* ***Sippai, that was of the children of the giant****: and they were subdued. And there was war again with the Philistines; and Elhanan the son of Jair slew* ***Lahmi the brother of Goliath the Gittite*** *[note: a Gittite is someone who comes from the city of Gath], whose spear staff was like a weaver's beam. And yet again there was war at Gath, where was* ***a man of great stature, whose fingers and toes were four and twenty, six on each hand, and six on each foot and he also was the son of the giant****. But when he defied Israel, Jonathan the son of Shimea David's brother slew him.* ***These were born unto the giant in Gath****; and they fell by the hand of David, and by the hand of his servants.* (1 Chronicles 20:4-8)

In the Table of Nations, Moses also revealed Nimrod's other cousins from the house of Canaan — a group of people God seems unusually hostile toward (unless you reckon them among the Nephilim).

> *When the Lord thy God shall have brought thee into the land, which thou art going in to possess, and shall have* ***destroyed*** *many nations before thee, the* ***Hethite****, and the* ***Gergezite****, and the* ***Amorrhite****, and the* ***Chanaanite****, and the* ***Pherezite****, and the* ***Hevite****, and the* ***Jebusite****, seven nations much more numerous than thou art, and stronger than thou:* (Deuteronomy 7:1 Douay-Rheims Bible)

> ***But thou shalt utterly destroy them****; namely, the* ***Hittites****, and the* ***Amorites****, the* ***Canaanites****, and the* ***Perizzites****, the* ***Hivites****, and the* ***Jebusites****; as the LORD thy God hath commanded thee:* (Deuteronomy 20:17)

If Canaan was the father of all of these "ites," then there were indeed a great deal of giant cousins for Nimrod to rule over! Presumably, in order for them to have been born from women, they must have started out as normal sized humans and grew larger from there. This may be possible simply by virtue of eliminating or turning off the growth inhibitor genes through the hybridization process.[16] If that theory is true, then they would have all "grown up" together. At some point in the process, Nimrod must have risen to a prominent position of power, authority and respect — even amongst those who may have later outgrown him in stature — in order for him to have been the ruler of this emerging world of giants. Regardless of speculation, the biblical text indicates that Nimrod was a giant, and so were most of his cousins — at least from the lineage of Canaan anyway.

In Genesis 11, we meet Abram for the first time. He was born approximately 350 years after the Flood. In Genesis 12, God calls Abram out of Ur and thus he went forth from there by faith, until God stopped him in Shechem. Note what the text says:

> *Abram traveled through the land as far as Shechem. There he set up camp beside the oak of Moreh. At that time,* ***the area was inhabited by Canaanites****.* (Genesis 12:6 NLT)

Here Moses tells us that the land was *already* inhabited by Canaanites. As an Amorite, Moreh was one of them. The Amorite giants are often compared with both the cedar tree (in height) and the oaks (in strength).[17] The giants seemed to really like being amongst those trees. Both Moreh and Mamre were owners of oak groves. Moreh's name means, "teacher" and "former rain."[18] I'm not entirely sure what, if any significance there is in that, but the Holy Spirit draws our attention to him and his oaks a few times in the Scriptures,[19] so I suspect there's probably something to be gleaned from that fact. At any rate, during those short 350 years

16. See my DVD, ***Archon Invasion And The Return of the Nephilim*** Part 1 for more on this.
17. See Amos 2:9
18. ***A Dictionary of Scripture Proper Names*** by J.B. Jackson, page 67
19 See: Genesis 12:6, Deuteronomy 11:30, Judges 7:1

following the Flood, Canaan's children began to settle, multiply and fill the land, which would come to bear his name.

Keep in mind that those early generations lived between 200 and 500 years of age. So, although they did indeed multiply, we aren't necessarily talking about multiple generations. There were likely generations living in the land who were the immediate sons and grandsons of Ham. After all, Shem was still alive at that time (serving as the Melchizedek[20] of *Genesis* 14) and living in the land as well.

In Genesis 13, Moses again draws our attention to the inhabitants of the land when Abram and Lot have their little dispute between Bethel and Ai:

> *And there was a strife between the herdmen of Abram's cattle and the herdmen of Lot's cattle: and the* ***Canaanite*** *and the* ***Perizzite*** *dwelled then in the land.* (Genesis 13:7)

Regarding this "new" people group we suddenly encounter called the Perizzites, *Gill's Exposition of the Entire Bible* states:

> *The Canaanite, though it was a general name for the people of the whole land, yet was given to a particular family in it, and was derived from their first founder Canaan, the son of Ham; the* ***Perizzite was another family or tribe of the same nation****, who had their name from "a village"; these being Pagans or villagers, living in huts, or houses, or tents scattered up and down in the fields,* ***and were a rough, <u>inhuman</u>, and unsociable sort of people...***

20 Shem was still alive and was believed to be about 500 years old at the time and Abram was 75 years of age. Chazalic literature, unanimously identifies Melchizedek as Shem son of Noah (Targum Yonathan to Genesis chap. 14, Genesis Rabbah 46:7, Babylonian Talmud to Tractate Nedarim 32b) and also Jasher 16:11,12 (as Adonizedek).

The Perizzites and Canaanites are often mentioned together in the Scriptures. Genesis 13:7 suggests that they lived together near Bethel and Ai. In Joshua 11:3, we see that they dwelt with the Jebusites in the hill country. Later in Joshua 17:5, we see that the tribe of Joseph took the land of the Rephaim and Perizzites. The tribes of Judah and Simeon attacked and defeated the Perizzites and Canaanites to take the territory of Judah, capturing King Adonibezek and cutting off his thumbs and toes. They were also among those who were still left in the land by the time of Ezra (Ezra 9:1).

I can't help wondering what Gill really meant by a "*rough and inhuman*" sort of people? It certainly makes you take notice of Scriptures such as these:

> *Benaiah the son of Jehoiada, the son of a valiant man of Kabzeel, who had done many acts;* ***he slew two lionlike men of Moab****: also he went down and slew a lion in a pit in a snowy day.* (1 Chronicles 11:22)

> *So they shall no more sacrifice their sacrifices to* ***goat demons*** [Hebrew: "sa'iyr" or satyrs], ***after whom they whore.***[21] *This shall be a statute forever for them throughout their generations.* (Leviticus 17:7 ESV)

> *He set up priests of his own for the high places, for the* ***satyrs*** *and for the calves which he had made.* (Chronicles 11:15 NASB)[22]

> *But wild beasts of the desert shall lie there; and their houses shall be full of doleful creatures; and owls shall dwell there, and* ***satyrs shall dance there****. And the wild beasts of the islands shall cry in their desolate houses, and dragons in their pleasant palaces: and her time*

21. Note: the text says people were mating with satyrs!
22. Note: the KJV translates satyrs in that passage as "devils."

> *is near to come, and her days shall not be prolonged.* (Isaiah 13:21,22)

The Septuagint version of these same Isaiah verses is worth noting:

> *But wild beasts shall rest there; and the houses shall be filled with howling;* ***and monsters shall rest there, and devils shall dance there, and satyrs shall dwell there****; and hedgehogs shall make their nests in their houses. It will come soon, and will not tarry.* (Isaiah 13:21,22 LXX)

Yes, the Bible has a lot of very interesting things in it! In fact, the more I dig, the more I find that the truth is far stranger than fiction — and often what we think of as myth or fiction is proven to be true. Thus, when considering Scriptures such as those listed above, I can not help but suspect that Gill was on to something when he described the Perizzites as "*rough and inhuman.*"

By the end of Genesis 13, Abram moves his camp to Hebron — a city we later discover (in Genesis 23 and elsewhere) was for some time named *Kiriath-Arba* (the city of Arba - who was the massive, giant ancestor of the Anakim). This is where things get very interesting. An event occurs in the next chapter of Genesis that I'm going to refer to as the *real* World War 1.

Chapter Eight

THE GENESIS 14 WAR

And it came to pass in the days of Amraphel king of Shinar, Arioch king of Ellasar, Chedorlaomer king of Elam, and Tidal king of nations; That these made war with Bera king of Sodom, and with Birsha king of Gomorrah, Shinab king of Admah, and Shemeber king of Zeboiim, and the king of Bela, which is Zoar. All these were joined together in the vale of Siddim, which is the salt sea. Twelve years they served Chedorlaomer, and in the thirteenth year they rebelled. (Genesis 14:1-4)

The Genesis 14 War was quite literally World War 1. It was an epic battle like something out of a Hollywood movie such as *Lord of the Rings* or *Clash of the Titans*. It was a war of giants. Four kings against five.

The on-line Jewish Encyclopedia makes mention of the identity of king Amraphel of Shinar, stating that this was Nimrod.

> *The punishment visited on the builders of the tower did not cause Nimrod to change his conduct; he remained an idolater. He particularly persecuted Abraham, who by his command was thrown into a heated furnace; and it was on this account, according to one opinion, that Nimrod was called "Amraphel" (= "he said, throw in")* (Targum pseudo-Jonathan to Gen. xiv. 1; Gen. R. xlii. 5; Cant. R. viii. 8)

Shlomo Yitzhak, also known as the great Torah scholar, "Rashi" agrees—as do a variety of other ancient commentators. So, by many accounts, here we have the first biblical reappearance of Nimrod after the Tower of Babel.

According to Jackson's, *A Dictionary of Scripture and Proper Names* (pg. 8), the name Amraphel means: "a sayer of darkness." This dark sayer is going to be joined in battle by a king named Arioch, whose name means "lion-like"(pg. 10). Considering 1 Chronicles 11:22, I have to wonder if Arioch is a predecessor to (or an ancient king of) the "lion-like men" of Moab. Could be. At any rate, Amraphel and Arioch are joined by another warrior named Chedorlaomer, whose name (according to Jackson) means, "binding for a sheaf" (pg. 22). As I dug deeper into this particular individual, I found that his name may be Elamite and breaks down to Kudur Lagamar or a servant of Lagamaru, who was the Akkadian Ninurta, the god of war (also associated with being another name for Nimrod). If this is true, that would essentially make him a great general serving under Nimrod. The fourth king was Tidal whose name means, "you shall be cast out from above" (pg. 93). Clearly, this is a motley crew of very dark characters.

These four made war with Bera king of Sodom, Birsha king of Gomorrah, Shinab king of Admah, Shemeber king of Zeboiim, and the king of Bela (Zoar). According to Jackson, Bera means "in the evil" (pg. 17), Birsha means, "in wickedness" (pg. 20), Shinab means, "father's tooth" (pg. 87), Shemeber means, "name of wing" (pg. 85) and though the name of the fifth king is not given, Bela means, "swallowing" (pg. 16). Again, we have some interesting characters listed here.

In Moses' account of the Genesis 14 War, we see that Nimrod and his evil gang were victorious over the offspring of other giants!

> *And in the fourteenth year came Chedorlaomer, and the kings that were with him, and smote the* ***Rephaims*** *in Ashteroth Karnaim, and the* ***Zuzims*** *in Ham, and the* ***Emins*** *in Shaveh Kiriathaim, And theHorites in their mount Seir, unto Elparan, which is by the wilderness. And they returned, and came to Enmishpat, which is Kadesh, and smote all the country of the* ***Amalekites****, and also the* ***Amorites****, that dwelt in Hazezontamar. And there went out the king of* ***Sodom****, and the king of* ***Gomorrah****, and the king of* ***Admah****, and the king of* ***Zeboiim****, and the king of Bela (the same is Zoar;) and they joined battle with them in the vale of Siddim;* (Genesis 14:5-10)

In addition to the new names seen above, notice where the opposing army of kings came from: Sodom, Gomorrah, Admah, Zoboiim and Bela. With the exception of Bela (Zoar: a "tiny town"), these are all areas settled by the children of Canaan.[1] Thus, this entire hoard of giants are all descendents of Noah's grandson! Again, I must point out the fact that there are no fallen angels anywhere in this picture. In the Genesis 14 War, we are dealing exclusively with the grandchildren of Noah — specifically the offspring of Canaan (and in the case of Nimrod/Amraphel, the offspring of Cush).

> *With Chedorlaomer the king of Elam, and with Tidal king of nations, and Amraphel king of Shinar, and Arioch king of Ellasar; four kings with five.* ***And the vale of Siddim was full of slimepits; and the kings of Sodom and Gomorrah fled, and fell there;***

1 See Genesis 10:15-19

> ***and they that remained fled to the mountain.*** (Genesis 14:9,10)

This is an extraordinary war! It took place just 450 years (or so) after the Flood. It was a war waged by and against mature giants! How do we know this? Consider what Moses (the same guy who wrote Genesis 14) says elsewhere:

Concerning the Raphaims (the healed ones): the word "raphaim" is used <u>at least 25 times as a reference to giants</u> in the Old Testament.

Concerning the Zuzims (the achievers)**:** presumed by many Bible commentators to be short for the Zamzummim):

> *(It is also regarded as the land of the Rephaim, for Rephaim formerly lived in it, but the Ammonites call them* ***Zamzummin, a people as great, numerous, and tall as the Anakim, but the LORD destroyed them*** *before them. And they dispossessed them and settled in their place, just as He did for the sons of Esau, who live in Seir, when He destroyed the Horites from before them; they dispossessed them and settled in their place even to this day. And the Avvim, who lived in villages as far as Gaza, the Caphtorim [Philistines] who came from Caphtor [Crete], destroyed them and lived in their place.)* (Deuteronomy 2:20-23 NASB)

Note here that the Raphaim giants of Ammon were reckoned as having formerly dwelt there. The *King James Version* says, "*That also was accounted a land of giants: giants dwelt therein in old time.*" So, this shows that those giants have been around for a while: since the "old times." Moses wrote that toward the end of the wandering in the wilderness after their Exodus from Egypt. That was only about 850 years after the Flood. Moses is looking back on those "old days" and telling us how long these giants have been around.

This passage is also very interesting in that it shows a series of dispossession. The Zamzummim were great and many and as tall as the Anakim, but the Anakim had previously been taken out by YHVH Himself some time prior. The Zamzummin (Zuzim) replaced the Anakim (who were Amorites). Their name means, "achievers" and may be related to city building and megalithic structures. Next we see that YHVH helped out the children of Esau just as He did the sons of Jacob. YHVH destroyed the Horites and the sons of Esau settled in their place. And finally, we see that the Caphtorim (who themselves may have been giants), came from Crete, destroyed the Avim (the perverters) and settled in their place.

Gill's Exposition of the Entire Bible describes the Zamzummim giants as follows:

> *Zamzummims; they are thought to be the same with the Zuzims in Genesis 14:5 who had their name, as Hillerus thinks, from Mezuzah, a door post, from their tall stature, being as high as one; and for a like reason Saph the giant might have his name, 2 Samuel 21:18. The word Zamzummims, according to him, signifies contrivers of evil and terrible things; they were inventors of wickedness, crafty and subtle in forming wicked and mischievous designs, which struck terror into people, and made them formidable to them. and goes on to say:* ***A people great and many, and tall as the Anakims,****.... As the Emims were, Deuteronomy 2:10 but the Lord destroyed them before them; destroyed the Zamzummims before the children of Amman; or otherwise they would have been an too much for them, being so numerous, and of* ***such a gigantic stature****:* [emphasis mine]

Note the repeated references to Anak, the son of Arba in these texts. Hold that thought. We'll come back to this interesting family in Chapter Ten. Just remember that they were extremely tall and very numerous in the land! Moving on to what Moses had to say...

Concerning the Emims (the terrors)**:**

> *The Emims dwelt therein in times past, a* ***people great, and many, and tall, as the Anakims; Which also were accounted giants****, as the Anakims; but the Moabites called them Emims.* (Deuteronomy 2:10,11)

Concerning the Horites[2] (the cave dwellers/troglodytes)**:**

> *The Horims also dwelt in Seir beforetime; but the children of Esau succeeded them, when they had destroyed them from before them, and dwelt in their stead; as Israel did unto the land of his possession, which the LORD gave unto them.* (Deuteronomy 2:12)

Concerning the Amorites (the sayers)**:** these early Amorites were given a massive height in the book of Amos:

> *But as my people watched, I destroyed the Amorites,* ***though they were as tall as cedars and as strong as oaks****. I destroyed the fruit on their branches and dug out their roots.* (Amos 2:9 NLT)

As you can see, we have quite a bit of supporting Scripture to show that the Genesis 14 War was a war against giants. Commenting on this passage, Josephus simplifies the issue by plainly stating:

> ***These kings had laid waste all Syria, and overthrown the offspring of the giants.***
>
> — Flavius Josephus[3]

He identifies Syria with Ham's offspring:

> ***The children of Ham possessed the land from Syria***

---

2. As cave-dwellers, it may be that the Horites were the ones who built Petra.
3. ***Antiquities of the Jews*** *1.9.*

> *and Amanus, and the mountains of Libanus; seizing upon all that was on its sea-coasts, and as far as the ocean, and keeping it as their own.*
>
> — Flavius Josephus[4]

This is also reflected in Genesis 14:5 where Moses writes, "the Zuzims in Ham." So here we are just 450 years after the Flood and about 350 years or so after the Tower of Babel and we see all out warfare between the sons of men and the ***offspring*** of giants!

GREATEST ARCHAEOLOGICAL FIND OF ALL TIME

Moses tells us the five kings were defeated by the four kings and that many of them fell into "slime pits."

> *And **the vale of Siddim was full of slimepits; and the kings of Sodom and Gomorrah fled, and fell there;** and they that remained fled to the mountain.*
> (Genesis 14:10)

Once again, Josephus gives us more details:

> *"These kings had laid waste all Syria, and overthrown the offspring of the giants. And when they were come over against Sodom, they pitched their camp at the vale called **the Slime Pits, for at that time there were pits in that place; but now, upon the destruction of the city of Sodom, that vale became the Lake Asphaltites [the Dead Sea], as it is called.***
>
> — Flavius Josephus[5]

Could it be that the greatest archaeological find of all time is waiting for us somewhere under the edge of the Dead Sea (which

4. ***Antiquities of the Jews*** *1.6.2*
5. ***Antiquities of the Jews*** *1.9*

is drying up)? With all that salt, I would think the remains of this giant army would be quite well preserved. I have already talked to Dr. Judd Burton about this and we are currently making plans to do a survey (YHVH and the government of Israel willing) to see what we might find. If you are interested in helping to sponsor our research, please contact me at **rob@babylonrisingbooks.com**.

THE ORIGINAL 300

In 2006, an epic movie called, *300* came out. It depicted intense, graphic battle scenes of King Leonidas and his force of 300 fighting men as they went to war with the Persians at Thermopylae circa 480 BC. As intense as that was, I'd like to suggest that the *original* story of 300 goes back to a time much further back in the historical record — to the time of Abram and the Genesis 14 War.

The four kings led by Amraphel (Nimrod) defeated five kings and their giant armies. They took Lot and his family away from Sodom and Gomorrah as spoils of war. In response, Abram basically said, *"Oh, I don't think so!"* and went after them.

> *And they took all the goods of Sodom and Gomorrah, and all their victuals, and went their way.*
>
> *And they took Lot, Abram's brother's son, who dwelt in Sodom, and his goods, and departed.*
>
> ***And there came one that had escaped, and told Abram the Hebrew; for he dwelt in the plain of Mamre the Amorite, brother of Eshcol, and brother of Aner: and these were confederate with Abram.***
>
> ***And when Abram heard that his brother was taken captive, he armed his trained servants, born in his own house, three hundred and eighteen, and pursued them unto Dan.***
>
> *And he divided himself against them, he and his servants, by night, and smote them, and pursued them unto Hobah, which is on the left hand of Damascus.*

And he brought back all the goods, and also brought again his brother Lot, and his goods, and the women also, and the people. (Genesis 14:11-16)

Most bible scholars focus on the meeting of Abram and Melchizedek that took place upon his return, but I'd like to suggest that an amazing story has been seriously overlooked. If we pause for a moment to think about it, we see that Abram was one fearless and tough dude! When he found out that his nephew Lot and his family had been taken, Abram assembled a band of 318 "trained servants" and went after them. Their victory was described as a "slaughter."

And the king of Sodom went out to meet him ***after his return from the slaughter of Chedorlaomer, and of the kings that were with him****, at the valley of Shaveh, which is the king's dale.* (Genesis 14:17)

Abram and his men *slaughtered* Nimrod's general Chedorlaomer and the kings that were with him! Melchizedek acknowledges that Abram's victory was from YHVH and blesses him. Then, the king of Sodom says Abram can keep all the spoils of war accept his people. Abram only accepts the food that had already been eaten by his men and requests that a fair share of the goods be given to his *Amorite* (giant) allies, Aner, Eshcol and Mamre. This is an incredibly epic story!

I'm thinking that the typical view of Abram as an old guy with a long beard needs a serious face-lift. Abram was a warrior and a man well respected — apparently by giants (and as we will see in Chapter Eleven, *possibly* even animal-human hybrids as well). He was a man of great faith, who served a great Creator who loved and blessed him for it.

After these things the word of the Lord came to Abram in a vision, saying, "Do not fear, Abram, I am a shield to you; Your reward shall be very great." (Genesis 15:1)

Chapter Nine

PROTECTING THE LINE OF CHRIST

And I will put enmity between you and the woman, and between your offspring and hers; he will crush your head, and you will strike his heel."
(Genesis 3:15 NIV)

One of the reasons why I named my TV series ***SEED*** is because of the above verse. When you look at history, the Bible and prophecy, you will see that it really is all about the two seeds. One will bruise the heel and the other will crush the head of his opponent. If you are the one receiving the prophecy that your head will be crushed by the seed of the woman, what do you think you will do to her seed? You are going to want to destroy it. Thus, the "Cosmic Chessmatch" (as L.A. Marzulli would say)[1] of move and counter-move began.

In my view of this concept, after the Tower of Babel incident, the game really started to move at a fast pace right about the time

1. See ***The Cosmic Chessmatch***, by L.A. Marzulli (© 2011 Spiral of Life)

Abram (one of Shem's descendents) was called out of Ur of the Chaldeans (part of Nimrod's kingdom and a land whose patron god was named "Sin" of all things) to go to the land of Canaan. Have you ever stopped to ask yourself, of all the places on the planet that God could have chosen, why did He tell Abram to go to Canaan?

> *As for you, you shall go to your fathers in peace; you will be buried at a good old age. Then* ***in the fourth generation*** *they will return here,* ***for the iniquity of the Amorite is not yet complete****." It came about when the sun had set, that it was very dark, and behold, there appeared a smoking oven and a flaming torch which passed between these pieces. On that day the Lord made a covenant with Abram, saying, "To your descendants I have given this land, From the river of Egypt as far as the great river, the river Euphrates: the Kenite and the Kenizzite and the Kadmonite and the Hittite and the Perizzite and the Rephaim and the Amorite and the Canaanite and the Girgashite and the Jebusite."* (Genesis 15:15-17 NASB)

As promised in Genesis 15:15-17, the land was quickly filling up with *generations* of Canaan's corrupt Nephilim seed. All those "ites" were there. Yet, that's where God had specifically told Abram to go. Then, to make matters even more confusing, why did God later have Abraham's descendents *leave* Canaan for Egypt, where they would eventually become slaves?

When my wife and I were first introduced to Torah study, we entered at the point in the readings that dealt with the life of Joseph. The things we learned and discovered in that first class were absolutely amazing! It is especially amazing when you come at the text from the frame of mind that we've had regarding our studies of the Nephilim and the false gods of this world.

Right after Joseph is sold into slavery, Moses interrupts that story to tell us another little story about what Judah was doing in the meantime. Then, he goes right back to telling us more about Joseph. It is the Genesis 38 interruption that gives us a key for understanding what God is doing. We must understand that Yeshua is modeled in Joseph, but descended from Judah. So, it is quite appropriate that these two stories are linked.

In Genesis 38, we learn that Judah married a Canaanite woman and has three sons: Er, Onan and Shelah. There's just one ***major*** problem here. Judah is the one through whom the Messiah is to come. Remember? Yeshua is the *"Lion of the Tribe of Judah."* Well, we've just established that the Canaanites are all of corrupted, Nephilim seed. Can the Messiah have Nephilim blood in his ancestry? No way! As soon as I read that Judah had married a Canaanite woman, I freaked out and my wife and I started to dig. We spent an entire day researching. This is what we found:

Judah sought out a wife for his oldest son. Her name was Tamar. In our Torah class there was some debate as to whether or not she was also a Canaanite woman. The text made it plain that Judah had married a Canaanite, but when it came to Tamar, it was silent about her ancestry. Our study guide said:

> *According to long standing Jewish tradition (at least as old as the Targums), Tamar was not a daughter of the Canaanites. She was a Shemite. The Torah remains silent regarding Tamar's nationality, but it is noteworthy that while both the Torah and the Chronicler felt compelled to point out that Bat-Shua (Judah's wife) was a Canaanite, neither refer to Tamar as a Canaanite.*
>
> *Torah Club Volume One* [we were reading Volume Five] *supposes that Tamar was a Canaanite. After all, her father's house was in Timnah, and Timnah was certainly a Canaanite city. Yet it seems inconceivable that the Torah would so casually accept Tamar the Canaanite when we went through such hand-wringing over the notion of Isaac*

> *marrying a Canaanite, such disdain for Esau's choices, such trepidation regarding Jacob's potential wives and so on.*[2]

Indeed, we see in several places in the Scriptures that the chosen people were not to mingle seed with the Canaanites!

> *And Abraham said unto his eldest servant of his house, that ruled over all that he had, Put, I pray thee, thy hand under my thigh: And* ***I will make thee swear by the LORD, the God of heaven, and the God of the earth, that thou shalt not take a wife unto my son of the daughters of the Canaanites,*** *among whom I dwell: But thou shalt go unto my country, and to my kindred, and take a wife unto my son Isaac.* (Genesis 24:2-4)

> *And Isaac called Jacob, and blessed him, and charged him, and said unto him,* ***Thou shalt not take a wife of the daughters of Canaan.*** (Genesis 28:1)

From Abraham to Jacob, no one chose a wife from the Canaanites. But then, Jacob has twelve sons. Hard to keep track of everyone I guess. One slips through the cracks and marries a Canaanite, and wouldn't you know it — of all the twelve sons — the one to do such a terrible thing was Judah; the man whose descendents were the ones through whom God planned to bring His Son! Do you think the Devil was trying to mess that plan up? You bet he was.

IT'S ALWAYS ABOUT THE SEED

It is my belief that this issue of not mixing seed was the whole purpose of circumcision. A covenant is always sealed in blood. Circumcision is a blood covenant, made in the "dispenser of seed" as a permanent reminder to stay pure.

---

2. First Fruits of Zion's ***Torah Club, Volume 5: Rejoicing of the Torah*** on Vayeshev, page 173

Abram Is Named Abraham

When Abram was ninety-nine years old, the Lord appeared to him and said, "I am El-Shaddai—'God Almighty.' Serve me faithfully and live a blameless life. I will make a covenant with you, by which I will guarantee to give you countless descendants."

At this, Abram fell face down on the ground. Then God said to him, "This is my covenant with you: I will make you the father of a multitude of nations! What's more, I am changing your name. It will no longer be Abram. Instead, you will be called Abraham, for you will be the father of many nations. I will make you extremely fruitful. Your descendants will become many nations, and kings will be among them!

"I will confirm my covenant with you and your descendants after you, from generation to generation. This is the everlasting covenant: I will always be your God and the God of your descendants after you. And I will give the entire land of Canaan, where you now live as a foreigner, to you and your descendants. It will be their possession forever, and I will be their God."

The Mark of the Covenant

Then God said to Abraham, "Your responsibility is to obey the terms of the covenant. You and all your descendants have this continual responsibility. This is the covenant that you and your descendants must keep: Each male among you must be circumcised. You must cut off the flesh of your foreskin as a sign of the covenant between me and you. From generation to generation, every male child must be circumcised on the eighth day after his birth. This applies not only to members of your family but also to the servants born in your household and the foreign-born servants

> *whom you have purchased. All must be circumcised. Your bodies will bear the mark of my everlasting covenant. Any male who fails to be circumcised will be cut off from the covenant family for breaking the covenant."*
> (Genesis 10:1-14 NLT)

Even though Judah most certainly was circumcised, he violated the meaning of that covenant when He married a Canaanite. But no worries. God will redeem even this failure.

In Torah class, we discussed this idea (at length) of whether or not Tamar was a Canaanite. In the end, the room was fairly divided, with some thinking she was and others saying she wasn't. No one had definitive proof for their position. That drove me crazy. So home we went. The next morning, my wife suggested we look up what her name meant because we remembered from our trip to Israel in 2005, that there was a place called Tamar. Strong's Concordance (# 8558) yielded the meaning of this word as: *"palm tree, date palm"*

The word also carries with it the connotation of "erect" or "upright." OK. So, either she was upright, or she was... a palm tree. Hmm. Keep looking. What about Jasher? Yes, let's check the "upright" book. It was there (once again) that a Genesis gap got filled in.

> *And in those days Judah went to the house of Shem and took* ***Tamar the daughter of Elam, the son of Shem,*** *for a wife for his first born Er.* (Jasher 45:23)

Mystery solved! Judah chose Tamar from the lineage of Shem (who had lived in Jerusalem as Melchizidek) to be the wife of his oldest son, Er. It would appear that she was *destined* to be an ancestor of the Messiah. Notice however, how Er was described:

> *And Judah took a wife for Er his firstborn, whose name was Tamar. And* ***Er, Judah's firstborn, was wicked in the sight of the LORD****; and the LORD slew him.*
> (Genesis 38:6,7)

There is no mention of why Er was considered ***"wicked in the sight of the LORD."*** Could it be that it wasn't anything he *did*, but rather who/what he was? If he was the offspring of a tainted female Canaanite (Judah's wife), could he have fallen into the 50% (of the Nephilim Punnett Square) that was corrupt? It is pure speculation on my part, but I strongly suspect that he was.

Er does not produce any children by Tamar because he was considered wicked in the sight of the LORD, and was therefore killed by Him. What does Judah do with Tamar next? He follows a tradition that would later become law:

> *If two brothers are living together on the same property and one of them dies without a son, his widow may not be married to anyone from outside the family. Instead, her husband's brother should marry her and have intercourse with her to fulfill the duties of a brother-in-law. The first son she bears to him will be considered the son of the dead brother, so that his name will not be forgotten in Israel.* (Deuteronomy 25:5,6 NLT)

Judah gets his second son, Onan to marry Tamar in order to produce an heir for his brother. But Onan doesn't want to produce an heir for his brother, so even though he has sex with her, he always pulls out and spills his semen on the ground. In context, the *real* "sin of Onan" therefore was not masturbation as many a Sunday School teacher would have us believe. No. It was the fact that he broke the law and dishonored his family.

> *But if the man refuses to marry his brother's widow, she must go to the town gate and say to the elders assembled there, 'My husband's brother refuses to preserve his brother's name in Israel—he refuses to fulfill the duties of a brother-in-law by marrying me.' The elders of the town will then summon him and talk with him. If he still refuses and says, 'I don't want to marry her,' the widow must walk*

> *over to him in the presence of the elders, pull his sandal from his foot, and spit in his face. Then she must declare, 'This is what happens to a man who refuses to provide his brother with children.' Ever afterward in Israel his family will be referred to as 'the family of the man whose sandal was pulled off'!* (Deuteronomy 25:7-10 NLT)

Onan took Tamar as his wife according to levirate tradition, but he refused to impregnate her. Instead he used her for pleasure. And God killed him for this. Could it be that Onan was of the 50% who (according to the Nephilim Punnett Square) may have been pure? If so, could it be that had he not done what he did, he may have been a forefather of the Messiah? We will never know. What we do however know is that unlike the issue of Er, who simply *was* something wicked, Onan appears to have been killed for something he *did*.

This left Tamar as something akin to "used goods." Judah has now lost two sons. His youngest son, Shelah is still too young for marriage at this point, so Judah sends Tamar back to her father's house to wait for Shelah to grow older. Poor Tamar has been used twice. She will never get another husband. Her only hope is in Shelah. So, she waits for him to get older.

Judah however begins to have second thoughts, because of what happened to his two oldest sons. Maybe Tamar is cursed? He doesn't want to take a chance on losing his only remaining son, so he decides not to call for Tamar when Shelah is of age. Realizing this, Tamar feels robbed and wants what is rightfully hers. She comes up with a plan.

OPERATION LEVERAGE

> *Some years later Judah's wife died. After the time of mourning was over, Judah and his friend Hirah the Adullamite went up to Timnah to supervise the shearing of his sheep. Someone told Tamar, "Look, your father-in-law is going up to Timnah to shear his sheep."*

> *Tamar was aware that Shelah had grown up, but no arrangements had been made for her to come and marry him. So she changed out of her widow's clothing and covered herself with a veil to disguise herself. Then she sat beside the road at the entrance to the village of Enaim, which is on the road to Timnah. Judah noticed her and thought she was a prostitute, since she had covered her face. So he stopped and propositioned her. "Let me have sex with you," he said, not realizing that she was his own daughter-in-law.* (Genesis 38:12-16a NLT)

This is one wild *Soap Opera* that begins to play out here! When she hears that Judah is coming to a nearby town, she puts on a veil (essentially dressing up as a prostitute) and gets his attention. Apparently quite interested, he offers a goat in payment for her "services." Knowing Judah is obviously not a man of his word, she wants an assurance that he will make good on the payment. She asks for his signet, chord and staff. Judah agrees and has sex with her. She then goes back home.

Later, Judah sends a friend (Hirah) with the promised goat looking for the prostitute (probably because he didn't want to get caught). The people of Shem say, *"We have no prostitutes!"* So, when he returns, he tells Judah that he couldn't find the woman and Judah basically says, *"Oh well, let her keep it then!"* He gives up on the matter probably because any further pursuance of it would have likely brought public shame upon him.

Three months later, word gets back to Judah that his daughter-in-law is pregnant as a result of prostitution! Not putting two and two together, Judah gets ticked off and becomes an extreme hypocrite. He shouts, *"Bring her out and burn her!"* Just as they are going to take her out and kill her, she pulls out the signet, chord and staff and says, *"The man who owns these is the one who made me pregnant!."* Judah is thus caught, admits that she is more right than he is and acknowledges that he wronged her. Judah never slept with her again. Now, here is the amazing part (my wife calls it "Operation Leverage"): YHVH leverages this whole affair in order for the promise to be fulfilled. The Messiah would come through the completely *uncorrupted* seed of Judah and Tamar!

Tamar has twins. One starts to come out, and the midwife ties a scarlet chord around his wrist. But then, he goes back inside and Perez comes out first. Perez then becomes an ancestor to Jesus! His name in Hebrew means, "breaking forth."

BUILDING A PURE NATION

This is the reason why YHVH removed his people, the sons of Israel, from Canaan and brought them to Egypt. Judah had gone astray and mingled pure seed with corrupt seed. That trend would have likely continued and the infant Hebrew nation would have become just like all the others. YHVH wanted a pure nation, separated from the influences of the cultures around them and one not tainted with Nephilim genetics. Apparently, Joseph also knew this:

> *"God has sent me here to keep you and your families alive so that you will become a great nation."*
> (Genesis 45:7 NLT-1996 edition)

This fact is reiterated when YHVH reassures Jacob that it is His will that they should go down to Egypt:

> *And God spake unto Israel in the visions of the night, and said, Jacob, Jacob. And he said, Here am I.*
>
> *And he said, I am God, the God of thy father: fear not to go down into Egypt; for* ***I will there make of thee a great nation:*** (Genesis 46:2,3)

Now, once in Egypt, the danger of them mixing with Mizraim's potentially corrupt seed was also present for a time. However, the fact that the house of Jacob was all together in Goshen, limited exposure to the native population. When they were eventually made into a colony of slaves, they were even more limited. So, in reality their slavery forced them to interbreed within their own (pure) gene pool. Essentially, they became a forced reproductive science experiment in YHVH's lab. In that lab, they reproduced like rabbits, spawning a nation that consisted of nearly 2 million genetically pure Israelites by the time of their Exodus!

Indeed, as Joseph noted, what men meant for evil, God meant for good! Once YHVH had His nation fully formed, it was time to release them back into the land that He had promised... to wipe out the Nephilim, and begin the process of cleansing the earth once again.

Israelite vs. Og of Bashan

Figure 35

Chapter Ten

FACING THE GIANTS

As the giants exhibited their size and power in physical confrontation, the Lord supernaturally empowered His people to defeat them. After their defeat in Canaan, the "giants" scattered to the winds of the west. Only camp fire stories of occasional sightings would remain.

— James R. Spillman[1]

There are repeated statements in the Bible of massive giants who were great and many and as tall as the Anakim. The Anakim were sons of Anak, who was a son of Arba, who was a (distant?) son of Amorreus, son of Canaan, son of Ham.

I like to depict things in visual format as I think it helps to see what is really going on. Therefore, I've created the following chart to show the steady line of giants from the time of the Flood, leading all the way up to the time of Abraham:

1. From ***A Conspiracy of Angels*** by James R. Spillman (© 2006 True Potential Publications, Inc., 2nd Print Edition), page 3

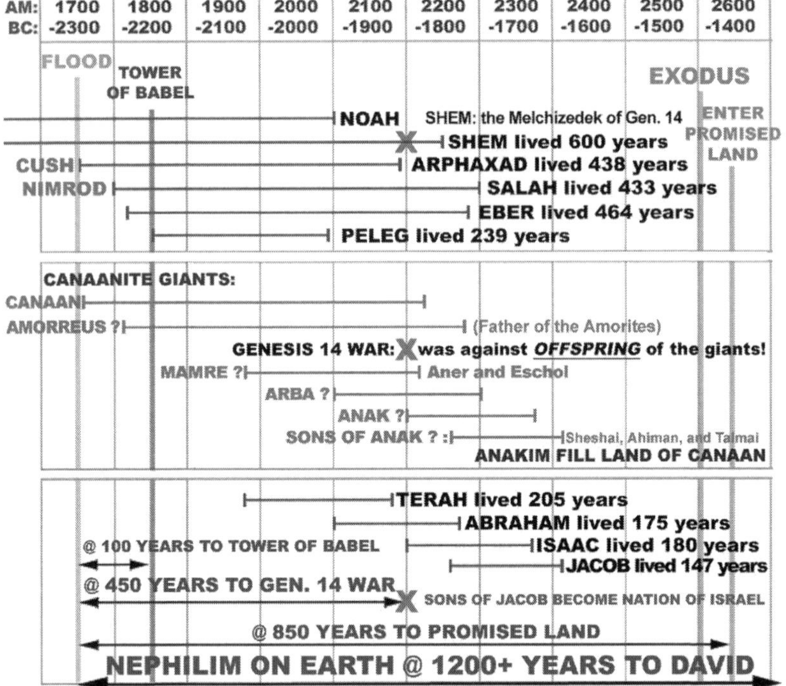

Figure 36

I believe that God was using his prophet Moses to put very specific names into his chronology in order to help us clearly see what was going on in the land of Canaan. We know that our faith was built upon the faith of our fathers, Abraham, Isaac and Jacob. The sons of Jacob, later became the children (the 12 tribes) of Israel. Looking at Genesis 12-15, we can see an interesting paralleled chronology of giants.

In Genesis 15, Moses tells us about God's covenant with Abraham.

> *And when the sun was going down, a deep sleep fell upon Abram; and, lo, an horror of great darkness fell upon him. And he said unto Abram, Know of a surety that thy seed shall be a stranger in a land that is not theirs, and shall serve them; and they shall afflict them four hundred years;*

> *And also that nation, whom they shall serve, will I judge: and afterward shall they come out with great substance.*
>
> *And thou shalt go to thy fathers in peace; thou shalt be buried in a good old age. But* ***in the fourth generation they shall come hither again: for the iniquity of the Amorites is not yet full****. And it came to pass, that, when the sun went down, and it was dark, behold a smoking furnace, and a burning lamp that passed between those pieces.*
>
> *In the same day the LORD made a covenant with Abram, saying,* ***Unto thy seed have I given this land****, from the river of Egypt unto the great river, the river Euphrates: The* ***Kenites****, and the* ***Kenizzites****, and the* ***Kadmonites****, And the* ***Hittites****, and the* ***Perizzites****, and the* ***Rephaims****, And the* ***Amorites****, and the* ***Canaanites****, and the* ***Girgashites****, and the* ***Jebusites****.* (Genesis 15:12-21)

At this point in Genesis, the names Kenites, Kenizzites and Kadmonites are new to us, so I will refer you to *Barnes Notes on the Bible* regarding them:

> *The ten principal nations inhabiting this area are here enumerated. Of these five are Kenaanite, and the other five probably not. The first three are new to us, and seem to occupy the extremities of the region here defined. The Kenite dwelt in the country bordering on Egypt and south of Palestine, in which the Amalekites also are found Numbers 24:20-22; 1 Samuel 15:6. They dwelt among the Midianites, as Hobab was both a Midianite and a Kenite Numbers 10:29; Judges 1:16; Judges 4:11. They were friendly to the Israelites, and hence some of them followed their fortunes and settled in their land 1 Chronicles 2:55. The Kenizzite dwelt apparently in the same region, having affinity with the Horites, and subsequently with Edom and Israel Genesis 36:11, Genesis 36:20-23; Joshua 15:17;*

> *1 Chronicles 2:50-52. The Kadmonite seems to be the Eastern, and, therefore, to hold the other extreme boundary of the promised land, toward Tadmor and the Phrat. These three tribes were probably related to Abram, and, therefore, descendants of Shem. The other seven tribes have already come under our notice.*

Indeed they have! Do those other seven tribal names sound familiar? Here God is telling Abram that He is going to give him the land of the giants — but only after four generations of them have had time to reproduce. I believe that is what is being referred to when God says, "*for the iniquity of the Amorites is not yet full.*" What is this "iniquity" that needs to become full? I believe it is the spreading of Nephilim seed for four generations.

> *But in the fourth generation they shall come hither again: for the iniquity of the Amorites is not yet full.* (Genesis 15:16)

Some would suggest that the four generations referred to in this passage are of Abraham's seed. The problem I have with this idea is that it will be another *seven* generations before anyone of Abraham's offspring returns to the land of promise after their time of slavery. Therefore, I am thinking the notion of four generations has more to do with the seed of the Amorites than the seed of Abraham.

ARBA AND SONS

The question, "*Who was Arba?*" has been asked in more than a few debates that I've had with my peers concerning the post-Flood giants. I suspect he was a contemporary of Abraham. This giant is clearly a significant figure in that he is the father of Anak, from whom came the Anakim, which are the giants so many are referred to and compared with in the land of Canaan.

The town of Hebron was once known as Kiriath-arba (or the city of Arba). When Abraham first arrives there, Moses records it as Hebron. Whether Hebron was the original name or not is debatable. Regardless, by the time of Sarah's death, the place was known as Kiriath-Arba:

> *Sarah died in Kiriath-arba (that is, Hebron) in the land of Canaan; and Abraham went in to mourn for Sarah and to weep for her.* (Genesis 23:1 NASB)

The name, Kiriath-arba appears to have remained at least until the time of Joshua:

> *Now the name of Hebron was formerly Kiriath-arba; for Arba was the greatest man among the Anakim. Then the land had rest from war.* (Joshua 14:15 NASB)

The name Arba means "four" in Hebrew. *The International Standard Bible Encyclopedia* states:

> *ar'-ba ('arba`, "four"): Variously described as "the greatest man among the Anakim" (Joshua 14:15), "the father of Anak" (Joshua 15:13), "the father of Anak" (Joshua 21:11 margin). Thus he seems to have been regarded as the ancestor of the Anakim, and as the most famous hero of that race. He was the reputed founder of the city called after him, on the site of which Hebron was built (Joshua 21:11).*

Clarke's Commentary on the Bible gives us more insight:

> *And the name of Hebron before was Kirjath-arba - That is, the city of Arba, or rather, the city of the four, for thus kiryath arba may be literally translated. It is very likely that this city had its name from four Anakim, gigantic or powerful men, probably brothers, who built or conquered it. This conjecture receives considerable strength from Joshua 15:14, where it is said that Caleb drove from Hebron the three sons of Anak, Sheshai, Ahiman, and Talmai: now it is quite possible that Hebron had its former name, Kirjath-arba, the city of the four, from these three sons and their father, who, being men of uncommon*

> *stature or abilities, had rendered themselves famous by acts proportioned to their strength and influence in the country. It appears however from Joshua 15:13 that Arba was a proper name, as there he is called the father of Anak.*

In his commentary on Joshua 14:15, Clarke also writes:

> *Sarah died in Kirjath-arba - Literally in the city of the four. Some suppose this place was called the city of the four because it was the burial place of Adam, Abraham, Isaac, and Jacob; others, because according to the opinion of the rabbins, Eve was buried there. with Sarah, Rebekah, and Leah. But it seems evidently to have had its name from a Canaanite, one of the Anakim, probably called Arba.*

Clarke describes Arba as being both the father of Anak and a Canaanite. No surprise there. Canaan is truly the father of many races of giants, but I strongly suspect Arba was a direct descendent of Canaan's son, Amorreus, from whom came the Amorites—if for no other reason than due to the way the Bible consistently describes the massive height of this particular people group and how in the same breath, nearly every giant race is compared to this particular family (Arba and Anak). Plus, it appears that Hebron has always had a strong affiliation with the Amorites. Beyond all that, consider what Barne's has to say concerning the Amorites:

> *The Amorite - These, as one of the mightiest of the Canaanite tribes, stand in Moses for all. Moses, in rehearsing to them the goodness of God and their backsliding, reminds them, how he had said, "Ye have come to the mountain of the Amorites, which the Lord your God giveth you" Deuteronomy 1:20; and that they, using this same word, said, "Because the Lord hateth us, He hath brought us forth out of the land of Egypt, to give us into the hand of the Amorite to destroy us"Deuteronomy 1:27. The aged Joshua, in rehearsing God's great deeds for Israel, places first by itself*

the destruction of the Amorite before them, with the use of this same idiom , "I brought you into the land of the Amorites which dwelt on the other side of Jordan - and I destroyed them before you." The Amorites were descended from the 4th son of Canaan Genesis 10:16.

At the invasion of Chedorlaomer, a portion of them [the Amorites] dwelt at Hazezon-Tamar or Engedi, half way on the west side of the Dead Sea, and at Hebron near it (Genesis 14:7, Genesis 14:13; compare Genesis 13:18; 2 Chronicles 20:2). ***Their corruption had not yet reached its height, and the return of Israel was delayed to the four hundredth year, "because the iniquity of the Amorite was not yet full" Genesis 15:16****. When Israel returned, the Amorites, (together with the Hittites and the Jebusites) held the hill country Numbers 13:29;Deuteronomy 1:7, Deuteronomy 1:44, Jerusalem, Hebron, Gibeon 2 Samuel 21:2, and, on the skirts of the mountains westward Jarmuth, Lachish, and Eglon Joshua 10:3,Joshua 10:5. They dwelt on the side of the Jordan westward Joshua 5:1, besides the two kingdoms which they had formed east of Jordan, reaching to Mount Hermon Deuteronomy 3:8 and Bashan up to the territory of Damascus. Afterward a small remnant remained only in the portion of Dan, and in the outskirts of Judah, from the south of the Dead Sea, Maaleh Akrabbim (Scorpion-pass) and Petra Judges 1:35-36. Those near Idumea were probably absorbed in Edom; and the remnant in Dan, after becoming tributary to Ephraim Judges 1:35-36, lost their national existence perhaps among the Philistines, since we have thenceforth only the single notice in the days of Samuel after the defeat of the Philistines, "there was peace between Israel and the Amorites" 1 Samuel 7:14.*

Whose height was like the height of the cedars - <u>The giant sons of Anak were among the Amorites</u> at "Hebron" Numbers 13:22 (called for a time

Kiriath Arba Joshua 14:15; Joshua 15:13-14 from their giant father) *"Debir, Ahab, and the mountains of Judah and Israel Joshua 11:21. The valley of Rephaim" 2 Samuel 5:18, southwest of Jerusalem, connects this giant race with the Amorites, as does the fact that Og, king of the Amorites in Basan, was "of the remnant of the Rephaim"Deuteronomy 3:11; Joshua 12:4; Joshua 13:19. Basan and Argob were, in Moses' time, still called "the land of Rephaim" Deuteronomy 3:13. The Rephaim, with the Perizzites, dwelt still in woody mountains near Ephraim; from where, on the complaint that the lot of the sons of Joseph was too narrow, Joshua bade his tribe to expel them Joshua 17:15, Joshua 17:18. The Rephaim are mentioned between the Perizzites and the Amorites Genesis 15:20-21, in God's first promise of the land to Abraham's seed, and perhaps some intermixture of race gave the giant stature to the Amorites. It is clear from Amos that the report of the spies, "**all the people that we saw in it were men of stature" Numbers 13:32, was no exaggeration, nor did Joshua and Caleb deny "this." The name of the Amorite is probably connected with "commanding," describing some quality of their forefather, which descended to his race**.*

Whose height was like the height of cedars - Giant height is sometimes a cause of weakness. Amos, in a degree like Hosea combines distinct images to make up the idea of stateliness and strength. The cedar is the ideal of eastern trees for height Isaiah 2:13; Ezekiel 17:22; Ezekiel 31:3; 1 Kings 4:33; 2 Kings 14:9, stretching forth its arms as for protection , "It groweth to an exceeding height, and with increasing time ever riseth higher." The oak has its Hebrew name from strength. The more majestic the tall strength of the Amorite, the more manifest that Israel "got not the land in possession by their own sword" Psalm 44:3, who had counted themselves, in sight of the Amorite, "as grasshoppers" Numbers 13:33. God, who gave him that

> *strength, took it away, as we say, "root and branch," leaving him no show above, no hope of recovered life below (see Hosea 9:16; Job 18:16; Ezekiel 17:9). Having compared each Amorite to a majestic tree, he compares the excision of the whole nation to the cutting down of that one tree, so swift, so entire, so irrecoverable. Yet the destruction of the Amorite, a mercy to Israel in the purpose of God, was a warning to israel when it became as they. God's terrors are mercies to the repentant; God's mercies are terrors to the impenitent. "Ye shall keep My statutes and My judgments and shall not commit any of these abominations," was the tenure upon which they held the Lord's land, "that the land spue not you out also, when ye defile it, as it spued out the nations that were before you" Leviticus 18:26, 38.*
>
> — Barnes Notes on the Bible (Amos 2:9)[2]

I think there is an abundance of evidence to show for the fact that "Arba & Co." are of Amorite stock.[3] Of all the sons of Canaan, the Amorites are mentioned the most in the Scriptures. And of all the families of giants that are specifically named, the family of Arba and Anak are by far the most famous. Note how the Hebrew spies described what they saw upon entering the land of Canaan:

> *So they brought to the people of Israel a bad report of the land that they had spied out, saying, "The land, through which we have gone to spy it out, is a land that devours its inhabitants, and* ***all the people that we saw in it are of great height. And there we saw the Nephilim (the sons of Anak, <u>who come from the Nephilim</u>)****, and we seemed to ourselves like grasshoppers, and so we seemed to them."* (Numbers 13:32,33 ESV)

2. http://barnes.biblecommenter.com/amos/2.htm
3. For more on the Amorites, see:
http://www.bible.ca/archeology/bible-archeology-exodus-amorites.htm
For more on Hebron and Arba, see:
http://biblicalgeography.wordpress.com/tag/amorites/
http://en.wikipedia.org/wiki/Amorites

The first thing we *must* acknowledge is that Moses described the Nephilim the spies had encountered in the land of Canaan as being giants who ***came from*** other Nephilim giants. Again, there is absolutely no mention of fallen angels mating with women to produce the giants that they saw, roughly 850+ years after the Flood. These Nephilim giants were the sons of another Nephilim giant named Anak. The great giant-producing Anak was himself fathered by an individual named Arba.

> *And unto Caleb the son of Jephunneh he gave a part among the children of Judah, according to the commandment of the LORD to Joshua, even the city of* ***Arba the father of Anak****, which city is Hebron.* (Joshua 15:13)

Arba means four. Does that mean that either he or Anak were one of four brothers? I don't know, but watch what happens when we pull together a timeline of four generations from Amorreus:

1. **Amorreus** The father of the Amorites was a son of Canaan and thus a contemporary cousin of Nimrod, Caphtor and Shem's grandson, Selah. That places his birth sometime between 35 and 70 years after the Flood.
2. **Arba**: As an Amorite and a contemporary of Abraham, Arba would have been born sometime between 150 and 350 years after the Flood.
3. **Anak**: Arba had a son named Anak who must have been born sometime prior to Joseph being sold into slavery or the house of Jacob going down to Egypt. His descendants filled the land of Canaan while the Israelites were in Egypt.
4. **Sons of Anak**: Immediately following the Exodus from Egypt, the Hebrew spies described the sons of Anak as being so big that they felt like grasshoppers by comparison. If the sons of Anak, who was a son of Arba were that big, those genes must have been passed down from their great grand dad, Amorreus who was a direct descendant of Canaan!

Here's a simplified family tree and timeline chart to further illustrate my point:

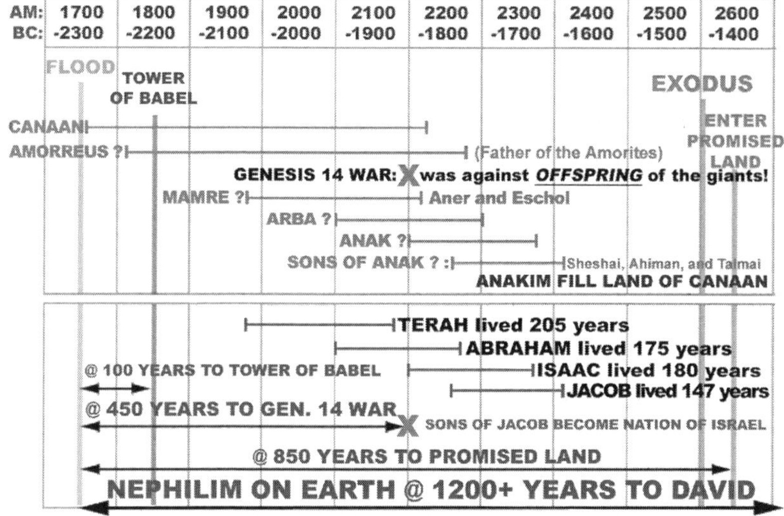

Figure 37

We cannot know for certain when Arba was born because the Scriptures are silent. We do however know that he lived at a time when normal humans were living between 200 (Terah's generation) and 438+ years (Canaan/Arphaxad's generation). I chose to depict him in the lower end of the age scale (200 years). Looking at the timelines above, and based on what we've learned so far, it would seem to be a safe conclusion to suggest that Abraham and the kings of the Genesis 14 War may have been fighting against either contemporaries of Arba or of one of his immediate ancestors. Whether that's true or not, one thing we know for sure is that Arba had to have been around at the time of or prior to the time of Abraham in order to have had a city named after him by the time of Sarah's death.

Previously, that area had been known as Hebron and specifically, the area of the oaks of Mamre. Mamre, interestingly enough appears to have been a "good Amorite." If so, this is the first time I've seen any Nephilim offspring that was good by any standard. Or maybe that's jumping to conclusions? At best, we know from Scripture that he and his brothers were considered by Abram to be allies.

> *Then a fugitive came and told Abram the Hebrew. Now he was living by the oaks of Mamre the Amorite, brother of Eshcol and brother of Aner, and **these were allies with Abram**.* (Genesis 14:13 NASB)

At some point around that time or shortly thereafter, Arba (who may have been a close relative of Mamre) had a son named Anak, who must have been known to the sons of Abraham as they would have been contemporaries. In fact, if this (**Figure 37**) timeline is accurate, it would appear that there is a direct parallel between the sons of Anak who were of Nephilim seed and the sons of Jacob who were of Abraham's seed. The race for whose sons would occupy the Promised Land was on! The parallels are uncanny, but this helps to explain how the Hebrew spies (who were of the generation of Jacob's great, great, great grandchildren) knew who those giants were when they saw them in the land! They probably heard the stories passed down from their fathers before them.

> *And there we saw the giants, the sons of Anak, **which come of the giants**: and we were in our own sight as grasshoppers, and so we were in their sight.* (Numbers 13:33)

The giants the Hebrew spies saw must have been upwards of 30 feet tall or more in order for them to have felt like "grasshoppers" by comparison. As I said at the beginning of this book, I'm choosing to take the Scriptures literally. To make that kind of comparison means those giants had to have been quite massive. Thus, **Figure 38** may be a fairly accurate representation of what they were up against.[4] If so, Caleb's statement really shows how much faith he actually had!

4. For a good representation of what that kind of battle might have looked like, watch this clip from the movie ***Wrath of the Titans***: http://babylonrisingbooks.com/book2/videosC104.html

Nevertheless, the people who live in the land are strong, and the cities are fortified and very large; and moreover, ***we saw the descendants of Anak there.*** *Amalek is living in the land of the Negev and the Hittites and the Jebusites and the Amorites are living in the hill country, and the Canaanites are living by the sea and by the side of the Jordan."*

Figure 38

Then Caleb quieted the people before Moses and said, ***"We should by all means go up and take possession of it, for we will surely overcome it."*** (Numbers 13:28-30 NASB)

Beyond the obvious size difference, there may have been even more reason to fear the Anakim. In one of his *Mysterious World* on-line articles, Doug Elwell notes:

> *The "sons of Anak", the Anakim were the next generation of Gibborim giants produced by the Rephaim in the land of Canaan. Stronger, faster, and fiercer than the rest of the giants before or during that time, the Anakim were greatly feared by all — including, probably, other giant types.*
>
>> *At this time, many Rephaim and some Horim, Avvim and Anakim giants occupied the hill country of northern Canaan, while the Anakim completely dominated the south. The spies must therefore have seen these frightening fellows every place they went. But in their later report to Moses they mentioned only the Anakim giants — apparently because they struck more terror in them than all the rest. For ferociousness and daring, the Anakim set the standard. Against them, in fact, all the other giants were measured. Moses himself confirmed their superiority when he wrote in his book this famous proverbial saying: "Who can stand against the sons of Anak?"* [Deut. 9:2][5]

Even though the Israelites had just seen the Red Sea opened for them, and they had experienced all the miracles associated with their deliverance (Exodus) from Egypt, and even though they witnessed the awesome power of God at Sinai, I can certainly see why the spies were still much afraid when they saw the Anakim.

> *But the men who had gone up with him* [Caleb] *said, "We are not able to go up against the people, for they are too strong for us." So they gave out to the sons of Israel a*

5. Doug was quoting from ***Giants: A Reference Guide from History, the Bible and Recorded Legend,*** by Charles DeLoach, ***"Canaan's Anakim"*** (pages 45 & 46). See full article here: http://www.mysteriousworld.com/Journal/2003/Spring/Giants/

> *bad report of the land which they had spied out, saying, "The land through which we have gone, in spying it out, is a land that devours its inhabitants; and all the people whom we saw in it are men of great size. There also we saw the Nephilim (the sons of Anak are part of the Nephilim); and we became like grasshoppers in our own sight, and so we were in their sight."* (Numbers 13:31-33)

They were not exaggerating. All of the terminology used in Numbers 13, clearly reveals to us that the Israelites encountered fierce giants of enormous size.

THE GRAPES OF ESHCOL (MAMRE)

In Chapter Two, we learned that the scale of the giants may have actually been confirmed by the size of the grapes given earlier in the "added details" of the spies' account:

> *And they came unto the brook of Eshcol, and cut down from thence a branch with one cluster of grapes, and they bare it between two upon a staff; and they brought of the pomegranates, and of the figs.* (Numbers 13:23)

Remember Abram's allies from the Genesis 14 War? Mamre, Aner and Eshcol were Amorite giants. Apparently Eschcol was into growing genetically modified grapes to feed his enormous appetite (possibly to match his name, which means "a cluster" and perhaps that of his brother Mamre, who's name means "causing fatness").

Notice that these grapes came from the brook (or valley) of Eschcol. Eschol was a brother of Mamre—the Amorite. None of this is by accident. It's not mere coincidence that YHVH gives us these details to consider. He is showing us connection after connection, helping us to see the "bigger" picture. As I began to realize this, I took a closer look at the grapes. As I did, I saw that the grapes actually confirmed the size of the giants who were eating them!

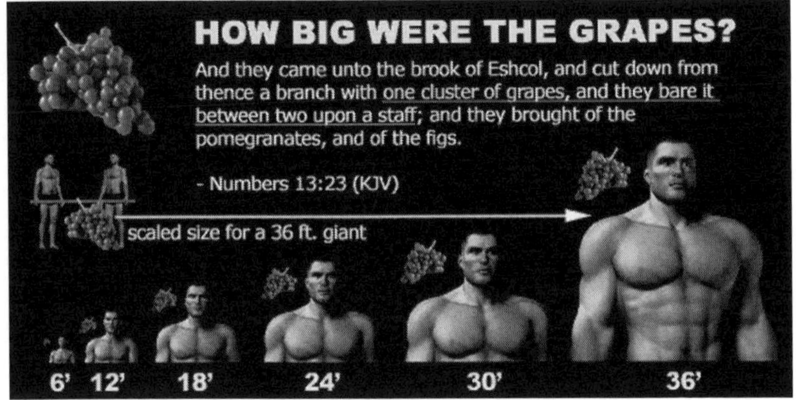

Figure 39

Looking at **Figure 39**, we can see that a 6 foot tall man would have no trouble carrying a cluster of grapes scaled to anything smaller than that which a 30 foot giant would have been eating. Much bigger than that, and you can see why it took two men to carry one cluster on a pole. The grapes are showing us that these giants were indeed massively huge! This fact is of course later confirmed by the prophet Amos who wrote about the giant Amorites as being tall as cedar trees:

> *"But as my people watched,* ***I destroyed the Amorites, though they were as tall as cedars and as strong as oaks****. I destroyed the fruit on their branches and dug out their roots."* (Amos 2:9 NLT)

The Hebrew spies identified them as the sons of Anak. How did they know who they were? Obviously, there had to have been some memory of Anak in their minds from times past. This would lead us to believe that either Isaac's or Jacob's generation knew who Anak was. As we've seen above, it is easy to see how this could be true. Notice how the Amos passage says that YHVH destroyed the Amorites before them. What's that all about?

If we imagine the giants the Israelite spies saw as being 36 foot *small* cedar trees, and these being sons (and perhaps grandsons) of Anak, could this imply that the previous generations may have been even bigger? Maybe, but let's just stick with the 36 footers for now. That's a serious foe! Looking at the scaled representation of **Figure 37**, it is very easy to understand why the spies gave a "bad report." Again, I must stress that Caleb's faith was extraordinary!

> *And Caleb stilled the people before Moses, and said, Let us go up at once, and possess it;* ***for we are well able to overcome it.*** (Numbers 13:30)

Perhaps he understood the deeper meaning behind the names of the spies who were with him.

SPYING OUT CALEB'S FAITH

Remember, names mean things in the Bible. My friend Kevin Roberts encouraged me to look at the name list for the Hebrew spies given to us by Moses. Once again, something amazing emerges from the text. I have assembled these names into a chart that gives the biblical reference, the name of the tribe, the spy and the father of the spy, listed in the order found in Numbers 13:4-16. In the right hand column, I have provided the meaning of each name.

Ref.	Relation	Name	Meaning
Nu 13:4	Tribe	Reuben	See Ye, a son
	Spy	Shammua	A careful listener - listen carefully
	Father	Zaccur	Remember
Nu 13:5	Tribe	Simeon	Hearkening - listening
	Spy	Shaphat	Judge
	Father	Hori	my noble
Nu 13:6	Tribe	Judah	He shall be praised
	Spy	Caleb	Whole Hearted
	Father	Jephunneh	He will be turned / prepared
Nu 13:7	Tribe	Issachar	He will bring a reward
	Spy	Igal	He will redeem
	Father	Joseph	Let Him add

Ref.	Relation	Name	Meaning
Nu 13:8	Tribe	Ephraim	I shall be doubly fruitful
	Spy	Oshea	To save
	Father	Nun	Perpetuity/Eternal Life
Nu 13:9	Tribe	Benjamin	Son of my right hand
	Spy	Palti	My escape
	Father	Raphu	Healed
Nu 13:10	Tribe	Zebulun	Dwelling
	Spy	Gaddiel	My fortune is God
	Father	Sodi	My confidant
Nu 13:11	Tribe	Joseph	Let Him add
	Tribe	Manasseh	Causing him to forget
	Spy	Gaddi	My invader/troop /fortune
	Father	Susi	My horse
Nu 13:12	Tribe	Dan	Judge
	Spy	Ammiel	My people of God
	Father	Gemalli	My camel
Nu 13:13	Tribe	Asher	Happy
	Spy	Sethur	Hidden
	Father	Michael	Who is as God?
Nu 13:14	Tribe	Naphtali	My wrestling
	Spy	Nahbi	My hiding
	Father	Vophsi	Wherefore vanish thou?
Nu 13:15	Tribe	Gad	Invader / troop / fortune
	Spy	Geuel	Exalt Ye God
	Father	Machi	My Poverty
Nu 13:16		Moses	Drawing out
		Oshea	To save
		Joshua	Yah is Salvation

Table 4

A rough translation of these names put together, might be:

Verse	Meaning of the names as a sentence
Nu 13:4	See a Son! Listen and Remember!
Nu 13:5	Listen to my noble judge.
Nu 13:6	He shall be praised whole-heartedly. He will be prepared.
Nu 13:7	He will bring a reward, and he will redeem. Let Him increase,
Nu 13:8	for He shall be doubly fruitful to save for eternity.
Nu 13:9	Son of my right hand, He will escape and be healed.
Nu 13:10	Dwelling in God - His fortune, my confidant.
Nu 13:11	Let Him add forgetfulness of my invader (while) on my horse
Nu 13:12	Judge my people of God. My camel is
Nu 13:13	happy and hidden. Who is as God?
Nu 13:14	My wrestling. My hiding. Where have you vanished?
Nu 13:15	My fortune is to exalt God in my poverty.
Nu 13:16	Drawing out to save; Yah is salvation!

Table 5

Simplified as a paragraph:

> *See a Son! Listen and Remember! Listen to my noble judge. He shall be praised whole-heartedly. He will be prepared. He will bring a reward, and he will redeem. Let Him increase, for He shall be doubly fruitful to save for eternity. Son of my right hand, He will escape and be healed. Dwelling in God - His fortune, my confidant. Let Him add forgetfulness of my invader (while) on my horse. Judge my people of God. My camel is happy and hidden.*[6]

6. The camel was associated with wealth, which in this case is hidden.

> *Who is as God? My wrestling. My hiding. Where have you vanished? My fortune is to exalt God in my poverty.* ***Drawing out to save; Yah is salvation!***

Did Caleb know this? Had he reasoned this out as he left to spy out the land? I don't know, but I do find that list to be quite interesting and prophetic! Regardless, Caleb had the faith to take the giants out and possess the promises of God. Aside from Joshua, the others did not and as a result the Israelites had to wander in the desert for 40 years. Then, at about 80 years of age, Caleb was given the opportunity to fight—and that he did!

> *Now he gave to Caleb the son of Jephunneh a portion among the sons of Judah, according to the [c]command of the Lord to Joshua, namely, Kiriath-arba, Arba being the father of Anak (that is, Hebron).* ***Caleb drove out from there the three sons of Anak: Sheshai and Ahiman and Talmai, the children of Anak.*** (Joshua 15:13,14)

May we have the same kind of faith and confidence in the God we serve! Not only did Caleb take Kiriath-Arba (Hebron), wiping out the giant offspring of Anak, but he also went after Debir. This is interesting. Debir means "oracle" and it must have been important, as Caleb offered up a reward for anyone who would help him take that place.

> *Then he went up from there against the inhabitants of Debir; now the name of Debir formerly was Kiriath-sepher. And Caleb said, "The one who attacks Kiriath-sepher and captures it, I will give him Achsah my daughter as a wife." Othniel the son of Kenaz, the brother of Caleb, captured it; so he gave him Achsah his daughter as a wife.* (Joshua 15:15-17)

Barne's says:

> *Debir probably is equivalent to "oracle," and Kirjath-sepher means "city of books." This plurality of names marks*

> *the importance of the town, as the inducement held out in Joshua 15:16, by Caleb, to secure its capture (compare 1 Samuel 17:25; 1 Samuel 18:17), points to its strength.*
>
> —Barne's Notes on the Bible (Joshua 15:15)

Keil and Delitzsch expand on that idea:

> *From Hebron Caleb went against the Inhabitants of Debir, to the south of Hebron. This town, which has not yet been discovered (see at Joshua 10:38), must have been very strong and hard to conquer; for Caleb offered a prize to the conqueror, promising to give his daughter Achzah for a wife to any one that should take it, just as Saul afterwards promised to give his daughter to the conqueror of Goliath (1 Samuel 17:25; 1 Samuel 18:17).*
>
> —Keil and Delitzsch Biblical Commentary on the Old Testament (Joshua 15:15)

I confess that this story *really* intrigues me as Caleb had no trouble taking out the Anakim. So why did he need help with this city? What's the deal with the oracle? What kind of books were housed there? Many questions. I'm thinking this is the kind of stuff that would make for a really great fantasy/mystery story plot! The Bible is loaded with *great* story-telling material. It's a shame so few have tapped into it.

SEED
www.seedtheseries.com
The keys to the FUTURE LIE buried in the past...

Figure 40

Someone needs to write us a check for $4 million to help get ***SEED*** [7] off the ground so that we can start putting these kinds of (biblical) stories

7. ***SEED*** is the 72 episode Internet-based TV series I'm developing. See *Appendix D* for more on this.

out into the mainstream media, with cool special effects and jaw dropping scenes that all depict the truth in a way the masses (who watch 4 to 5 hours of TV per day and spend $9 billion a year going to the movies) can receive.

FACING THE (SHRINKING) GIANTS

I used to think Numbers 13:33 provided the first mention of the post-Flood Nephilim. However, as we can now see, there is a well documented stream of giants producing giants starting almost immediately after the Flood and continuing all the way up to when the Israelites returned to the land of Canaan — after the time of "the iniquity" of the four generations of Amorites was complete. Thus, from within a hundred years after the Flood (as in Nimrod and Amorreus) all the way up until this Numbers 13 account following the Israelite Exodus from Egypt, we can see a solid 850 to 900 years worth of trackable giant lineage. This is a well documented, biblically supported fact! And this "generational linking" continued all the way up to the time of David.

Because the people lacked the faith of Caleb, and did not believe that YHVH would deliver these giants into their hand, the Israelites were made to wander in the wilderness for 40 years until that entire generation died off. By the time they faced and engaged the later generation Amorite kings — namely the King of Sihon and Og of Bashan — the giants they fought were about half the size of those they had encountered 40 years prior! What happened?

> *"But as my people watched,* ***I destroyed the Amorites, though they were as tall as cedars and as strong as oaks****. I destroyed the fruit on their branches and dug out their roots."* (Amos 2:9 NLT)

I believe Amos 2:9 is stating that it was YHVH who supernaturally wiped out the big ones. Perhaps this is what the Scriptures meant when God said:

> *Behold,* ***I send an Angel before thee****, to keep thee in the way, and to bring thee into the place which I have prepared.*(Exodus 23:20)

> *And the LORD said unto Moses, Depart, and go up hence, thou and the people which thou hast brought up out of the land of Egypt, unto the land which I sware unto Abraham, to Isaac, and to Jacob, saying, Unto thy seed will I give it: And I will send an angel before thee; and* ***I will drive out the Canaanite, the Amorite, and the Hittite, and the Perizzite, the Hivite, and the Jebusite****: Unto a land flowing with milk and honey: for I will not go up in the midst of thee; for thou art a stiffnecked people: lest I consume thee in the way.* (Exodus 33:1-3)

> *"When the LORD your God brings you into the land where you are entering to possess it, and clears away many nations before you, the Hittites and the Girgashites and the Amorites and the Canaanites and the Perizzites and the Hivites and the Jebusites, seven nations greater and stronger than you, and* ***when the LORD your God delivers them before you and you defeat them,*** *then you shall utterly destroy them. You shall make no covenant with them and show no favor to them.* (Deuteronomy 7:1,2 NASB)

Although sick and tired of dealing with this "stiff-necked people," YHVH still gave them some advantage going into the land. They obviously lacked the faith to go up against 30+ footers, so it looks like God pounded the big ones out and left the small ones — the 15 to 18 footers — for those who had the faith of Joshua and Caleb to take out. And that's exactly what they did!

Even though Og of Bashan was quite a bit smaller than the Anakim the Israelites had originally encountered in Canaan, he was still someone worthy of respect. Just to put things into perspective, have you ever stopped to think about how much a giant had to eat just to stay alive? Doug Hamp did. He wrote about Og's dietary needs in his book *Corrupting the Image,* where he estimates (based on what the Scriptures have to say concerning his height) that Og probably would have weighed about 3,125 pounds:

> *If we use the more conservative weight calculation then he would have needed to consume at least 22,657 calories per day just to stay alive as per the Basel Metabolic Rate which calculates, based on a person's height and weight, how many calories they need to live if they are not doing any significant work per day.*[8]

That's just to keep his heart beating! However, Doug reminds us that Og was a warrior. In modern terms, he estimates that Og would have had to eat more than 30 pizzas or about 150 cheeseburgers per day in order to get the needed calories to maintain the lifestyle of a warrior! With so many giants in the land, is it any wonder that the Hebrew spies would say, *"the land devours itself"*? This may also shed some light on a plausible reason for why there were so many famines in the land too![9]

POSSESSING THE LAND

Remember, YHVH had promised Abraham that he would be given the land of the Kenites, Kenizzites, Kadmonites, Hittites, Perizzites, Rephaim, Amorites, Canaanites, Girgashites, and the Jebusites (Genesis 15:17-21). God appears to have wiped out most of the Amorites. Among the remaining problematic tribes, there are essentially six core people groups mentioned in the Old Testament: the Hittites, Perizzites, Ammonites, Hivites, Canaanites, and Jebusites. These six are listed in: Exodus 3:8&17, 13:5 (omits Perizzites), 23:23, 33:2, and 34:11, Deuteronomy 20:17, Joshua 9:1, 12:8, and Judges 3:5. There is one shorter list, consisting only

8. ***Corrupting the Image***, by Douglas Hamp (©2011 Defender Publishing, LLC) page 153
9. See the video on ligers: http://www.babylonrisingbooks.com/book2/videosC105.html

of the Hittites, Canaanites and Hivites in Exodus 23:28. Some of the lists add the Girgashites to the above mentioned six as in: Deuteronomy 7:1, Joshuah 3:10, 24:11, Nehemiah 9:8 (who omits Hivites). So clearly, they still had quite a lot to do!

Moses sums up their battles in Deuteronomy 2 and 3, and I think it is worth it to read these two chapters in their entirety.

Deuteronomy 2 - Wanderings in the Wilderness:

"Then we turned and set out for the wilderness by the way to the Red Sea, as the Lord spoke to me, and circled Mount Seir for many days. And the Lord spoke to me, saying, 'You have circled this mountain long enough. Now turn north, and command the people, saying, "You will pass through the territory of your brothers the sons of Esau who live in Seir; and they will be afraid of you. So be very careful; do not provoke them, for I will not give you any of their land, even as little as a footstep because I have given Mount Seir to Esau as a possession. You shall buy food from them with money so that you may eat, and you shall also purchase water from them with money so that you may drink. For the Lord your God has blessed you in all that you have done; He has known your wanderings through this great wilderness. These forty years the Lord your God has been with you; you have not lacked a thing."'

"So we passed beyond our brothers the sons of Esau, who live in Seir, away from the Arabah road, away from Elath and from Ezion-geber. And we turned and passed through by the way of the wilderness of Moab. Then the Lord said to me, 'Do not harass Moab, nor provoke them to war, for I will not give you any of their land as a possession, because I have given Ar to the sons of Lot as a possession.' ***(The Emim lived there formerly, a people as great, numerous, and tall as the Anakim. Like the Anakim, they are also regarded as Rephaim, but the Moabites***

call them Emim. The Horites formerly lived in Seir, but the sons of Esau dispossessed them and destroyed them from before them and settled in their place, just as Israel did to the land of their possession which the Lord gave to them.) *'Now arise and cross over the brook Zered yourselves.' So we crossed over the brook Zered. Now the time that it took for us to come from Kadesh-barnea until we crossed over the brook Zered was thirty-eight years, until all the generation of the men of war perished from within the camp, as the Lord had sworn to them. Moreover the hand of the Lord was against them, to destroy them from within the camp until they all perished.*

"So it came about when all the men of war had finally perished from among the people, that the Lord spoke to me, saying, Today you shall cross over Ar, the border of Moab. When you come opposite the sons of Ammon, do not harass them nor provoke them, for I will not give you any of the land of the sons of Ammon as a possession, because I have given it to the sons of Lot as a possession.' ***(It is also regarded as the land of the Rephaim, for Rephaim formerly lived in it, but the Ammonites call them Zamzummin, <u>a people as great, numerous, and tall as the Anakim</u>, but the Lord destroyed them before them. And they dispossessed them and settled in their place, just as He did for the sons of Esau, who live in Seir, when He destroyed the Horites from before them; they dispossessed them and settled in their place even to this day. And the Avvim, who lived in villages as far as Gaza, the Caphtorim who came from Caphtor, destroyed them and lived in their place.)*** *'Arise, set out, and pass through the valley of Arnon. Look! I have given Sihon the Amorite, king of Heshbon, and his land into your hand; begin to take possession and contend with him in battle.* ***This day I will begin to put the dread and fear of you upon the peoples everywhere under***

the heavens, who, when they hear the report of you, will tremble and be in anguish because of you.' [10]

"So I sent messengers from the wilderness of Kedemoth to Sihon king of Heshbon with words of peace, saying, 'Let me pass through your land, I will travel only on the highway; I will not turn aside to the right or to the left. You will sell me food for money so that I may eat, and give me water for money so that I may drink, only let me pass through on foot, just as the sons of Esau who live in Seir and the Moabites who live in Ar did for me, until I cross over the Jordan into the land which the Lord our God is giving to us.' But Sihon king of Heshbon was not willing for us to pass through his land; for the Lord your God hardened his spirit and made his heart obstinate, in order to deliver him into your hand, as he is today. The Lord said to me, 'See, I have begun to deliver Sihon and his land over to you. Begin to occupy, that you may possess his land.'

"Then Sihon with all his people came out to meet us in battle at Jahaz. ***The Lord our God delivered him over to us, and we defeated him with his sons and all his people. So we captured all his cities at that time and <u>utterly destroyed the men, women and children</u> of every city. We left no survivor.*** *We took only the animals as our booty and the spoil of the cities which we had captured. From Aroer which is on the edge of the valley of Arnon and from the city which is in the valley, even to Gilead, there was no city that was too high for us; the Lord our God delivered all over to us. Only you did not go near to the land of the sons of Ammon, all along the river Jabbok and the cities of the hill country, and wherever the Lord our God had commanded us.*

10. This is why I believe God allowed the Nephilim to continue to exist after the Flood: So that He could get the glory through his people, and so that all the pagan, false god worshipping nations would know who YHVH was and who His people were. See also Joshua 2:8-11.

Deuteronomy 3 - Conquests Recounted:

"Then we turned and went up the road to Bashan, and Og, king of Bashan, with all his people came out to meet us in battle at Edrei. But the Lord said to me, 'Do not fear him, for I have delivered him and all his people and his land into your hand; and you shall do to him just as you did to Sihon king of the Amorites, who lived at Heshbon.' ***So the Lord our God delivered Og also, king of Bashan, with all his people into our hand, and we smote them until no survivor was left. We captured all his cities at that time; there was not a city which we did not take from them: sixty cities, all the region of Argob, the kingdom of Og in Bashan. All these were cities fortified with high walls, gates and bars, besides a great many unwalled towns. We utterly destroyed them, as we did to Sihon king of Heshbon, utterly destroying the men, women and children of every city.*** *But all the animals and the spoil of the cities we took as our booty.*

"Thus we took the land at that time from the hand of the two kings of the Amorites who were beyond the Jordan, from the valley of Arnon to Mount Hermon (Sidonians call Hermon Sirion, and the Amorites call it Senir): all the cities of the plateau and all Gilead and all Bashan, as far as Salecah and Edrei, cities of the kingdom of Og in Bashan. ***(For only Og king of Bashan was left of the remnant of the Rephaim. Behold, his bedstead was an iron bedstead; it is in Rabbah of the sons of Ammon. Its length was nine cubits and its width four cubits by ordinary cubit.)***

"So we took possession of this land at that time. From Aroer, which is by the valley of Arnon, and half the hill country of Gilead and its cities I gave to the Reubenites and to the Gadites. The rest of Gilead and all Bashan,

the kingdom of Og, I gave to the half-tribe of Manasseh, all the region of Argob (concerning all Bashan, it is called the land of Rephaim. Jair the son of Manasseh took all the region of Argob as far as the border of the Geshurites and the Maacathites, and called it, that is, Bashan, after his own name, Havvoth-jair, as it is to this day.) To Machir I gave Gilead. To the Reubenites and to the Gadites I gave from Gilead even as far as the valley of Arnon, the middle of the valley as a border and as far as the river Jabbok, the border of the sons of Ammon; the Arabah also, with the Jordan as a border, from Chinnereth even as far as the sea of the Arabah, the Salt Sea, at the foot of the slopes of Pisgah on the east.

"Then I commanded you at that time, saying, 'The Lord your God has given you this land to possess it; all you valiant men shall cross over armed before your brothers, the sons of Israel. But your wives and your little ones and your livestock (I know that you have much livestock) shall remain in your cities which I have given you, until the Lord gives rest to your fellow countrymen as to you, and they also possess the land which the Lord your God will give them beyond the Jordan. Then you may return every man to his possession which I have given you.' I commanded Joshua at that time, saying, 'Your eyes have seen all that the Lord your God has done to these two kings; so the Lord shall do to all the kingdoms into which you are about to cross. ***Do not fear them, for the Lord your God is the one fighting for you.'***

"I also pleaded with the Lord at that time, saying, 'O Lord God, You have begun to show Your servant Your greatness and Your strong hand; for ***what god is there in heaven or on earth who can do such works and mighty acts as Yours?*** *Let me, I pray, cross over and see the fair land that is beyond the Jordan, that good hill country and Lebanon.' But the Lord was angry with me on your account, and*

would not listen to me; and the Lord said to me, 'Enough! Speak to Me no more of this matter. Go up to the top of Pisgah and lift up your eyes to the west and north and south and east, and see it with your eyes, for you shall not cross over this Jordan. But charge Joshua and encourage him and strengthen him, for he shall go across at the head of this people, and he will give them as an inheritance the land which you will see.' So we remained in the valley opposite Beth-peor.

Wow! What an incredible story of epic battles and victories over giants. Here we see that in order for them to posses the land God had promised their ancestors, Abraham, Isaac and Jacob, the Isrealites had to completely cleanse the land of Nephilim seed. For the most part, they did a pretty good job. However Joshua and his boys failed to get them all. After a number of victorious battles, we find this report concerning the giant sons of Anak that remained:

There was none of the Anakim left in the land of the children of Israel: only in Gaza, in Gath, and in Ashdod, any remained. (Joshua 11:22)

For the better part of the next 400 years or so, these remaining false god worshipping giants would pose a constant threat and prove to be very problematic for the children of Israel — especially the Philistines (who were descendants of Mitraim's son Caphtor from Crete). These giants and their offspring were mentioned even more times in the Bible than the Amorites. They became one of Israel's primary enemies with about 270 references in the Bible. They were a constant problem for God's chosen people. Then along came a shepherd boy, filled with the Holy Spirit and the fire of YHVH running through his veins. He went out to meet the giant.

A champion named Goliath, who was from Gath, came out of the Philistine camp. He was over nine feet tall.
(1 Samuel 17:4 NIV)

Various scholars place Goliath at a mere 9 to 12 feet in height. That's significantly smaller than the massive Anakim, and not what you would expect if there really were multiple incursions producing first generation Nephilim. Still, even at 9 feet, that's one big dude! But David was not afraid.

> *Your servant has struck down both lions and bears, and this uncircumcised Philistine shall be like one of them, for he has defied the armies of the living God.*
> (1 Samuel 17:36 ESV)

We all know how the battle went down. David killed the giant. Later his mighty men took out Goliath's brothers. Then, the cleansing of the land continued where Joshua left off:

> *Now after this it came about that David defeated the Philistines and subdued them and took Gath and its towns from the hand of the Philistines.*
> (1 Chronicles 18:1 NASB)

> *And it came to pass after this, that there arose war at Gezer with the Philistines; at which time Sibbechai the Hushathite slew Sippai, that was of the children of the giant: and they were subdued. And there was war again with the Philistines; and Elhanan the son of Jair slew Lahmi the brother of Goliath the Gittite, whose spear staff was like a weaver's beam. And yet again there was war at Gath, where was a man of great stature, whose fingers and toes were four and twenty, six on each hand, and six on each foot and he also was the son of the giant. But when he defied Israel, Jonathan the son of Shimea David's brother slew him. These were born unto the giant in Gath; and they fell by the hand of David, and by the hand of his servants.* (1 Chronicles 20:4-8)

Years later, King Uzziah continued to wipe them out in Ashdod and elsewhere...

> *Uzziah declared war on the Philistines and broke down the walls of Gath, Jabneh, and Ashdod. Then he built new towns in the Ashdod area and in other parts of Philistia.* (2 Chronicles 26:6)

Sometime after that, King Hezekiah went after the Philistines of Gaza:

> *He also conquered the Philistines as far distant as Gaza and its territory, from their smallest outpost to their largest walled city.* (2 Kings 18:8 NLT)

Regarding the latter two accounts, we don't see mention of giants amongst the Philistines. It would seem that David and his mighty men took out the last of them in the land.

IN SUMMARY:

As you can see, the Bible gives us a great deal of information concerning the return of the Nephilim: *after* the Flood. What it does *not* give us is anything whatsoever concerning angels ever again mating with women to produce these giants — not one single Scripture reference. Whereas, we have an abundance of Scriptures referring to the offspring of the sons of Ham, beginning very soon after the Flood and continuing on for just over 1,200 years to the time of David. In every single case, the Bible refers to the post-Flood giants as the offspring of previous giants, who all descended from the people in the list given in Genesis 10 (not fallen angels or Watchers). The Multiple Incursions Theory is therefore completely un-biblical and totally unnecessary to explain the post-Flood giants. The post-Flood Nephilim came from other Nephilim, and YHVH's people wiped them out.

Chapter Eleven

GOG, MAGOG, CHIMERAS AND THE SECOND INCURSION

"Extraordinary claims require extraordinary evidence."

— Carl Sagan

I once heard Steve Quayle say something to the effect of, *"The understanding of the Nephilim is literally the Rosetta Stone for understanding all of history."* Indeed. The more I study the subject of the Nephilim, the more I find that it is literally woven into nearly every thread of civilization. I would even go so far as to say that without a proper understanding of the Nephilim, you really cannot truly understand much of anything from history, to the Bible, genetics, science, prophecy and even global politics. Regarding the latter two, I have found some rather interesting facts concerning...

GOG AND MAGOG

So far, I have spent a lot of time addressing the giant offspring of Ham, but along the way, I did make mention of the fact that there appears to be historical evidence for giants in Japheth's line as well.

I actually discovered this as a result of going on a missionary trip to China in 2006. There, I was privileged to stand on the Great Wall of China. What I didn't know however was that this amazing structure was originally known as the *Ramparts of Gog and Magog.*

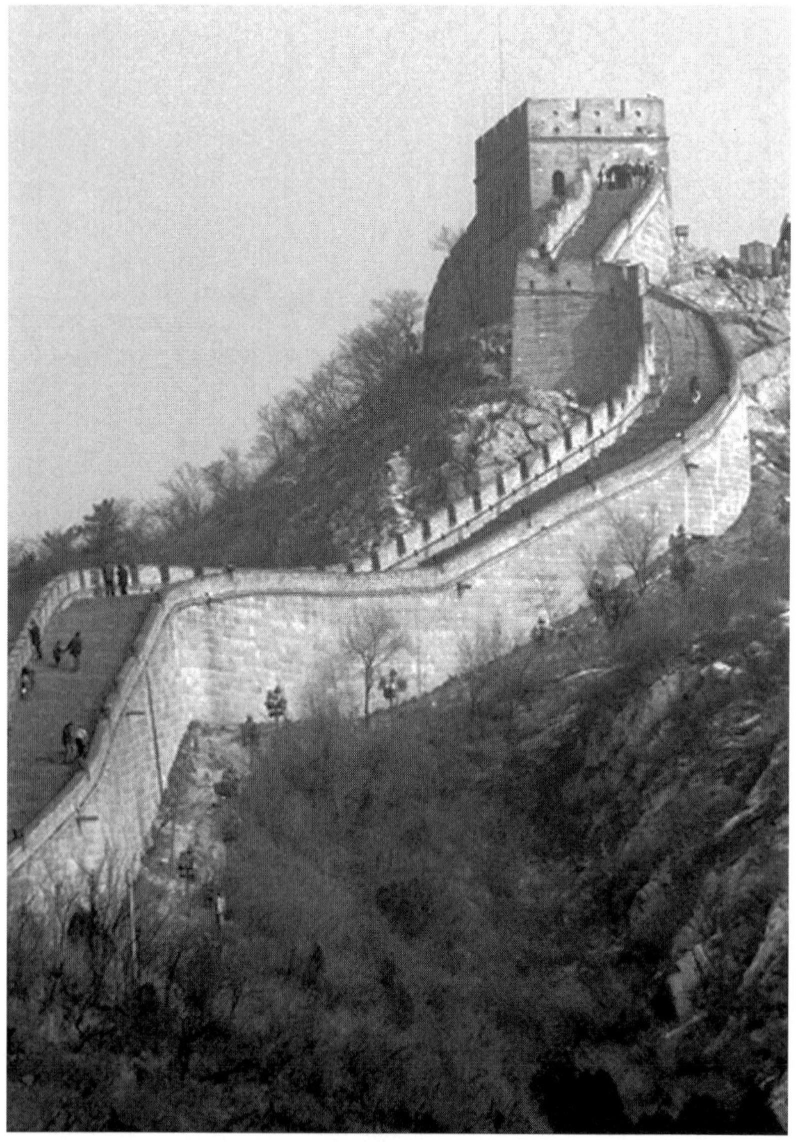

Figure 41

When I discovered that, all of a sudden, I realized there was a possibility this incredibly long and massive wall may have been built to keep out giants! You may ask, *"How did you come to that conclusion?"* Keep reading.

In my research, I found that Gog and Magog were historically considered to have been giants.

> *Corineus and Gogmagog were two brave giants who richly valued their honour and exerted their whole strength and force in the defence of their liberty and country; so the City of London, by placing these, their representatives in their Guildhall, emblematically declare, that they will, like mighty giants defend the honour of their country and liberties of this their City; which excels all others, as much as those huge giants exceed in stature the common bulk of mankind.*
>
> — Thomas Boreman, *Gigantick History*, 1741

Figure 42

The picture to the left is from the *Romance of Alexander* (at Trinity College, Cambridge). It depicts Gog and Magog (and others) as horrible, cannibalistic giants who were thought to be the ancestors of the Mongols.

Here they are depicted as evil and ugly. However elsewhere, they are depicted as jolly good giants who help people (such as in **Figure 43**).

Gog and Magog were considered to be warrior giants. As such, they are almost always depicted as one having a long pole with a mace attached to it and the other holding a long spear and a shield.

GOG AND MAGOG GIVING PADDY A LIFT OUT OF THE MIRE.

Figure 43

Did you know that even to this day, Gog and Magog are celebrated as "patron saints" and "protectors" of London?

Every year, on the second Saturday of November, their giant statues are paraded through the streets of the city in what is called the Lord Mayor Parade.[1] They just celebrated the last one on November 10, 2012. Wikipedia describes the Lord Mayor account of Gog and Magog as follows:

> *The Lord Mayor's account of Gog and Magog says that the Roman Emperor Diocletian had thirty-three wicked daughters. He found thirty-three husbands for them to curb their wicked ways; they chafed at this, and under the leadership of the eldest sister, Alba, they murdered their husbands. For this crime they were set adrift at sea; they washed ashore on a windswept island, which they named "Albion" - after Alba. Here they coupled with demons and gave birth to a race of giants, whose descendants included Gog and Magog.*[2]

> *An even older British connection to Gog and Magog appears in Geoffrey of Monmouth's influential 12th century Historia Regum Britanniae, which states that Goemagot was a giant slain by the eponymous Cornish hero Corin or Corineus. The tale figures in the body of unlikely lore that has Britain settled by the Trojan soldier Brutus and other fleeing heroes from the Trojan War. Corineus supposedly slew the giant by throwing him into the sea near Plymouth; Richard Carew notes the presence of chalk figures carved on Plymouth Hoe in his time. Wace*

1. See: www.lordmayorsshow.org and www.reformation.org/en-gog-and-magog1.jpg
2. Gog and Magog at the Lord Mayor's Show: official website. Retrieved August 3, 2007.

(Roman de Brut), Layamon (Layamon's Brut) (who calls the giant Goemagog), and other chroniclers retell the story, which was picked up by later poets and romanciers. John Milton's "History of Britain" gives this version:

> *The Island, not yet Britain, but Albion, was in a manner desert and inhospitable, kept only by a remnant of Giants, whose excessive Force and Tyrannie had consumed the rest. Them Brutus destroies, and to his people divides the land, which, with some reference to his own name, he thenceforth calls Britain. To Corineus, Cornwall, as now we call it, fell by lot; the rather by him lik't, for that the hugest Giants in Rocks and Caves were said to lurk still there; which kind of Monsters to deal with was his old exercise.*
>
> *And heer, with leave bespok'n to recite a grand fable, though dignify'd by our best Poets: While Brutus, on a certain Festival day, solemnly kept on that shore where he first landed (Totnes), was with the People in great jollity and mirth, a crew of these savages, breaking in upon them, began on the sudden another sort of Game than at such a meeting was expected. But at length by many hands overcome, Goemagog, the hugest, in hight twelve cubits, is reserved alive; that with him Corineus, who desired nothing more, might try his strength, whom in a Wrestle the Giant catching aloft, with a terrible hugg broke three of his Ribs: Nevertheless Corineus, enraged, heaving him up by main force, and on his shoulders bearing him to the next high rock, threw him hedlong all shatter'd into the sea, and left his name on the cliff, called ever since Langoemagog, which is to say, the Giant's Leap.*

Michael Drayton's Poly-Olbion preserves the tale as well:

> *Amongst the ragged Cleeves those monstrous giants sought:*
> *Who (of their dreadful kind) t'appal the Trojans brought*

Great Gogmagog, an oake that by the roots could teare;
So mighty were (that time) the men who lived there:
But, for the use of armes he did not understand
(Except some rock or tree, that coming next to land,
He raised out of the earth to execute his rage),
He challenge makes for strength, and offereth there his gage,
Which Corin taketh up, to answer by and by,
Upon this sonne of earth his utmost power to try.

Figure 44

Figure 44 depicts Gog and Magog as clock guarding statues in the Royal Arcade in Melbourne, Australia.

Figure 45

Growing up listening to teachers of eschatology, I always heard of Gog and Magog as representations of China and Russia. Yet, if you continue to dig, you will find many paintings, sculptures, effigies and stories all depicting these two characters as apparently members of real giants who were descended from Japheth.

Suddenly, it starts to make sense why someone would want to build such a massive structure as the Ramparts of Magog. As I stood on the Great Wall of China (**Figure 45**), I had to admit, it did seem a bit "over-kill" if it was simply meant to keep out armies of 6 foot tall invaders. On the other hand, if we're talking about giants... well, that's a different story. I might also suggest that if this theory is true, it sure puts a whole new spin on the Ezekiel 38 war, doesn't it?

One of the things that really caught my attention regarding the Lord Mayor Parade though is when and how it got started. According to the official website:[3]

> *In 1215 King John, keen to win the support of the City in his baronial feuds, made the Mayor of London one of England's first elected offices.*
>
> *The Mayor was a powerful figure, equal to any of John's unruly Barons. Only two months later William Hardel, the new Mayor of London, would put his signature to the Magna Carta. He was probably responsible for the inclusion of part 13:*
>
> > *13. The city of London shall enjoy all its ancient liberties and free customs, both by land and by water. We also will and grant that all other cities, boroughs, towns, and ports shall enjoy all their liberties and free customs.*
>
> *Perhaps it suited the King for the city to have more influence, but he also wanted to keep it close to him. It was a condition of the new Charter that every year the newly elected Mayor would have to present himself at court and*

3. http://www.lordmayorsshow.org/history/

> *swear loyalty to the Crown*. And so it began: every year, the newly elected Mayor of London would travel upriver to the small town of Westminster and give his oath. The Lord Mayor has made that journey almost every year since, despite plague and fire and countless wars, and given his loyalty to 34 kings and queens of England.*

This "King John" is King John Lackland. Is it just a *coincidence* that nearly all of our U.S. presidents are related to him? I wrote about this issue in my book, *Babylon Rising: And The First Shall Be Last* (Chapter Seven):

> *What am I talking about? Among other things, I'm talking about the whole facade of supposedly electing presidents who are "of the people, by the people, for the people." I believe that simply is not true. If it were, let me ask you (once again) what are the statistical odds that 43 out of 44 of our presidents would all be related to each other; many of them tracing directly back to the same man (King John Lackland of the House of Plantagenet)?*[4] *Further, why is it that nearly all (if not all) of them have been members of secret societies—all of which have practices that trace directly back to Nimrod and ancient Babylon? All of our presidents have been either Freemasons, Bonesmen, members of the CFR, the Trilateral Commission, the Bohemian Grove, the Bilderbergers, or any number of other "Round Table"*[5] *secret societies, fraternities and/or special interest groups that don't allow the general public to know what they are truly about. It gets to the point where "coincidence" just doesn't cut it anymore. Sooner or later we must face the facts. The*

---

4. Visit http://weareallrelated.com for more
5. A U.S. and British-based group of secret societies and government think tanks that consists of the Council on Foreign Relations (CFR), the United Nations, the Bilderberg Group, the Club of Rome, the Royal Institute of International Affairs and the Trilateral Commission. David Icke calls this network *"the most powerful expression of the Illuminati"* and says that these are dominated by the Rothschilds and Rockefellers, with major manipulators in play like Henry Kissinger. To read more from Mr. Icke go to: http://www.bibliotecapleyades.net/sociopolitica/esp_sociopol_roundtable_5.htm

> *Elite don't like to share power. Once they have it, they keep it in the family. No outsiders are allowed to crash their power party. That's the way it has always been, and that's the way it is today.*
>
> *It appears to me we have presidents who are "of the Masons (and other secret societies), by the Illuminati, for the Elite."*

How interesting that the elite of London would celebrate something with a parade that honors Nephilim — and that all of our presidents can be traced back to the one who started it? Could it be that there is something to all of those "blue blood" theories after all? King John Lackland was of the House of Plantagenet . In Chapter Four of *Babylon Rising: And The First Shall Be Last* I wrote:

> *The House of Plantagenet is a branch of the Angevins.*
>
>> ***Popular legends surrounding the Angevins suggested that they had corrupt or <u>demonic origins</u>.*** *While the chronicler Gerald of Wales is the key contemporaneous source for these stories, they often borrowed elements of the wider Melusine legend. For example, Gerald wrote in his* De instructione principis *of "a certain countess of Anjou" who rarely attended mass, and one day flew away, never to be seen again. A similar story was attached to Eleanor of Aquitaine in the thirteenth century romance* Richard Coeur-de-lion. *Gerald also presents a list of sins committed by Geoffrey V and Henry II as further evidence of their "corrupt" origins.*
>>
>> *According to Gerald, these legends were not always discouraged by the Angevins. Richard the Lionheart was said to have often remarked of his family that they "**come of the devil, and to the devil they would go.**"*
>>
>> *A similar statement is attributed to St. Bernard regarding Henry II. Henry II's sons reportedly*

> *defended their frequent infighting by saying* ***"Do not deprive us of our heritage; we cannot help acting like devils."*** *The legends surrounding the Angevins grew into English folklore and led some historians to give them the epithet* ***"The Devil's Brood."***
>
> —Wikipedia[6]

The *"Devil's Brood"* is an interesting epithet, wouldn't you say? Could there be some truth to that notion? What if there really was/is Nephilim seed being passed along amongst those believed to have descended from Japheth? Time does not afford me the opportunity to cover that subject in more detail in this book. If interested in tracing down more Nephilim who may have originated within Japeth's lineage, I would suggest you read the following excellent books:

- ***Genesis 6 Giants*** by Steve Quayle
- ***Giants and Dwarfs*** by Edward J. Wood
- ***Ancient Post Flood History*** by Dr. Ken Johnson
- ***Genes, Giants, Monsters and Men*** by Josephy P. Farrell

ENGINEERING THE ÜBERMENSCH

I have already stated that I do not subscribe to the idea that all whites come from Japheth, all Asians and Middle Easterners come from Shem and all blacks come from Ham. What I find quite intriguing in this regard, concerns the reality that most of the giants that have been found in both history as well as the present are described as basically Caucasian: Often white with blond or red hair, with piercing, light colored eyes. How interesting that those same traits were most desired by Hitler and the Nazis as proof of "Aryan blood."

6. http://en.wikipedia.org/wiki/Plantagenet citing various sources: Meade 1991, p. viii, Gerald of Wales, *Instructione Principis,* Fordham University, Warren 1978, p. 2 and http://www.cardiff.ac.uk/share/currentstudents/history/undergradmodulesyear2/module-HS1713.html

Hitler was basically trying to backwards engineer the Nephilim by finding traits common to the "gods" and isolating them into control-groups for selective breeding experiments. The Übermensch (Superman) was not considered to be a dark-skinned person, but rather someone with light colored hair and blue eyes (which by the way, are recessive gene traits) and fair skin. Thus, Hitler and the Nazis were not looking for specimens in the traditional territories of Ham, but rather those of Japheth (and in some cases, Shem).

The notion of an "Aryan race" comes from an early 20th century racialist thought, which was most notably embraced by the Nazi ideology of a so-called "master race." They believed that the "Nordic peoples" (a.k.a. the "Germanic peoples") represent an ideal and "pure race," declaring that the Nordics were the true Aryans because they claimed they were less "racially mixed" than other peoples.

Famed occultist, Helena Blavatsky argued that humanity had descended from a series of "Root Races," naming the fifth root race (out of seven) the Aryan Race. She thought that the Aryans originally came from Atlantis and described them this way:

> *"The Aryan races, for instance, now varying from dark brown, almost black, red-brown-yellow, down to the whitest creamy colour, are yet all of one and the same stock -- the Fifth Root-Race -- and spring from one single progenitor, (...) who is said to have lived over 18,000,000 years ago, and also 850,000 years ago -- at the time of the sinking of the last remnants of the great continent of Atlantis."* [7]

She also claimed that Semitic (those who come from Shem) are an offshoot of the Aryans who have become *"degenerate in spirituality*

7. Blavatsky, ***The Secret Doctrine, the Synthesis of Science, Religion and Philosophy***, Vol.II, pg. 249

and perfected in materiality." Others have become *"semi-animal creatures."* [8] To Hitler and the Nazis, the Semetic people came to be seen as an alien presence within the Aryan societies and that as such, they were the cause of all social disorder, which (in their mind) could lead to civilization's downfall. Thus, they worked to purify their race through eugenics programs, following concepts and practices that actually originated in the United States (such as mandatory sterilization of the mentally ill and physically handicapped). Eventually, Heinrich Himmler, under Hitler's direction, implemented the "Final Solution," which became known as "The Holocaust."

What I want you to pay attention to in all of this, is that people's *genetics* were the primary focus.

ENGINEERING ANIMAL-HUMAN CHIMERAS

Hitler tried to backward engineer the Nephilim through eugenics. Modern scientists may be trying to bring about their return through genetic engineering by way of blending species (as in Noah's day).[9]

Figure 46

8. Ibid, pg. 200
9. **Figure 45** depicts the famous "Chimera of Arezzo" as an Etruscan bronze sculpture.

Messing with the genome is becoming more and more prevalent in our day. Curiously enough, just like in the latter days of Methuselah, scientists are once again blending "kinds" that were never meant to be blended together. The genetic codes of animals, insects, fish, plants and yes, even people are being mixed together in labs. This is corrupting the image(s) YHVH originally created.

In Chapter Five, we saw that this practice started in the last 120 years leading up to the Flood. There is evidence that it continued after the Flood as well. We have a number of overt and a few not so overt examples in Scripture, which prove this fact.

The first possible example may be that of one of the four kings who served with Amraphel (Nimrod) in the Genesis 14 War: Arioch. His name means "lion-like." In Chapter Eight, I considered the possibility that he may have been a predecessor to (or an ancient king of) the "lion-like men of Moab" that Benaiah was said to have killed in 1 Chronicles 11:22.

> *Benaiah the son of Jehoiada, the son of a valiant man of Kabzeel, who had done many acts;* ***he slew two lionlike men of Moab****: also he went down and slew a lion in a pit in a snowy day.* (1 Chronicles 11:22)

Figure 47

Could these lion-like men of Moab be the similar to the strange chimera depicted (**Figure 47**) on the Black Obelisk of Shalmaneser III, tied to leashes, and apparently escorted by giants walking behind an elephant?

Similar "lion-men" are depicted on other artifacts from the ancient world such as the one shown here in **Figure 48**. This stone relief depicts a chimera with a human *and* a lion's head on a lion's body with wings! This is from Herald's Wall, Carchemish and is in the late Hittite style under Aramaean influence. It is from the Museum of Anatolian Civilizations in Ankara, Turkey.

Figure 48

Figure 49

What about this relief (**Figure 49**) from the same wall, depicting satyr-like beings along with lion-headed people?

Could it be that we really need to rethink our view of the ancient world, to include such strange creatures—even in the biblical record? We've looked at the possibility of lion-men in Genesis 14 and 1 Chronicles. Now, consider the possibility of satyrs. Take Genesis 23 for instance, Here we read about the death of Abraham's wife, Sarah and some interesting funeral guests/arrangements.

> *And Sarah was an hundred and seven and twenty years old: these were the years of the life of Sarah. And Sarah died in Kirjatharba;*[10] *the same is Hebron in the land of Canaan: and Abraham came to mourn for Sarah, and to weep for her. And Abraham stood up from before his dead, and spake unto the sons of Heth,*[11] *saying, I am a stranger and a sojourner with you: give me a possession of a buryingplace with you, that I may bury my dead out of my sight.*
>
> *And the children of Heth answered Abraham, saying unto him, Hear us, my lord: thou art a mighty prince among us: in the choice of our sepulchres bury thy dead; none of us shall withhold from thee his sepulchre, but that thou mayest bury thy dead.*
>
> *And Abraham stood up, and bowed himself to the people of the land, even to the children of Heth. And he communed with them, saying, If it be your mind that I should bury my dead out of my sight; hear me, and intreat for me to Ephron the son of Zohar, That he may give me the cave of Machpelah, which he hath, which is in the end of his field; for as much money as it is worth he shall give it me for a possession of a buryingplace amongst you.*
>
> *And* ***Ephron dwelt among the children of Heth: and Ephron the Hittite answered Abraham in the audience of the children of Heth****, even of all that went in at the gate of his city, saying, Nay, my lord, hear me:*

10. Or the "city of Arba," who was the father of Anak, the father of the Anakim.
11. Heth means "terror." The Hittites mean "the terrors."

> *the field give I thee, and the cave that is therein, I give it thee; in the presence of the sons of my people give I it thee: bury thy dead.*
>
> *And Abraham bowed down himself before the people of the land. And he spake unto Ephron in the audience of the people of the land, saying, But if thou wilt give it, I pray thee, hear me: I will give thee money for the field; take it of me, and I will bury my dead there.*

In this story, we see a character named Ephron who dwelt among the children of terror (the Hittites). Curiously, Ephron means "fawn-like." Was he a satyr living amongst other terrifying creatures? Satyrs do appear in our Bible from time to time.[12] Also, remember, the images in the reliefs depicted in **Figures 48** and **49** are of Hittite origin, so this is not beyond the realm of possibility.

The first direct mention of a satyr-like creature that I could find in the Hebrew record is in the book of Jasher:

> *And it was one day that Zepho*[13] *lost a young heifer, and he went to seek it, and he heard it lowing round about the mountain.*
>
> *And Zepho went and he saw and behold there was a large cave at the bottom of the mountain, and there was a great stone there at the entrance of the cave, and Zepho split the stone and he came into the cave and he looked* ***and behold, a large animal was devouring the ox; from the middle upward it resembled a man, and from the middle downward it resembled an animal****, and Zepho rose up against the animal and slew it with his swords.*
>
> *And the inhabitants of Chittim heard of this thing, and they rejoiced exceedingly, and they said, What shall we do unto this man who has slain this animal that devoured*

12. See Isaiah 13:21 and Isaiah 34:14 for instance.
13. According to Genesis 36:11, Zepho was a son of Eliphaz, Esau's son.

> *our cattle?*
>
> *And they all assembled to consecrate one day in the year to him, and they called the name thereof Zepho after his name, and they brought unto him drink offerings year after year on that day, and they brought unto him gifts.* (Jasher 61:14-17)

That's right, satyrs are not limited to the Greek myths. They find their way into both the Scriptures as well as extra-biblical Hebrew texts too.

I went on a missionary trip to Cyprus back in 2009. As part of that trip, I also went to Athens, Greece. That was actually the second time I had been there (the first in 2005). I began to notice that nearly everywhere I looked, I saw the toppled remains of temples, and gods as well as depictions of animal-human hybrids such as satyrs, minotaurs, centaurs and the like. I thought to myself, *"There must be some truth to these creatures."* I came home from that trip and told my theory to my wife. We had an interesting talk and then went to bed. The next morning, Sheila woke up and went to check her e-mail. She ended up seeing a news article on one of the RSS feeds in her e-mail software that said, ***"Scientists have successfully cloned a sheep with a human heart."*** The article went on to state that if they kept doing this type of research, eventually the genes will fuse together and then we'll have animal-human hybrids — and all the ethical issues to deal with that will naturally come from the creation of such things. I took that as confirmation: those so-called mythological creatures were real and I believe they were Nephilim.

THE RETURN OF THE NEPHILIM

It is my belief that giants and chimeras are here among us today. I also believe that at least the animal-human variety of chimeric Nephilim were prophesied to return.

> *A fire devoureth before them; and behind them a flame burneth: the land is as the garden of Eden before them, and behind them a desolate wilderness; yea, and nothing shall escape them.* ***The appearance of them is as the appearance of horses; and as horsemen, so shall they run.*** *Like the noise of chariots on the tops of mountains shall they leap, like the noise of a flame of fire that devoureth the stubble, as a strong people set in battle array. Before their face the people shall be much pained: all faces shall gather blackness. They shall run like mighty men* [gibbor]*; they shall climb the wall like men of war; and they shall march every one on his ways, and they shall not break their ranks: Neither shall one thrust another; they shall walk every one in his path: and when they fall upon the sword, they shall not be wounded.* (Joel 2:3-8)

Contrary to what some[14] in the Body of Christ think and teach, the "Joel 2 Army" is not made up of Believers! The Joel 2 Army are Nephilim chimeric "locusts" which come up out of the Bottomless Pit. John elaborates on these creatures in Revelation:

> ***The appearance of the locusts was like horses prepared for battle****; and on their heads appeared to be crowns like gold, and* ***their faces were like the faces of men****. They had hair like the hair of women, and* ***their teeth were like the teeth of lions****. They had breastplates like breastplates of iron; and the sound of* ***their wings*** *was like the sound of chariots, of many horses rushing to battle. T****hey have tails like scorpions, and stings****; and in their tails is their power to hurt men for five months.* (Revelation 9:7-10)

If ever there was a biblical description of a chimera, this is it! We see multiple animals represented, along with some human characteristics, all essential described as a locust-like centaur. What I find most interesting about that is the Bible describes Apollyon

14. Like those in the "New Apostolic Reformation."

as their king.[15] Apollyon is a derivative spelling of Apollo, who is Nimrod. Among other things, Apollo was known as "the giver and stayer of plagues and pestilence" in Greek mythology. All through the Bible, pestilence is usually associated with locusts. The word locust is also often used to describe vast multitudes. So, here we have a vast multitude of plague-causing chimeras coming up out of the Bottomless Pit, led by their king, Apollo.

> *And the four angels, who had been prepared for the hour and day and month and year, were released, so that they would kill a third of mankind.* ***The number of the armies of the horsemen was two hundred million;*** *I heard the number of them.* (Revelation 9:15,16)

These locust are described as horsemen. Most teachers of eschatology look at the "200 million horseman army" and point to the Russians, Chinese and now Muslims. The problem is, you can check just about any equestrian website that tracks horse populations and find there are only about 60 to 70 million horses on the planet![16] So, how do you get 200 million men on only 70 million horses? Besides, these days, what army of any consequence uses *horses* to wage war anyway?

Figure 50

What if we were to simply take the Bible literally, and realize we are talking about 200 million centaurs, being led by Apollo/Nimrod

15. Revelation 9:11.
16. See: http://www.ultimatehorsesite.com/info/horsequestions/hq_numberofhorses.htm

and four fallen angels? Another interesting tie-in that supports this idea is the fact that Apollo was the father of Centaurus, who was the father of the centaurs. Suddenly, the word "horsemen" takes on an entirely different meaning: We're talking about horse-man-chimera.

The Bible also prophecies the return of satyrs:

> *But wild beasts of the desert shall lie there; and their houses shall be full of doleful creatures; and owls shall dwell there,* ***and satyrs shall dance there****. And the wild beasts of the islands shall cry in their desolate houses, and dragons in their pleasant palaces: and her time is near to come, and her days shall not be prolonged.* (Isaiah 13:21,22)

Satyrs and dragons are coming back? I bet you haven't heard too many pastors tell you about that! The Septuagint takes it even further:

> *But wild beasts shall rest there; and the houses shall be filled with howling; and* ***monsters shall rest there, and devils shall dance there, and satyrs shall dwell there****; and hedgehogs shall make their nests in their houses. It will come soon, and will not tarry.* (Isaiah 13:21,22 LXX)

As Babylon rises, I'd like to suggest these things need to be taken into consideration. According to the Jewish apocryphal text of 4th Esdras, the archangel Uriel informs us that in the Last Days, *"pregnant women will give birth to monsters."*[17] Putting the arguments of canon aside, let's just acknowledge this is an ancient Hebrew text that paints a very interesting and possibly accurate picture of our days and the days ahead. As soon as we realize animal-human hybrids are just as "Nephilim" as angel-human hybrids, it all becomes quite clear: These creatures are prophesied to return and if we are to believe the news reports, I'd say they already have.

17. See 4th Esdras 5:8,9

Figure 51

THE ONLY SECOND INCURSION

The official punishment for the crime (sin) that was committed in Genesis 6:1-4, is binding in chains of darkness and being cast into the prison of Tartarus. Of course, the book of 1 Enoch gives us the most detail, but we also find similar references in the canon of Scripture:

> *For if God spared not the angels that sinned, but cast them down to hell* [Tartarus=bottomless pit], *and delivered them into chains of darkness, to be reserved unto judgment;* (2 Peter 2:4)

> *And the angels which kept not their first estate, but left their own habitation, he hath reserved in everlasting chains under darkness unto the judgment of the great day.* (Jude 6)

As I have already stated, YHVH would not be just if He were to allow another "incursion" and not impose the same *exact* judgment on those who participated. Indeed, as we will now see, He *is* just and the judgment remains the same for the one and only second biblical incursion, which is the Archon invasion of the Last Days. It begins with a war in Heaven:

> ***And there was war in heaven: Michael and his angels fought against the dragon; and the dragon fought and his angels, And prevailed not; neither was their place found any more in heaven. And the great dragon was cast out, that old serpent, called the Devil, and Satan, which deceiveth the whole world: he was cast out into the earth, and his angels were cast out with him.***
>
> *And I heard a loud voice saying in heaven, Now is come salvation, and strength, and the kingdom of our God, and the power of his Christ: for the accuser of our brethren is cast down, which accused them before our God day and night.*
>
> *And they overcame him by the blood of the Lamb, and by the word of their testimony; and they loved not their lives unto the death.*
>
> *Therefore rejoice, ye heavens, and ye that dwell in them.* ***Woe to the inhabiters of the earth and of the sea! for the devil is come down unto you, having great wrath, because he knoweth that he hath but a short time.*** (Revelation 12:7-12)

More of the story is given in the book of Isaiah:

> *How art thou fallen from heaven, O Lucifer, son of the morning! how art thou cut down to the ground, which didst weaken the nations!*
>
> *For thou hast said in thine heart, I will ascend into heaven, I will exalt my throne above the stars of God: I will sit also upon the mount of the congregation, in the sides of the north: I will ascend above the heights of the clouds; I will be like the most High.*
>
> *Yet thou shalt be brought down to hell, to the sides of the pit. They that see thee shall narrowly look upon thee, and consider thee, saying, Is this the man that made the earth to tremble, that did shake kingdoms; That made the world as a wilderness, and destroyed the cities thereof; that opened not the house of his prisoners? All the kings of the nations, even all of them, lie in glory, every one in his own house.*
>
> *But thou art cast out of thy grave like an abominable branch, and as the raiment of those that are slain, thrust through with a sword, that go down to the stones of the pit; as a carcase trodden under feet. Thou shalt not be joined with them in burial, because thou hast destroyed thy land, and slain thy people: the seed of evildoers shall never be renowned.*
>
> ***Prepare slaughter for his children for the iniquity of their fathers; that they do not rise, nor possess the land, nor fill the face of the world with cities.***
> (Isaiah 14:12-21)

At last we see evidence of Lucifer's actual seed. Some suggest that his seed goes further back (to the beginning), stating that Cain was the offspring of some union between Eve and the Devil. The biggest problem I have with this idea is given in Genesis 4:1:

> *And* ***Adam knew Eve his wife; and she conceived, and bare Cain****, and said, I have gotten a man from the Lord.* (Genesis 4:1)

There are all sorts of wild theories put forth to try and get around that, but it seems pretty cut and dry to me. Cain was the offspring of Adam and Eve, not Satan and Eve.

Apart from a plain reading of Genesis 4, the other problem I have with this idea is that had the Serpent mated with her, he would have been bound in chains and cast into Tartarus just like those angels who came along hundreds of years later in the days of Jared. We know that Lucifer is not bound in chains, but rather is roaming about as a roaring lion, seeking people to devour. According to the Scriptures, is also quite busy accusing the brethren, killing, stealing and destroying. We know that he tempted Yeshua in the wilderness too. No, Satan did not have sex with Eve, but he will attempt to have sex with her offspring—sometime in the near future. How do I know this? Because the Bible tells us so in Isaiah 14. It says after he is cast down from Heaven (by Michael and his angels in Revelation 12), he will have children, that YHVH has already prepared for slaughter. These will not rise, nor posses the land to build cities like the Nephilim of old did. After this failed incursion, Lucifer will receive the *exact same judgment* as the Watchers!

> *And I saw an angel come down from heaven,* ***having the key of the bottomless pit and a great chain in his hand. And he laid hold on the dragon, that old serpent, which is the Devil, and Satan, and bound him a thousand years, And cast him into the bottomless pit,*** *and shut him up, and set a seal upon him, that he should deceive the nations no more, till the thousand years should be fulfilled: and after that he must be loosed a little season.* (Revelation 20:1-3)

Just like the Watchers before him, he will be bound in chains and thrown into the Bottomless Pit, which is Tartarus. He will serve a one thousand year prison sentence. Then, he will be released for some unspecified period of time, before finally being cast into the Lake of Fire.

> *And the devil that deceived them was cast into the lake of fire and brimstone, where the beast and the false prophet are, and shall be tormented day and night for ever and ever.* (Revelation 20:10)

There is more to this story, but I will save it for the next book.

FINAL THOUGHTS

Some may wonder why I have spent so much time trying to disprove the idea of multiple incursions. What's the big deal? Well, for one thing, as I stated at the beginning of this book, I am on a quest for truth, looking for evidence. There simply is no evidence for the idea that angels continued to mate with women after the initial incursion, which took place in the days of Jared. Whereas, the evidence we *do* find points to the disturbing practice of transhuman, genetic manipulation, which is exactly what we see happening in the news today. YHVH took care of the angel sex issue long ago, and will do so again when Lucifer tries it. Therefore, in my opinion, that's not the issue we need to be concerned about. For 120 years YHVH had His servant Noah preach repentance in order to prevent man from corrupting all flesh. The people would not listen. It was this act that brought down God's divine judgment. Yeshua said the Last Days would be just like those days.

> *When the Son of Man returns, it will be like it was in Noah's day.* (Matthew 24:37 NLT)

If you've stuck with me this far, I'm going to go out on a limb and make some bold claims here. These are just my opinions, based on observations I've been making for quite some time now. I believe Nephilim are already among us. I think they have held positions of power in the governments of the world for millennia, dating all the way back to Nimrod. Their motives have always been the same: To kill, steal and destroy that which YHVH created. You want to know why all of our U.S. presidents are related to each other and can be traced back to King John Lackland (of the house of Plantagenet), founder of the Lord Mayor Parade (with Gog and Magog)? Nephilim. You want to know why our skies are filled with toxic chemtrails?[18] Nephilim. You want to know why the Georgia Guidestones clearly state that the Elite want to kill more than 6.5 *billion* people?[19] Nephilim. You want to know why we see Agenda 21[20] moving forward? Nephilim. You want to know why our food is being genetically modified and our drinking water is being filled with toxic chemicals? Nephilim. You want to know why laboratories around the world are blending species?[21] Nephilim. I could go on and on.

Maybe I am wearing a tin-foil hat and drinking too much of the Conspiracy Kool-Aid. Then again, maybe I'm right. Either way, the Scriptures clearly state that it is only going to get worse — much worse. Thus, it is easy to understand why the Apostle Paul said:

---

18. There is a big difference between chemtrails and contrails. A contrail is nothing more than vapor from the exhaust of a plane. It is usually quite small and trails behind a plane as it flies, dissipating into the air quickly. Whereas, a chemtrail is a very long trail (of toxic chemicals and metals) that goes from one end of the horizon to the other and tends to hang in the sky for hours, often in grid-like patterns.
19. The first of the "new 10 commandments" carved into the Georgia Guidestones is, *"Maintain humanity under 500,000,000 in perpetual balance with nature."* The second is, *"Guide reproduction wisely — improving fitness and diversity."* The third, reminiscent of the Tower of Babel is, *"Unite humanity with a living new language."*
20. "Agenda 21 is a non-binding, voluntarily implemented action plan of the United Nations with regard to sustainable development. It is a product of the UN Conference on Environment and Development (UNCED) held in Rio de Janeiro, Brazil, in 1992. It is an action agenda for the UN, other multilateral organizations, and individual governments around the world that can be executed at local, national, and global levels. The "21" in Agenda 21 refers to the 21st century. It has been affirmed and modified at subsequent UN conferences." [wikipedia] You owe it to yourself and your loved ones to research all you can into the sinister *agendas* contained in Agenda 21. See also: http:// babylonrisingbooks.com/book2/videosC106.html
21. In 2011, the U.K. announced the (previously secret) creation of 150 animal-human hybrids in the laboratory. See: http://www.dailymail.co.uk/sciencetech/article-2017818/Embryos-involving-genes-animals-mixed-humans-produced-secretively-past-years.html

> "...***behold, now is the accepted time; behold, now is the day of salvation.***" (2 Corinthians 6:2b)

Whether I am right or wrong about the things put forth in this book is irrelevant. All I have tried to share with you is what I have found in my research. I would encourage you to do your own research and come to your own conclusions. I believe as you do this, you will see — if nothing else — that history is repeating itself and our time is running out. Judgment is coming just as it did in the days of Noah, only this time, it will be by fire.

If you do not know where you will spend eternity, please do not wait to settle that issue. Being wrong about the Nephilim is one thing. Being wrong about eternity is another. You are not going to be held accountable to me. You will be held accountable to YHVH. As I've said before, I could be wrong about some or all of this. Or I could be right about some or all of it. I don't know. Please ask the Holy Spirit to lead you to all truth. Check out the things I have written for yourself. Try the spirits to see whether they be of YHVH or man or devil, because now more than ever, I believe we need to know the truth that sets men free.

The **greatest truth of all** is that Yeshua (Jesus) is the only path to salvation. The Fallen Ones tried to prevent Him from coming many times, but they failed. He came, He died, He rose from the dead and heralded His victory to those who are now in the prison of Tartarus!

> *For Christ also hath once suffered for sins, the just for the unjust, that he might bring us to God, being put to death in the flesh, but quickened by the Spirit: By which also* ***he went and preached***[22] ***unto the spirits in prison****; Which sometime were disobedient, when once the longsuffering of God waited in the days of Noah, while the ark was a preparing, wherein few, that is, eight souls were saved by water.* (1 Peter 3:18-20)

22. The Greek word used for "preached" is *kérussó,* which is actually better understood to mean, *proclaimed or heralded in victory.*

Yeshua has already won the war, and He paid the ultimate price for you to share in that victory with Him for all eternity. Therefore, I will leave you with a prayer that is much like the one I once sincerely prayed for myself. If you would like to receive the salvation that only Christ can offer, it is not about the words below, but rather it is about your heart's desire to repent and be made right with your Creator.

> *Father in Heaven, Yahovah, please forgive me. I know I am a sinner. I believe You sent Your Son, Yeshua (Jesus), to die a horrible death on the cross to pay the price for my sin and to draw me out of Lucifer's grasp in order that I may spend eternity with You. I accept Yeshua's sacrifice and ask Him to come and live in my heart right now. Yahovah, please cleanse me of my sins and save me by the blood of the Lamb. Father, send Your Holy Spirit to help me know and do right. Please empower me to share the truths You reveal to me in love so that others may be saved as well. Help me to be a bold witness for you in these Last Days. For it is in Yeshua's holy name I pray, Amen.*

If you prayed that prayer and this is the first time you've asked Yeshua (Jesus Christ) to be your Lord and Savior, please send us an e-mail[23] and let us know. We'd love to celebrate and pray with you!

23. E-mail: RobSkiba@seedtheseries.com

ENOCH'S ANIMAL APOCALYPSE DREAM

In 1 Enoch chapters 85-90, we find what some have called the "Animal Apocalypse Dream" of Enoch. It covers the whole of human existence (as recorded in the Bible) from Adam to the Final Judgement and describes men, kingdoms and events in allegorical terms. As you read this, take note of the fact that after *The Genesis Six Experiment* (first incursion) there is no mention of any other incursions of "stars" in the entire record. The first incursion is described as follows:

> *And again I saw in the vision, and looked towards heaven, and behold I saw many stars descend and cast themselves down from heaven to the first start, and they became bulls among those cattle and pastured with them. And I looked at them and saw that they let out their private* [sexual] *members, like horses, and began to mount the cows of the bulls, and they all became pregnant and bore elephants, camels and asses.* (1 Enoch 86:3,4)

Later, we will see that those "stars" are judged, bound and cast into the abyss. From that point on in Enoch's *all encompassing*, prophetic dream, we find no further mention any other stars (angels) "mounting" cows (women), producing elephants, camels and asses (different varieties of Nephilim).

1 ENOCH 85

1. And after this I saw another dream, and I will show the whole dream to thee, my son.

2. And Enoch lifted up (his voice) and spake to his son Methuselah: 'To thee, my son, will I speak: hear my words--incline thine ear to the dream-vision of thy father.

3. Before I took thy mother Edna, I saw in a vision on my bed, and behold a bull came forth from the earth, and that bull was white; and after it came forth a heifer, and along with this (latter) came forth two bulls, one of them black and the other red.

4. And that black bull gored the red one and pursued him over the earth, and thereupon I could no longer see that red bull.

5. But that black bull grew and that heifer went with him, and I saw that many oxen proceeded from him which resembled and followed him.

6. And that cow, that first one, went from the presence of that first bull in order to seek that red one, but found him not, and lamented with a great lamentation over him and sought him.

7. And I looked till that first bull came to her and quieted her, and from that time onward she cried no more.

8. And after that she bore another white bull, and after him she bore many bulls and black cows.

9. And I saw in my sleep that white bull likewise grow and become a great white bull, and from Him proceeded many white bulls, and they resembled him. And they began to beget many white bulls, which resembled them, one following the other, (even) many.

1 ENOCH 86

1. And again I saw with mine eyes as I slept, and I saw the heaven above, and behold a star fell from heaven, and it arose and eat and pastured amongst those oxen.

2. And after that I saw the large and the black oxen, and behold they all changed their stalls and pastures and their cattle, and began to live with each other.

3. And again I saw in the vision, and looked towards the heaven,

and behold I saw many stars descend and cast themselves down from heaven to that first star, and they became bulls amongst those cattle and pastured with them amongst them.

4. And I looked at them and saw, and behold they all let out their privy members, like horses, and began to cover the cows of the oxen, and they all became pregnant and bare elephants, camels, and asses.

5. And all the oxen feared them and were affrighted at them, and began to bite with their teeth and to devour, and to gore with their horns.

6. And they began, moreover, to devour those oxen; and behold all the children of the earth began to tremble and quake before them and to flee from them.

1 ENOCH 87

1. And again I saw how they began to gore each other and to devour each other, and the earth began to cry aloud.

2. And I raised mine eyes again to heaven, and I saw in the vision, and behold there came forth from heaven beings who were like white men: and four went forth from that place and three with them.

3. And those three that had last come forth grasped me by my hand and took me up, away from the generations of the earth, and raised me up to a lofty place, and showed me a tower raised high above the earth, and all the hills were lower.

4. And one said unto me: 'Remain here till thou seest everything that befalls those elephants, camels, and asses, and the stars and the oxen, and all of them.'

1 ENOCH 88

1. And I saw one of those four who had come forth first, and he seized that first star which had fallen from the heaven, and bound it hand and foot and cast it into an abyss: now that abyss was narrow and deep, and horrible and dark.

2. And one of them drew a sword, and gave it to those elephants and camels and asses: then they began to smite each other, and the whole earth quaked because of them.

3. And as I was beholding in the vision, lo, one of those four who had come forth stoned (them) from heaven, and gathered and took all the great stars whose privy members were like those of horses, and bound them all hand and foot, and cast them in an abyss of the earth.

1 ENOCH 89

1. And one of those four went to that white bull and instructed him in a secret, without his being terrified: he was born a bull and became a man, and built for himself a great vessel and dwelt thereon; and three bulls dwelt with him in that vessel and they were covered in.

2. And again I raised mine eyes towards heaven and saw a lofty roof, with seven water torrents thereon, and those torrents flowed with much water into an enclosure.

3. And I saw again, and behold fountains were opened on the surface of that great enclosure, and that water began to swell and rise upon the surface, and I saw that enclosure till all its surface was covered with water.

4. And the water, the darkness, and mist increased upon it; and as I looked at the height of that water, that water had risen above the height of that enclosure, and was streaming over that enclosure, and it stood upon the earth.

5. And all the cattle of that enclosure were gathered together until I saw how they sank and were swallowed up and perished in that water.

6. But that vessel floated on the water, while all the oxen and elephants and camels and asses sank to the bottom with all the animals, so that I could no longer see them, and they were not able to escape, (but) perished and sank into the depths.

7. And again I saw in the vision till those water torrents were removed from that high roof, and the chasms of the earth were levelled up and other abysses were opened.

8. Then the water began to run down into these, till the earth became visible; but that vessel settled on the earth, and the darkness retired and light appeared.

9. But that white bull which had become a man came out of that vessel, and the three bulls with him, and one of those three was white like that bull, and one of them was red as blood, and one black: and that white bull departed from them.

From the Death of Noah to the Exodus.

10. And they began to bring forth beasts of the field and birds, so that there arose different genera: lions, tigers, wolves, dogs, hyenas, wild boars, foxes, squirrels, swine, falcons, vultures, kites, eagles, and ravens; and among them was born a white bull.

11. And they began to bite one another; but that white bull which was born amongst them begat a wild ass and a white bull with it, and the wild asses multiplied.

12. But that bull which was born from him begat a black wild boar and a white sheep; and the former begat many boars, but that sheep begat twelve sheep.

13. And when those twelve sheep had grown, they gave up one of them to the asses, and those asses again gave up that sheep to the wolves, and that sheep grew up among the wolves.

14. And the Lord brought the eleven sheep to live with it and to pasture with it among the wolves: and they multiplied and became many flocks of sheep.

15. And the wolves began to fear them, and they oppressed them until they destroyed their little ones, and they cast their young into a river of much water: but those sheep began to cry aloud on account of their little ones, and to complain unto their Lord.

16. And a sheep which had been saved from the wolves fled and

escaped to the wild asses; and I saw the sheep how they lamented and cried, and besought their Lord with all their might, till that Lord of the sheep descended at the voice of the sheep from a lofty abode, and came to them and pastured them.

17. And He called that sheep which had escaped the wolves, and spake with it concerning the wolves that it should admonish them not to touch the sheep.

18. And the sheep went to the wolves according to the word of the Lord, and another sheep met it and went with it, and the two went and entered together into the assembly of those wolves, and spake with them and admonished them not to touch the sheep from henceforth.

19. And thereupon I saw the wolves, and how they oppressed the sheep exceedingly with all their power; and the sheep cried aloud.

20. And the Lord came to the sheep and they began to smite those wolves: and the wolves began to make lamentation; but the sheep became quiet and forthwith ceased to cry out.

21. And I saw the sheep till they departed from amongst the wolves; but the eyes of the wolves were blinded, and those wolves departed in pursuit of the sheep with all their power.

22. And the Lord of the sheep went with them, as their leader, and all His sheep followed Him: and his face was dazzling and glorious and terrible to behold.

23. But the wolves began to pursue those sheep till they reached a sea of water.

24. And that sea was divided, and the water stood on this side and on that before their face, and their Lord led them and placed Himself between them and the wolves.

25. And as those wolves did not yet see the sheep, they proceeded into the midst of that sea, and the wolves followed the sheep, and [those wolves] ran after them into that sea.

26. And when they saw the Lord of the sheep, they turned to flee before His face, but that sea gathered itself together, and became as

it had been created, and the water swelled and rose till it covered those wolves.

27. And I saw till all the wolves who pursued those sheep perished and were drowned.

Israel in the Desert, the Giving of the Law, the Entrance into the Promised Land.

28. But the sheep escaped from that water and went forth into a wilderness, where there was no water and no grass; and they began to open their eyes and to see; and I saw the Lord of the sheep pasturing them and giving them water and grass, and that sheep going and leading them.

29. And that sheep ascended to the summit of that lofty rock, and the Lord of the sheep sent it to them.

30. And after that I saw the Lord of the sheep who stood before them, and His appearance was great and terrible and majestic, and all those sheep saw Him and were afraid before His face.

31. And they all feared and trembled because of Him, and they cried to that sheep with them [which was amongst them]: "We are not able to stand before our Lord or to behold Him."

32. And that sheep which led them again ascended to the summit of that rock, but the sheep began to be blinded and to wander from the way which he had showed them, but that sheep wot not thereof.

33. And the Lord of the sheep was wrathful exceedingly against them, and that sheep discovered it, and went down from the summit of the rock, and came to the sheep, and found the greatest part of them blinded and fallen away.

34. And when they saw it they feared and trembled at its presence, and desired to return to their folds.

35. And that sheep took other sheep with it, and came to those sheep which had fallen away, and began to slay them; and the sheep feared its presence, and thus that sheep brought back those sheep that had fallen away, and they returned to their folds.

36. And I saw in this vision till that sheep became a man and built a house for the Lord of the sheep, and placed all the sheep in that house.

37. And I saw till this sheep which had met that sheep which led them fell asleep: and I saw till all the great sheep perished and little ones arose in their place, and they came to a pasture, and approached a stream of water.

38. Then that sheep, their leader which had become a man, withdrew from them and fell asleep, and all the sheep sought it and cried over it with a great crying.

39. And I saw till they left off crying for that sheep and crossed that stream of water, and there arose the two sheep as leaders in the place of those which had led them and fallen asleep (lit. "had fallen asleep and led them").

40. And I saw till the sheep came to a goodly place, and a pleasant and glorious land, and I saw till those sheep were satisfied; and that house stood amongst them in the pleasant land.

From the Time of the Judges till the Building of the Temple.

41. And sometimes their eyes were opened, and sometimes blinded, till another sheep arose and led them and brought them all back, and their eyes were opened.

42. And the dogs and the foxes and the wild boars began to devour those sheep till the Lord of the sheep raised up [another sheep] a ram from their midst, which led them. 43. And that ram began to butt on either side those dogs, foxes, and wild boars till he had destroyed them †all†. 44. And that sheep whose eyes were opened saw that ram, which was amongst the sheep, till it †forsook its glory† and began to butt those sheep, and trampled upon them, and behaved itself unseemly. 45. And the Lord of the sheep sent the lamb to another lamb and raised it to being a ram and leader of the sheep instead of that ram which had forsaken its glory.

46. And it went to it and spake to it alone, and raised it to being a ram, and made it the prince and leader of the sheep; but during all these things those dogs oppressed the sheep.

47. And the first ram pursued that second ram, and that second ram arose and fled before it; and I saw till those dogs pulled down the first ram.

48. And that second ram arose and led the [little] sheep.

49. And those sheep grew and multiplied; but all the dogs, and foxes, and wild boars feared and fled before it, and that ram butted and killed the wild beasts, and those wild beasts had no longer any power among the sheep and robbed them no more of ought.

48b. And that ram begat many sheep and fell asleep; and a little sheep became ram in its stead, and became prince and leader of those sheep.

50. And that house became great and broad, and it was built for those sheep: (and) a tower lofty and great was built on the house for the Lord of the sheep, and that house was low, but the tower was elevated and lofty, and the Lord of the sheep stood on that tower and they offered a full table before Him.

The Two Kingdoms of Israel and Judah, to the Destruction of Jerusalem.

51. And again I saw those sheep that they again erred and went many ways, and forsook that their house, and the Lord of the sheep called some from amongst the sheep and sent them to the sheep, but the sheep began to slay them.

52. And one of them was saved and was not slain, and it sped away and cried aloud over the sheep; and they sought to slay it, but the Lord of the sheep saved it from the sheep, and brought it up to me, and caused it to dwell there.

53. And many other sheep He sent to those sheep to testify unto them and lament over them.

54. And after that I saw that when they forsook the house of the Lord and His tower they fell away entirely, and their eyes were blinded; and I saw the Lord of the sheep how He wrought much slaughter amongst them in their herds until those sheep invited that slaughter and betrayed His place.

55. And He gave them over into the hands of the lions and tigers, and wolves and hyenas, and into the hand of the foxes, and to all the wild beasts, and those wild beasts began to tear in pieces those sheep.

56. And I saw that He forsook that their house and their tower and gave them all into the hand of the lions, to tear and devour them, into the hand of all the wild beasts.

57. And I began to cry aloud with all my power, and to appeal to the Lord of the sheep, and to represent to Him in regard to the sheep that they were devoured by all the wild beasts.

58. But He remained unmoved, though He saw it, and rejoiced that they were devoured and swallowed and robbed, and left them to be devoured in the hand of all the beasts.

59. And He called seventy shepherds, and cast those sheep to them that they might pasture them, and He spake to the shepherds and their companions: "Let each individual of you pasture the sheep henceforward, and everything that I shall command you that do ye.

60. And I will deliver them over unto you duly numbered, and tell you which of them are to be destroyed--and them destroy ye." And He gave over unto them those sheep.

61. And He called another and spake unto him: "Observe and mark everything that the shepherds will do to those sheep; for they will destroy more of them than I have commanded them.

62. And every excess and the destruction which will be wrought through the shepherds, record (namely) how many they destroy according to my command, and how many according to their own caprice: record against every individual shepherd all the

destruction he effects.

63. And read out before me by number how many they destroy, and how many they deliver over for destruction, that I may have this as a testimony against them, and know every deed of the shepherds, that I may comprehend and see what they do, whether or not they abide by my command which I have commanded them.

64. But they shall not know it, and thou shalt not declare it to them, nor admonish them, but only record against each individual all the destruction which the shepherds effect each in his time and lay it all before me."

65. And I saw till those shepherds pastured in their season, and they began to slay and to destroy more than they were bidden, and they delivered those sheep into the hand of the lions.

66. And the lions and tigers eat and devoured the greater part of those sheep, and the wild boars eat along with them; and they burnt that tower and demolished that house.

67. And I became exceedingly sorrowful over that tower because that house of the sheep was demolished, and afterwards I was unable to see if those sheep entered that house.

First Period of the Angelic Rulers--from the Destruction of Jerusalem to the Return from the Captivity.

68. And the shepherds and their associates delivered over those sheep to all the wild beasts, to devour them, and each one of them received in his time a definite number: it was written by the other in a book how many each one of them destroyed of them.

69. And each one slew and destroyed many more than was prescribed; and I began to weep and lament on account of those sheep.

70. And thus in the vision I saw that one who wrote, how he wrote down every one that was destroyed by those shepherds, day by day, and carried up and laid down and showed actually the whole book to the Lord of the sheep--(even) everything that they had done, and all that each one of them had made away with, and all that

they had given over to destruction.

71. And the book was read before the Lord of the sheep, and He took the book from his hand and read it and sealed it and laid it down.

Second Period--from the time of Cyrus to that of Alexander the Great.

72. And forthwith I saw how the shepherds pastured for twelve hours, and behold three of those sheep turned back and came and entered and began to build up all that had fallen down of that house; but the wild boars tried to hinder them, but they were not able.

73. And they began again to build as before, and they reared up that tower, and it was named the high tower; and they began again to place a table before the tower, but all the bread on it was polluted and not pure.

74. And as touching all this the eyes of those sheep were blinded so that they saw not, and (the eyes of) their shepherds likewise; and they delivered them in large numbers to their shepherds for destruction, and they trampled the sheep with their feet and devoured them.

75. And the Lord of the sheep remained unmoved till all the sheep were dispersed over the field and mingled with them (i.e. the beasts), and they (i.e. the shepherds) did not save them out of the hand of the beasts.

76. And this one who wrote the book carried it up, and showed it and read it before the Lord of the sheep, and implored Him on their account, and besought Him on their account as he showed Him all the doings of the shepherds, and gave testimony before Him against all the shepherds. And he took the actual book and laid it down beside Him and departed.

1 ENOCH 90

Third Period--from Alexander the Great to the Graeco-Syrian Domination.

1. And I saw till that in this manner thirty-five shepherds undertook the pasturing (of the sheep), and they severally completed their periods as did the first; and others received them into their hands, to pasture them for their period, each shepherd in his own period.

2. And after that I saw in my vision all the birds of heaven coming, the eagles, the vultures, the kites, the ravens; but the eagles led all the birds; and they began to devour those sheep, and to pick out their eyes and to devour their flesh.

3. And the sheep cried out because their flesh was being devoured by the birds, and as for me I looked and lamented in my sleep over that shepherd who pastured the sheep.

4. And I saw until those sheep were devoured by the dogs and eagles and kites, and they left neither flesh nor skin nor sinew remaining on them till only their bones stood there: and their bones too fell to the earth and the sheep became few.

5. And I saw until that twenty-three had undertaken the pasturing and completed in their several periods fifty-eight times.

Fourth Period--from the Graeco-Syrian Domination to the Maccabæan Revolt.

6. But behold lambs were borne by those white sheep, and they began to open their eyes and to see, and to cry to the sheep.

7. Yea, they cried to them, but they did not hearken to what they said to them, but were exceedingly deaf, and their eyes were very exceedingly blinded.

8. And I saw in the vision how the ravens flew upon those lambs and took one of those lambs, and dashed the sheep in pieces and devoured them.

9. And I saw till horns grew upon those lambs, and the ravens cast down their horns; and I saw till there sprouted a great horn of one of those sheep, and their eyes were opened.

10. And it looked at them [and their eyes opened], and it cried to the sheep, and the rams saw it and all ran to it.

11. And notwithstanding all this those eagles and vultures and ravens and kites still kept tearing the sheep and swooping down upon them and devouring them: still the sheep remained silent, but the rams lamented and cried out.

12. And those ravens fought and battled with it and sought to lay low its horn, but they had no power over it.

The Last Assault of the Gentiles on the Jews (where vv. 13-15 and 16-18 are doublets).

13. And I saw till the shepherds and eagles and those vultures and kites came, and they cried to the ravens that they should break the horn of that ram, and they battled and fought with it, and it battled with them and cried that its help might come.	16. All the eagles and vultures and ravens and kites were gathered together, and there came with them all the sheep of the field, yea, they all came together, and helped each other to break that horn of the ram.

19. And I saw till a great sword was given to the sheep, and the sheep proceeded against all the beasts of the field to slay them, and all the beasts and the birds of the heaven fled before their face.

14. And I saw till that man, who wrote down the names of the shepherds [and] carried up into the presence of the Lord of the sheep [came and helped it and showed it everything: he had come down for the help of that ram].	17. And I saw that man, who wrote the book according to the command of the Lord, till he opened that book concerning the destruction which those twelve last shepherds had wrought, and showed that they had destroyed much more than their predecessors, before the Lord of the sheep.

15. And I saw till the Lord of the sheep came unto them in wrath, and all who saw Him fled, and they all fell †into His shadow† from before His face.	18. And I saw till the Lord of the sheep came unto them and took in His hand the staff of His wrath, and smote the earth, and the earth clave asunder, and all the beasts and all the birds of the heaven fell from among those sheep, and were swallowed up in the earth and it covered them.

Judgement of the Fallen Angels, the Shepherds, and the Apostates.

20. And I saw till a throne was erected in the pleasant land, and the Lord of the sheep sat Himself thereon, and the other took the sealed books and opened those books before the Lord of the sheep.

21. And the Lord called those men the seven first white ones, and commanded that they should bring before Him, beginning with the first star which led the way, all the stars whose privy members were like those of horses, and they brought them all before Him.

22. And He said to that man who wrote before Him, being one of those seven white ones, and said unto him: "Take those seventy shepherds to whom I delivered the sheep, and who taking them on their own authority slew more than I commanded them."

23. And behold they were all bound, I saw, and they all stood before Him.

24. And the judgement was held first over the stars, and they were judged and found guilty, and went to the place of condemnation, and they were cast into an abyss, full of fire and flaming, and full of pillars of fire.

25. And those seventy shepherds were judged and found guilty, and they were cast into that fiery abyss.

26. And I saw at that time how a like abyss was opened in the midst of the earth, full of fire, and they brought those blinded sheep, and

they were all judged and found guilty and cast into this fiery abyss, and they burned; now this abyss was to the right of that house.

27. And I saw those sheep burning †and their bones burning†.

The New Jerusalem, the Conversion of the surviving Gentiles, the Resurrection of the Righteous, the Messiah.

28. And I stood up to see till they folded up that old house; and carried off all the pillars, and all the beams and ornaments of the house were at the same time folded up with it, and they carried it off and laid it in a place in the south of the land.

29. And I saw till the Lord of the sheep brought a new house greater and loftier than that first, and set it up in the place of the first which had beer folded up: all its pillars were new, and its ornaments were new and larger than those of the first, the old one which He had taken away, and all the sheep were within it.

30. And I saw all the sheep which had been left, and all the beasts on the earth, and all the birds of the heaven, falling down and doing homage to those sheep and making petition to and obeying them in every thing.

31. And thereafter those three who were clothed in white and had seized me by my hand [who had taken me up before], and the hand of that ram also seizing hold of me, they took me up and set me down in the midst of those sheep before the judgement took place.

32. And those sheep were all white, and their wool was abundant and clean.

33. And all that had been destroyed and dispersed, and all the beasts of the field, and all the birds of the heaven, assembled in that house, and the Lord of the sheep rejoiced with great joy because they were all good and had returned to His house.

34. And I saw till they laid down that sword, which had been given to the sheep, and they brought it back into the house, and it was sealed before the presence of the Lord, and all the sheep were invited into that house, but it held them not.

35. And the eyes of them all were opened, and they saw the good, and there was not one among them that did not see.

36. And I saw that that house was large and broad and very full.

37. And I saw that a white bull was born, with large horns and all the beasts of the field and all the birds of the air feared him and made petition to him all the time.

38. And I saw till all their generations were transformed, and they all became white bulls; and the first among them became a lamb, and that lamb became a great animal and had great black horns on its head; and the Lord of the sheep rejoiced over it and over all the oxen.

39. And I slept in their midst: and I awoke and saw everything.

40. This is the vision which I saw while I slept, and I awoke and blessed the Lord of righteousness and gave Him glory.

41. Then I wept with a great weeping and my tears stayed not till I could no longer endure it: when I saw, they flowed on account of what I had seen; for everything shall come and be fulfilled, and all the deeds of men in their order were shown to me.

42. On that night I remembered the first dream, and because of it I wept and was troubled--because I had seen that vision.'

I have often been asked what books I've read that have inspired me in my work. Therefore, I wanted to provide the following resources for you to check out for yourself. This list represents a selection of books either directly from my own research library or from authors I respect. Most of the books on this list were of tremendous value to me in the writing of this book series. They are not necessarily listed here in any particular order, but are categorized by author.

Recommended Reading:

Author	Book (Main) Title
Dr. Thomas Horn	• ***Nephilim Stargates*** • ***The Ahriman Gate*** • ***Apollyon Rising 2012*** • ***Forbidden Gates*** • ***Pandemonium's Engine*** • ***The Researcher's Library of Ancient Texts Volume I*** (Includes the Apocrypha as well as the books of Enoch, Jasher, Jubilees all in one volume!)
James R. Spillman	• ***A Conspiracy of Angels***
Steve Quayle	• ***Angel Wars*** • ***Genesis 6 Giants*** • ***Aliens & Fallen Angels*** • ***Genetic Armageddon***

David E. Flynn	• ***Cydonia: The Secret Chronicles of Mars*** • ***Temple at the Center of Time***
Jim Wilhelmsen	• ***Beyond Science Fiction***
I.D.E. Thomas	• ***The Omega Conspiracy***
L.A. Marzulli	• ***The Alien Interviews*** • ***Nephilim Trilogy*** • ***Politics, Prophecy and the Supernatural*** • ***The Cosmic Chess Match***
Charles DeLoach	• ***Giants: A Reference Guide From History, the Bible, and Recorded Legend***
Edward J. Wood	• ***Giants and Dwarfs***
Douglas Elwell	• ***Planet X: The Sign of the Son of Man and the End of the Age***
Russ Dizdar	• ***The Black Awakening***
Minister Dante Fortson	• ***The Serpent Seed: Debunked*** • ***As The Days of Noah Were*** • ***Beyond Flesh and Blood***
King Wells	• ***Ancient Myths and the Bible***
Douglas Hamp	• ***Corrupting the Image***
Immanuel Velikovsky	• ***Worlds in Collision*** • ***Ages in Chaos*** • ***Earth in Upheaval***
Dr. Ken Johnson	• ***Ancient Post Flood History***
G.H. Pember	• ***Earth's Earliest Ages***
Daniel Duval	• ***Noah's Ark and the End of Days***
Dr. A. Nyland	• ***Complete Books of Enoch***
Professor Edward Hull (Dorset Press)	• ***The Wall Chart of World History***
Randall Price	• ***Secrets of the Dead Sea Scrolls***

Joseph B. Lumpkin	• ***The First and Second Books of Enoch: The Ethiopic and Slavonic Texts*** • ***The Book of Jasher*** • ***The Book of Jubilees*** • ***Fallen Angels, The Watchers and the Origin of Evil***
Erik von Däniken	• ***Chariots of the Gods***
Stephanie Dalley (Oxford World's Classics)	• ***Myths from Mesopotamia***
Childress & Foerster	• ***The Enigma of Cranial Deformation***
Dr. Judd Burton	• ***Interview With The Giant***
Louis Ginzberg	• ***The Legends of the Jews***
J.B. Jackson	• ***A Dictionary of Scripture Proper Names***
Peter Goodgame	• ***The Giza Discovery***
Josephy P. Farrell	• ***Genes, Giants, Monsters and Men***
Arthur Cotterell & Rachael Storm	• ***The Ultimate Encyclopedia of Mythology***
Cliffnotes	• ***Mythology***
Gustav Davidson	• ***A Dictionary of Angels***
Rosemary Ellen Guiley	• ***Demons & Demonology***
Richard C. Hoagland	• ***The Monuments of Mars***
Graham Hancock	• ***The Mars Mystery***
Gwendolyn Leick	• ***A Dictionary of Ancient Near Eastern Mythology***
Jeremy Black and Anthony Green	• ***Gods, Demons and Symbols of Ancient Mesopotamia: An Illustrated Dictionary***
Michael Alouf	• ***History of Baalbek***
Rob Skiba	• ***Babylon Rising (Book 1)***

For additional resource material that goes along with this book series, please be sure to visit the Babylon Rising blog site:

www.babylonrisingblog.com

To order more copies of this book, visit:

www.babylonrisingbooks.com

Recommended Viewing:

The following is a list of videos I highly recommend watching in order to get a better understanding of some of the positions I take in this book and why. For those of you who are familiar with and know how to use the QR Code system, you can use the code provided to go directly to the videos online.

Do a YouTube search for the following Archon Invasion related videos:

- ***Nimrod and the post-Flood Nephilim***
- ***The Nephilim Agenda in Pop Culture***
- ***Evolution, Panspermia and the Alien Gospel***
- ***Corrupting all flesh and the Mark of the Beast***
- ***Genesis 6:12 is beginning to happen in our day***
- ***The Return of the Nephilim Now and in the Future***
- ***Who were the Anakim Nephilim***
- ***How did the Nephilim return BEFORE the Flood?***
- ***Proof of no 2nd Incursion***
- ***Have the Watchers been released?***
- ***The Omega Plan?***

You can also access all of these videos and more at:

babylonrisingbooks.com/book2/videos.html

Recommended Listening:

The following is a list of CD box sets and online radio shows I highly recommend you listen to in order to get a better understanding of some of the positions I take in this book and why.

Host and Guest	CD Box Set Title
Steve Quayle and Tom Horn	***The Days of Noah***
Spencer Bennett and Tom Horn	***Conspiracy Theory Special Edition***
RNN Radio and Tom Horn	***The Lost Symbol Revealed*** Each of the above titles are available at: survivormall.com/videosdvdsmusic.aspx
Host(s)	**Internet Radio Talk Shows**
Derek and Sharon Gilbert	***PID Radio:*** www.blogtalkradio.com/pidradio
Shannon Davis	***Omega Man Radio:*** www.blogtalkradio.com/omegamanradio
Richard Grund	***The Porch:*** www.onsolomonsporch.org
Matthew Miller, Brian Ingram	***The End Time Tribune:*** www.blogtalkradio.com/theendtimetribune
Dori Etheridge	***Doors of Deception:*** www.blogtalkradio.com/doorsofdeceptionradio
L.A. Marzulli	***Acceleration Radio:*** www.lamarzulli.net/listenlive.htm
Jim Wilhelmsen and Dave Ruffino	***Opposing the Matrix:*** www.blogtalkradio.com/opposing-the-matrix
Barry Meyer	***End Time Talk Radio:*** endtimesradio.spruz.com/end-time-talk-radio.htm
Randall and Stacy Harp	***Active Christian Media:*** www.activechristianmedia.com

Rozz	***Prepare for Battle*** www.blogtalkradio.com/preparing-for-battle
Minister Dante Fortson	***The Omega Hour*** www.blogtalkradio.com/ministerfortson
Russ Dizdar	***Shatter The Darkness*** http://www.shatterthedarkness.net
GeorgeAnne Hughes	***The Byte Show*** www.thebyteshow.com
Doug Riggs	***Morning Star Testimony Church*** http://www.dougriggs.org/AudioFiles.html

Listen to my Blog Talk Radio show,
The Revolutionary Radio Project

www.blogtalkradio.com/revolutionaryradio

OTHER PRODUCTS AVAILABLE FROM ROB SKIBA

DVDs:

- ***Mythology and the Coming Great Deception*** ($20)
- ***The Mount Hermon-Roswell Connection*** ($20)
- ***Babylon Rising: And The First Shall Be Last*** ($25)
- ***322, Tetrads and the Time of Jacob's Trouble*** ($25)
- ***Archon Invasion And The Return of the Nephilim 1*** ($25)
- ***Archon Invasion And The Return of the Nephilim 2*** ($22)

($25)

($20)

($20)

MP3 Sets:

- *Babylon Rising: And The First Shall Be Last Audio Book*
- *The Babylon Rising Blog Series*
- *The Revolutionary Radio Project: Supernatural Collection*

Get the Babylon Rising SEED Interactive DVD-Rom Super Collection For Just $50!

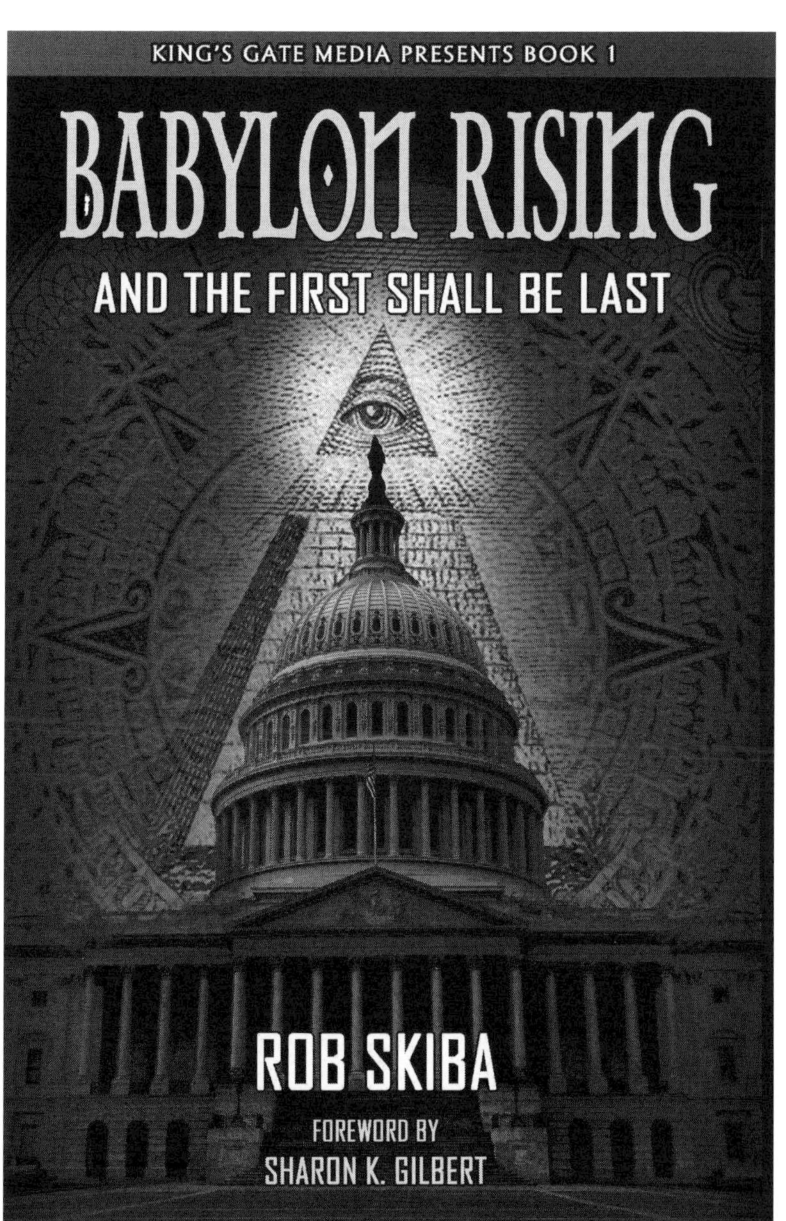

Get the book that started it all:
Babylon Rising: And The First Shall Be Last

You get Book 1, *Babylon Rising: And The First Shall Be Last*, as well as the 2hr. DVD and 7 hour audio book that goes with it, plus the Mythology and the Coming Great Deception & The Mt. Hermon-Roswell Connection Double Feature, and the Archon Invasion And The Return of the Nephilim Parts 1 &2 (3 hr. and 51 min.) DVDs along with the SEED: Why We Need To Be Culturally Relevant DVD as a bonus!

To order any of these products go to:

www.babylonrisingbooks.com/products.html

Appendix D

INTRODUCING SEED THE SERIES

The content of this book (and the others that will follow) provides the non-fiction foundation upon which the forthcoming science-fiction TV show we are currently developing called, ***SEED*** *the series* will be built. ***SEED*** really is *Lost* meets *Battlestar Galactica*, wrapped up in *The X-Files*. It will have the mystery and intrigue that made *Lost* so successful, combined with the sci-fi appeal of shows like *Battlestar Galactica* and *Star Trek*, mixed with the conspiracy and alien agenda themes of *The X-Files*.

SEED
www.seedtheseries.com
The keys to the FUTURE LIE buried in the past....

The reason we are creating this series is to get the message of books like this one (as well as those of the other authors mentioned in it) out to the masses. In my opinion, nothing has a greater impact on our culture than movies, television, music, the arts and entertainment. Statistics show that the average American watches 4 to 5 hours of TV per day and as a whole, we spend over $9 billion a year going to the movies.

In fact, that was the primary reason why filmmaker, Alex Kendrick started making movies like *Facing the Giants, Fireproof* and *Courageous*. He said:

> *"I found a (Barna Group) survey that basically said the top three most influential factors in our culture were movies, television, and the Internet. The church wasn't even in the top ten."*
>
> —Alex Kendrick[1]

When you realize how much time the average American spends going to church or reading their Bibles verses watching TV and going to the movies, it's not hard to understand why George Lucas once said:

> *"For better or worse, the influence of the church, which used to be all powerful, has been usurped by film. Films and television tell us the way we conduct our lives, what is right and wrong."*
>
> —George Lucas[2]

George Lucas captured my young imagination at age 7, and as I said in the Introduction to this book, *Star Wars* had a profound impact on my life growing up. Imagine if the stories of the Bible could capture an entire generation the way that one film did!

---

1. Read *War on the Airwaves* at: http://biblestudynow.webs.com/warontheairwaves.htm
2. *George Lucas: Interviews* by George Lucas and Sally Kline, page 143

One advantage of the science-fiction genre is that people go into it suspending their disbelief. Thus, if they have turned their disbelief filter off, that means they are open to believing whatever is being said. The devil has taken full advantage of this truth for too long! We believe it's time for the Church to become as good at telling the truth as the devil is at telling lies, and that is why we have developed this series called, ***SEED***.

The time has never been better for a series like ***SEED***. It seems as though nearly everyone is searching for answers concerning December 21, 2012 (and beyond). Unfortunately, the Church is largely silent on the subject and/or has no answers to provide. The world on the other hand, is offering up lots and lots of answers based on the ancient prophecies of people who were anything but godly (in the sense of worshippers of YHVH anyway).

The History Channel has run three seasons worth of their *Ancient Aliens* series, promoting the idea that we were the product of "seeding" and genetic tampering by beings known to some as the "Anunnaki," who were the gods of the ancient world. This concept is gaining more and more acceptance and the speculation is that our ancient, alien parents may be returning soon—possibly on December 21, 2012.

After watching two seasons worth of the *Ancient Aliens* series, a good friend of mine called me. He had recently finished going to a Bible college and had ambitions of starting his own Bible school when I got the call. To say he was shaken in his faith would be a little bit too strong of a statement, but he was quite disturbed by what he had seen nonetheless. Knowing that I was "into this stuff," he asked me what I thought about it. He is not alone. Many have asked:

> *"What do you do with this kind of evidence? I mean, it's real and we can't just ignore it, but how do all of these crop circles, megalithic structures, UFOs and 'ancient aliens' fit into what we believe to be true from the Scriptures?"*

It was at that moment, while talking with my seminary trained friend, that I knew there was a real need to educate the Body of Christ. Why? Because Jesus said that there was a deception coming that would be so great that even His elect could be deceived by it. The deception is already here dear friend, and I believe it is going to get much worse in the days ahead. Therefore, I began to think about that old saying, *"Find a need and fill it."*

I started going to lectures, seminars and conferences to learn from people like Tom Horn, LA Marzulli, Derek and Sharon Gilbert, Doug Woodward, Russ Dizdar and others who were already teaching on the subjects you never hear about in church. Soon, I was doing lectures of my own and producing CDs and DVDs that would later be sold through organizations like *Prophecy in the News* and *Cutting Edge Ministries*. However, in all of that, I kept noticing something that I found to be rather disturbing: there were always only a handful of people at those conferences and lectures and only a few thousand books, DVDs, and CDs were being sold.

There are over 300 million people in America and more than 7 billion on the planet! I began to wonder how in the world are we ever going to reach that many people if only a few hundred were going to these lectures and a few thousand were buying the books, CDs and DVDs? Then it hit me: the best way to reach the masses is through the media—specifically through the medium of science fiction television. Thus, ***SEED*** *the series* was born.

SEED will deal with the subjects from a Biblical worldview, but will be served on a secular palette. By that I mean, it will not be the next *Left Behind* series or a program that will only run on networks like *TBN* or *CBN*. ***SEED*** is designed to play to the same audiences that watch *V, The Event, Fringe, The X-Files, Heroes, Lost, Battlestar Galactica* and *Star Trek*. It will be just as "cool" and have the same production value, while providing another way to look at comparable subject matter, in a *non*-preachy format.

In my opinion, there are at least three major problems with most Christian movies and television shows:

1. They are usually severely underfunded, which leads to cheesy acting, poor lighting and sound and insufficient production value. Children of the King of the universe should surely be able to do better than that!
2. They attempt to preach in a venue that people go to be entertained. That will never work (and the financial statistics prove it doesn't). People do not go to the movies or watch episodic television to be preached to (they can surf to TBN and CBN if they want preaching), their desire is to be entertained.
3. Because Christian productions are so concerned with "closing the deal," they become overzealous with a "message" that they feel *must* be conveyed, to the point where they actually end up producing something that the world will never go see. As a result, they merely "preach to the choir," and completely miss the opportunity to reach the very audience they set out to give the message to in the first place.

The apostle Paul understood that the natural (or carnal, secular) man cannot receive the things of the Spirit, nor can he know them, because they are spiritually discerned:

> *But the natural man receiveth not the things of the Spirit of God: for they are foolishness unto him: neither can he know them, because they are spiritually discerned.* (1 Corinthians 2:14)

I believe this is why Jesus spoke in parables. **He taught culturally relevant stories that illustrated Kingdom principles.** He taught about fishing and farming... things the people could easily relate to in order to show them what the Kingdom is really like.

Jesus did not walk around with scrolls under His arms saying, *"Obadiah says... and Nahum says..."* like the characters in most Christian films do.

Come on, admit it: how many times have you seen a Christian film or show that was full of someone (usually with a bad southern accent) saying, *"The Bible says..."* every ten minutes? That does not compute in the average moviegoer's mind. They don't speak "Christianese" and neither should we—if we actually want to reach them.

Your friends and family are much more likely to come to faith in Jesus Christ as a result of conversations born out of a relationship with you than they ever will from a 60 minute television show or a 2 hour movie that is loaded with Scripture references.

I appreciate something Mel Gibson said while promoting his film, *The Passion of the Christ*. It was a very powerful film and many of the top evangelicals in the country got behind it. At one point, Gibson was basically asked to put an "invitation" at the end of the film. This is a paraphrase, but he basically said,

> *"No guys. That's not my job, that's your job. My job is to put compelling images up on the screen. Your job is to do the follow up."*

Following that same philosophy, our goal with ***SEED*** is to put compelling images on the screen, such that the secular world will become intrigued and want to continue watching it. Your job will then be to water the "seeds" we plant in ***SEED*** and use them as talking points—or a bridge—to lead others to the Truth.

There are a total of 72 episodes planned for ***SEED***, divided up over 6 seasons, with 12 episodes per season. The first two scripts have been written and a third one will be finished soon. If you want to read what has been done so far, you can download the two-part pilot episode by going to:

www.babylonrisingbooks.com/SEED.html

We cannot do this alone. If we go to any major studio or network, they will control our content, censor us, and have the power to cancel the series prematurely and own the rights, thus killing the project forever. The only way this can work is with your help. We are putting the control into the hands of our audience. This gives us total freedom and gives you the assurance that your favorite show will remain on the air, without being compromised.

Do you want the content that you've read in this book to get out to the masses? Do you want the messages of Tom Horn, Steve Quayle, LA Marzulli, Jim Wilhelmsen, S. Douglas Woodward, Russ Dizdar, Doug Hamp and others to get out to a much larger audience in a cool, science-fiction format? Well, ***SEED*** *the series* is how we intend to do it!

Please visit, **www.seedtheseries.com** and click the *"SEE"* link in order to learn more about this project. Click the *"SOW"* link to get involved and help make this show a reality.

> *"Christianity is not a religion. It is a revolution against the forces of darkness."*
>
> — Peter C. Spencer[3]
> Filmmaker, *Return to the Hiding Place*

3. Please support this incredible film: *Return to the Hiding Place:* http://www.imdb.com/title/tt1691153/

COMING SOON: SEED THE GRAPHIC NOVEL SERIES!
DALLAS, TEXAS
JANUARY 25, 2003
BLAM!
MY NAME IS
ZAK RANDALL.
EVERYONE THINKS
I'M DEAD...
BUT I'M NOT!
RANDALL

About The Author

Rob Skiba is the co-founder of King's Gate Media, LLC, the creator/writer of the forthcoming, science-fiction, Internet TV series ***SEED***, and the author the non-fiction books, *Babylon Rising: And The First Shall Be Last* and *Archon Invasion: The Rise, Fall and Return of the Nephilim.*

Rob is an award-winning documentary film-maker, entrepreneur, published author, artist, internationally recognized keynote speaker, motivational coach, Army veteran, former missionary and an active member of three charitable organizations, serving on several boards of directors.

He has written and directed numerous theatrical plays, including performances in New York, Connecticut and throughout western Massachusetts. He has been an actor ever since the founding of his High School Drama Club in 1986. Since then, he has helped to start several Community Theater groups as well as the Drama Ministry at his home church and has toured the country with a traveling acting troop.

A graduate of the Hollywood Film Institute, Rob Skiba's life-long dream has been to produce powerful television and motion picture productions. He is currently in pre-production on ***SEED*** the series and has numerous projects in various stages of development.

Rob is happily married, has a teenage son and lives in The Colony, Texas.

Made in the USA
San Bernardino, CA
23 April 2013